Education and Libraries

Selected Papers by

LOUIS ROUND WILSON

Photograph by Harold "Chips" Wea

Louis B. Wilson

Education and Libraries

Selected Papers by

LOUIS ROUND WILSON

Edited, with a Biographical
Sketch and Commentary, by

MAURICE F. TAUBER and JERROLD ORNE

THE SHOE STRING PRESS, INC., 1966

Contents

Foreword

Within the covers of this book Librarians Orne and Tauber have brought together in convenient form a series of papers which reveal the thinking of one man who by devotion primarily to the printed word in its many aspects has helped largely to establish a profession of surpassing importance.

This one man, Louis Round Wilson, has shown how a librarian can be not simply a bibliophile occupied in the acquisition, care and keeping of books, but also a scholarly historian, an editor, a promoter and an administrator of large educational enterprises, and through all this a teacher, and a mover of the minds and hearts of men.

In his youthful days spent as a printer's devil, Louis Wilson first found fascination in the printed word, in its physical limitations and in its inherent significance. He became more than a type-setting printer. He found that the exactness of observation required of a printer was required no less of one who wished to have recorded in print the results of his observation and thinking.

The knowledge stood him in good stead when he went to college He already knew the form, use, and import of words. He found suited to his natural cast of mind the steady classroom drill, under scholarly teachers, in the basic use of words: purity, propriety, and precision. He developed an ability to review his own composition, to practice the classical virtues of unity, coherence, and emphasis; to strive for excellence by removing the un-needed, the trite, and the commonplace. Here was training for a scholar, preparation for an editor. He taught school briefly and then left off teaching, with a realization that his interest was directly in books, that books in themselves created obligations as to presentation, protection, housing, handling, distribution—all of these essential to the diffusion of knowledge—and the promotion of understanding; that for such diffusion and promotion the printed word has been and still is, the principal means. Where else could all this lead a man of scholarly temperament and active imagination except to the precincts of a university library?

At Chapel Hill, in the University of North Carolina, he found his place. He literally "took over" the meager library. Supported by faculty friends of extraordinary foresight, he proceeded to build a collection of books and manuscripts designed not simply for use in temporary courses or in response to ephemeral fancy but for scholars in generations to come, a repository of knowledge. To this collection he contributed by his own successful editorship of scholarly journals and by his research as a historian.

Inevitably, however, his inclination to the classroom reasserted itself in the conviction that librarianship had to become a profession, not just an occupation for which an apprenticeship was sufficient. He advocated training for librarianship in an environment where other professional training was given.

After a period of organization and development he left North Carolina to become dean of the graduate library school at the University of Chicago. For more than a decade there he was able, possibly for the first time, to make full use of his unusual talents. He gathered about him, a group of young men and women— teachers and students—who came to share his vision of librarianship. Over them he wielded an extraordinary influence. With his wide range of knowledge and long experience as an administrator, editor, and scholar, he was able to strip from research in librarianship much of the scholarly "bunk" which threatened to become a prevalent and alleged scholarly attitude; he imparted to these young prospective librarians the idea that librarians should be educators as well as managers of great educational enterprises. How well he succeeded is indicated by the quality of college and university librarians now visible on academic campuses.

During these years, as in previous decades, he wrote, edited, and published; he organized librarians; he plotted the course of librarianship. He gave aim and direction to hundreds of libraries, public and academic.

Rarely moved to eloquence on the platform, he never lacked for words. In conversation, in consultation and in decision-making, he was articulate, and convincing. The listener listened with respect and admiration. He realized that the speaker knew what he was talking about, that what he said made sense, was important, should be done.

His sound judgment on many subjects whether of library administration or of educational policy, his intellectual as well as his moral integrity, his natural quality of kindly consideration and ready understanding, gave weight and value to his opinions. His personal and lovable qualities added strength to his professional attitudes and enhanced this influence. His opinions on library matters became determinants, a yard-stick, a touch-stone.

Thucydides once wrote

"It is men who make a city, not walls or ships without crews." In the minds of those who know him, Louis Round Wilson has made walls, ships, and crews.

As one who has admired him for some forty years, I am glad to have this book, but do not need it to make me mindful of him.

Robert M. Lester
Executive Director
Southern Fellowships Fund
Chapel Hill, North Carolina

Introduction: Louis Round Wilson

It is seldom possible to mark the 90th birthday of a man who continues as a living influence in his chosen field of endeavor. Not often can one document such a man's vital contributions in a broad spectrum of fields, and it is scarcely possible to bring greater honor to a man whose name is already honored in all parts of our land and beyond. In full awareness of the historic significance of his work and the unique opportunity of the occasion, we two, former acolytes of the teacher, have undertaken to bring together this collection of papers written by Dr. Louis Round Wilson over more than sixty years of professional life. Important as they are, these papers constitute only a modest sampling of literally hundreds from which they were selected. To better understand the man and his work, one should know his way of life.

Louis Round Wilson was born in Lenoir, North Carolina, on December 27, 1876, the year of the founding of the American Library Association, an organization for which he was to work earnestly in later years. The line of his ancestry goes back to John Howland, who arrived in America on the Mayflower.

As a young boy, Wilson attended the various local schools of Lenoir, and spent two years at Lenoir Academy. Like his father Jethro Reuben Wilson, young Louis was early involved in multiple responsibilities. In his teens in Lenoir he worked in the office of the *Lenoir Topic* as type setter and printer's devil. While working on the *Topic*, he was a boy-of-all-work at the Methodist Church. Since he was not at school during this period from 1891–1894, he spent his evenings studying at home and reciting to J. D. Minnick, of Davenport College.

A full scale biography of Louis Round Wilson is scheduled for publication by Columbia University Press, February 1967.

His earliest duty as a librarian was the responsibility he had for the Library of the Sunday School of the Methodist Church. Each Sunday he devoted an hour in charging off returned volumes and charging out books to the various classes in the Sunday School. In later life, he was one of the prime movers in the building of the University Methodist Church.

After spending a year preparing for college at Davenport College, he started his program at Haverford College in 1895. It was rough going at first, due largely to his relatively informal preparation, but he made such progress that he was awarded the Class of 1896 prize for his outstanding work in Latin. After three years at Haverford, Mr. Wilson transferred to the University of North Carolina, where he completed his work in 1899. On graduation, he was awarded the Hume Senior Essayist Medal.

Two years of teaching in private schools preceded his return to Chapel Hill as Librarian of the University in 1901. Again he was involved in both study and work; he received his Master's degree in 1902 and his Doctor of Philosophy degree in 1905. He was the first student in the Graduate School after its formal establishment in 1903 to receive the doctorate, and his dissertation was the first number of *Studies in Philology*.

In his first years as Librarian of the University, Dr. Wilson was not sure whether he would consider library work as a career or go into classroom teaching. As he worked with the Library and became more familiar with the complex organization that was essential to support an instructional and research program, he saw academic librarianship as a vital part of the teaching profession. Once he had made up his mind, he directed his attention to making the University of North Carolina Library one of the best in the country.

Dr. Wilson's success in building up the collections of the library is well known. When he took over the position of Librarian in 1901, there were 38,593 volumes in the Library. When he left to go to Chicago in 1932, the book collection totaled over 235,000 volumes. The few periodical titles which were being received in 1901 soared to 3,448 by 1932. He played the leading role in the planning of two library buildings. Twenty-three trained librarians were on the staff in 1932; he had worked with one assistant from 1907 until 1915, although he had introduced a successful system of student aides. He early saw the potential usefulness of a North Carolina Collection, and at his departure there were 47,000 items assembled for study and research. A Southern Historical Collection was on his agenda as early as 1904, and it has become an important body of materials for investigators on all phases of southern social, economic, and cultural life. In 1929, the Hanes Foundation for the Study of the Origin and Development of the Book was established. It foreshadowed the development of the Friends of the Library group three years later. His activities as a whole demonstrated his vision and his conception of the key role the Library had in the progress of a modern university.

Dr. Wilson's interest in librarianship as a profession did not stop with the building up of one library. He was early an enthusiast for library training. In 1904 he started offering courses in the summer, and later gave them in the regular terms. Convinced that a strong library school was essential for the training of professional librarians for school, college, university, and special libraries in the South, he worked tirelessly to establish a school at North Carolina. The School of Library Science was opened in the fall of 1931. The School was made possible by a grant from the Carnegie Corporation of $100,000 for its establishment and maintenance over a five-year period. It has had an important part in the training of librarians who have held ranking positions in southern and other American libraries.

It was not long after he began his work at the University Library that he realized that a librarian or the staff of a single library could only do so much to promote educational improvement and expansion. Librarians and libraries together had professional obligations which could be furthered by library agencies and associations. During 1904 Dr. Wilson worked actively for the establishment of the North Carolina Library Association. The Association came into being as a result of the vital influence of Miss Anne Wallace and the Carnegie Library of Atlanta. The influence was exerted through Mrs. Annie Smith Ross, who became librarian of the Carnegie Library at Charlotte in 1902. Mrs. Ross, impressed with what was done in Georgia, corresponded with Dr. Wilson and others concerning the possibility of a state library association. A meeting in Charlotte in 1904 won support from the press, librarians and others interested in library development. Dr. Wilson served as secretary-treasurer from 1904 to

1909, being elected president in the latter year. His interest in the Association has been constant. He also realized that development of libraries in North Carolina could be speeded up by an active state library commission. In 1907, as secretary of the North Carolina Library Association, he assisted in the drafting of the first proposed law for the establishment of the North Carolina Library Commission and worked untiringly for its enactment by the Legislature. The effort failed in 1907, but the ground-work had been carefully laid for a successful presentation in 1909. Dr. Wilson was elected chairman of the Commission in April, 1909, an office which he held until 1916. His duties were concerned with securing office space in the State Library building at Raleigh, establishing cordial relations with the State Librarian and the State Superintendent of Public Instruction, securing a versatile executive-secretary, and with her and other members of the Commission outlining a program of important activities which included the publication of *The North Carolina Library Bulletin*, the promotion of package and traveling libraries, assistance to schools, colleges, and communities in the development and improvement of libraries, securing the enactment of library legislation that would facilitate library development, and the collection and publication of library statistics. Thus, he played a distinguished role in placing the commission's program on a sound basis.

"Once get printer's ink on your fingers and it never comes off" was evidently true in Dr. Wilson's case. His early work on the *Lenoir Topic* was never forgotten. He obtained more experience with the publication of his doctoral dissertation, which he put through the press himself; his editorial work on the University *Record*; and with his editorship of the *Alumni Review*. As editor of the *Review*, he frequently wrote editorials concerning various phases of the university's development, one of which he particularly emphasized being the need of a University Press to bring together all the publications of the institution under one imprint. He worked closely with Dean Edwin Greenlaw in 1920 when the latter urged the establishment of a Press. When the Press was finally incorporated in 1922, Dr. Wilson was made Director, a position in which he served until he left for Chicago in 1932. During the decade that Dr. Wilson was Director, the Press published over 100 titles, covering various fields related to southern life and culture. Novels, short stories, drama, poetry, biography, history, regional sociology and economics, agriculture, botany, and zoology, as related to the South, were among the titles. Many prominent scholars were among the early contributors of manuscripts to the Press. Several of the volumes found their place in the annual list of the forty most important books published in the United States issued by the Committee on Intellectual Cooperation of the League of Nations. Dr. Wilson's building up of the Press has been one of his most valuable contributions to the University, the State, the Southeast, and the Nation.

It is not possible to list here every activity in which Dr. Wilson engaged. In addition to his work in establishing the North Carolina Library Association and the North Carolina Library Commission, he was among the founders of the Southeastern Library Association, serving as president from 1924 to 1926. He was active in the Department of Libraries, Southern Educational Association, and became president of the Department in 1911. For seven years, 1925–32, he was a member of the Board of Education for Librarianship of the American Library Association, serving as chairman, 1930–31. He was a member of various other committees of the American Library Association, and was elected president of the Association for the year 1935–36. His early interest in the training of teachers to make effective use of libraries and standards for school libraries was demonstrated by his membership on the Committee on Normal School Libraries of the Department of Libraries of the National Education Association, and on the Committee on High School Library Standards of the Southeastern Library Association in cooperation with a similar committee of the Southern Association of Colleges and Secondary Schools. He was a charter member of the National University Extension Association, and a member of such groups as the North Carolina Literary and Historical Association and the Bibliographical Society of America, as well as a fellow of the American Library Institute. He was a delegate of the American Library Association to the British Library Association Conference in 1931, meeting in Cheltenham, and to the Federation of International Library Associations, holding its second conference in Madrid and Barcelona, in 1935. He was a member of the Advisory Group on College Libraries for the Carnegie Corporation of New York, 1928–30, and of a special commiteee appointed by the American Medical Association to study Negro colleges for accreditation by American medical schools. The American Library Association commissioned him as the surveyor of southern Negro colleges in the selection of the location of a library school for Negroes.

Dr. Louis Round Wilson has always lived in the present—working every minute, generally for others. Such men are rare and deserve all the honors that their fellow men bestow upon them. Honorary doctorates have been given him by Haverford, North Carolina, Denver, and Catawba. He is an honorary life member of the American Library Association; in 1954 he was presented the Herbert Putnam Award by the Association. Many other awards were to follow. President Alvin R. Keppel of Catawba College in presenting Dr. Wilson for the degree of Doctor of Humane Laws remarked: "For almost fifty years Louis R. Wilson has labored without stint to provide greater opportunities for reading for all the people of his native State and of the South. Carrying the torch of truth, he has always been a soldier in the van in the greatest of all wars, the war against ignorance." Quiet, devout, simple, and outgiving, he is held in deep admiration and affection by all who know him. In every respect, he is one of the great sons of North Carolina. With these brief biographical notes in mind, the pattern of the selected papers can readily be understood. The first group of papers concerns the development of library service in the Southern states.

Dr. Wilson realized from the very beginnings of his professional life the limited range of educational development in his native part of our land. With characteristic vigor he set about informing every potential action group he could reach. His first paper, written for a popular national journal put libraries of the South into a national framework. Another placed the public library in the picture of adult education. His early grasp of the importance of the great foundations led him to press for greater attention to the region, with impressive results. The continuous reporting of his own studies on the effects of their investment undoubtedly provided bases for additional grants. As one paper sketches out the current library situation of the region, the next places it in contrast to the national scene. In the one, his counsel may be by implication; in another, it is positive and direct. He never failed to provide a clear set of recommendations, usually in a numbered logical sequence. Examples of this are found in the papers on "New Objectives for Southern Libraries" and "Restudying the Library Chart." In the first group of papers, one finds analysis in sharp detail of the modest provision of libraries or library resources in the South, the relationship of libraries to education at various levels, and the inter-relations between these and adult education. Wilson always saw the whole picture first, then its parts. It was this breadth of vision that early marked his quality; it is amply represented in the first group of papers.

The second group centers about the school library. It is typical of Wilson to make a major contribution in this area of education as sound preparation for further development on higher levels. Good teaching and learning in the early years was inbred in him and in his family. Although he moved rapidly into higher education and settled there, his was no ivory tower. He took an active part in promoting the establishment of good standards and the provision of some form of library service at all levels. These papers were delivered before large groups of education administrators and were published in education journals. While the program projected is clearly defined, what is not so apparent is the continuing campaign of which these few papers were only a small part. They represent another evidence of Wilson's broad-ranging interests.

Nonetheless, it is clear that his greater love is in the area of academic libraries. The papers in the third group are therefore more numerous. They place the library in its proper relationship to education from the first year of college through the highest levels. They record progress in recognition of the usefulness and purpose of libraries in educational institutions. They stress the importance of relating the library's resources and services to teaching. Here, as in other fields, he always took the broadest view. When he reports gains, he compares them to national norms; when he analyzes resources, he measures them against other areas, always at higher levels. Again he makes wide-ranging recommendations for improving resources, closer integration of library and teaching, and for great coordination and cooperation. It was in this field that the seeds of cooperation spread by Wilson brought the largest yield. The North Carolina-Duke University cooperative planning, initiated by Robert

B. Downs, remains even today one of the most illustrious examples of the kind of far-seeing concepts promoted by Dr. Wilson.

Professional training for librarianship was a wholly natural additional field for his attention. It was also typical that he addressed himself first to the problems of the South. In this field, as in others, he was a leader, and the very existence of most of the library schools in the southern states is associated with his early efforts. He saw clearly the glaring deficiencies in trained personnel at all levels in southern institutions. He was determined to improve the situation. It was not long after the establishment of recognized training at Emory, Peabody and North Carolina that his own predilection for higher education led him to leave North Carolina for the Deanship at the Graduate Library School of the University of Chicago. Over a period of ten years there, he developed the highest level of professional library education ever seen in this land. He brought together a talented faculty representing all aspects of library work, a brilliant group of graduate students, and the assurance of sound financial backing. He introduced the concept of research in library problems. His faculty applied the concept, each to his chosen field. He related his training to other fields of graduate study and research, notably the social sciences. He pillaged other fields for useful techniques and applications of research method. His own paper on "The Impact of the Graduate Library School upon American Librarianship" is a cogent review of his own work and the ever widening circles that spread out from it. This group of papers is closed characteristically with one which reviews the long historical development of training for librarianship and its relationship to the world in which it grew. The word "world" is used advisedly, for here, as elsewhere, one sees the amazing breadth of vision of the man. His view was always all-inclusive. First concerning himself with the local problems, then state and regional, he moved swiftly to the national and looked on to international levels. Yet he never failed to relate the larger to the smaller, the whole picture to its parts.

A small group of papers, closing this collection, is an example of one of those parts. Publishing was always essential to the Dean, and as his biographer says, he never could keep his fingers out of printer's ink. This interest, reflected concretely in the establishment of the

University of North Carolina Press, became an integral part of his work with libraries. He foresaw the importance of publishing to education and libraries and especially to graduate training in the South; he beat the drums for physical facilities far beyond anything then known in that region. The papers speak for themselves. This is only one more evidence of the catholicity of a great man.

We do not say this was a titan; he is a titan. Even today, with four score and ten behind him, he still holds forth on these and many other related matters, with lucidity and vigor. It is with pride and great affection that we offer this collection to him not only for ourselves, but in the name of all who have been touched by the magic of his intelligence.

Maurice Tauber
Jerrold Orne

The Library in the Social Order

The Growth of the Libraries

TEN YEARS AGO, IN A MAGAZINE descriptive of the general growth of the Southern States, a statement of the development of the library as an institution which largely affected the life of the South would scarcely have found a place. Then there was no clearly defined, well-organized library movement. The free public library, one of the latest products of library development, was little known in the region.

But the modern library—school, public, college, and traveling—has, since 1895, established itself as an institution making for saner life and broader culture.

One of the most notable steps taken has been the establishment of the rural school library. In North Carolina, when the educational qualification for suffrage was enacted early in the early 1900's, something very definite in the way of greater educational facilities for all the people had to be provided. The legislature of 1901 provided funds, with the aid of funds raised by the school districts and counties, for at least six rural school libraries in each of its ninety-seven counties. By means of further appropriations in 1903 and 1905, the number of libraries in each county was increased from six to eighteen, and on June 30th, 1906, 1,400 of these libraries, containing a total of 125,000 volumes, were in operation in the state.

In Virginia, the same idea has been carried out through a system of traveling school libraries, which has been operative since October, 1906, and 2,625 volumes have been put in immediate circulation. Libraries containing fifty volumes each are made up from it and sent out daily to the rural school stations throughout the state. Every station is allowed to keep its collection for four or six months, and then to send it back to the state library to receive a new collection.

At the close of December, 1906, twenty well equipped Carnegie

Reprinted from *The World's Work*, 14:8985–8986, June, 1907, by permission of the publishers.

libraries, representing $537,000 in buildings, were in operation in Texas. Since 1897, Durham, Raleigh, Greensboro, Asheville, Charlotte, and other North Carolina towns, a score or more in all, have established public libraries, and during the year 1906 the five towns just named recorded loans totaling 200,000 volumes among 25,000 borrowers. In 1905–06, Virginia and Arkansas each established its first three public libraries. Within the past six months, Atlanta has received $30,000 for two additional branch libraries, Louisville $200,000 for eight similar branch stations, and the New Orleans library is just finishing its $200,000 quarters.

The most significant fact growing out of the activities of these public libraries, however, is not that they have been placed on a sound financial basis and are recording a splendid total of loans, but rather that they have tended to reproduce themselves in other communities. In Charlotte, Atlanta, Austin, Louisville, Chattanooga, Nashville—in fact, in all the larger towns—the public library has been a fertile centre from which decidedly active influences have spread. In each of these libraries, a system of apprenticeship and general library instruction has been maintained which has quickened individual growth, and a publicity program has been carried on which has helped to form and crystallize a fine, general library sentiment.

Southern college libraries have also undergone a revolution in spirit, although their growth has not been so apparent as that of the school and public libraries. While they have not served the public directly, they have served it none the less effectively by impressing the student with the true importance of the library as an institution. Quietly, but at the same time enthusiastically, they have worked their way up to a place of dignity and power in college life. Ten years ago, the library was useful to the student of literature and history primarily, and not to the college as a whole; but, since then it has come to be more and more a perfectly equipped laboratory, and, in as much as the librarian is no longer a mere curator of books but a well-trained, professional man, the library has been recognized as an active force in college life.

Their growth, however, has also been extended in other ways. Since 1895, the University of Virginia has spent $60,000 in restoring its library building and has added 50,000 volumes to the 12,000 saved from the disastrous fire which destroyed its former library. In North

Carolina, Trinity College has received a splendid $50,000 building since 1899 and has increased its book collection from 11,000 to 37,000 volumes. In September of the present year, the University of North Carolina will house its present collection of 45,000 volumes in a new, fire-proof structure and will enjoy, in addition to its present library revenues, the income from a new $55,000 endowment fund for books. At the Universities of Georgia and Louisiana, $50,000 library buildings have been occupied in the last four years and material additions have been made to the original collections. South Carolina, Texas, Tennessee, and Alabama have each added one or more college library buildings since 1905; and since January of the present year, Florida has received a gift of $40,000 for library purposes at Stetson University.

The traveling library, too, has established itself in the South and has met with immediate success. Its general adoption in rural and sparsely settled communities is certain, being conditioned solely upon a proper provision by the states for its care and direction. Georgia inaugurated the movement in 1898. By 1905 twenty-three schools had been added to the traveling list; ninety-seven schools and forty-six rural communities had received circulating collections; 4,174 magazines and periodicals had been sent out; and since 1898, 800 schools have been influenced to make permanent improvements upon their schoolhouses or grounds; 400 have established libraries of their own; forty-six rural communities have founded village improvement societies, and a total of 5,468 books have been kept in constant circulation. In North Carolina and Texas, the movement has found strong support in the Federation of Women's Clubs. In Virginia the traveling libraries have been placed under direct state control. A fund of $7,500 was appropriated for their maintenance for two years. Free transportation was received from the railroads; and thus the small Virginia village, which hitherto has contented itself with its general store, post-office, school, and church, has been brought under the broadening, vitalizing influence of the open book.

The most conclusive proof of library development is the state library association. In seven of the Southern States, such an organization—composed of librarians, trustees, educators, members of social clubs, and others—has been formed. With a membership of 1,000, these associations have given serious consideration to various library

problems and have worked toward one common end—the populariza-
tion of the library movement and the creation of a public sentiment
sufficiently strong to insure every community some form of library
facilities. The state library commissions of Maryland, Virginia, Tennessee, and Georgia have grown out of the state associations and
have placed all forms of public library activity upon a permanent
basis. In North Carolina, Alabama, and Texas, the state associations
have not yet succeeded in securing definite legislation, but the need
has been clearly shown and the demand, sooner or later, will be met.

In Georgia and Texas, library progress of all kinds has been
longer lived and the results are more satisfying. In South Carolina,
Mississippi, and Florida, growth has been less evident. But everywhere throughout the South undisputed progress has been made.
Three facts in this connection are significant. The first is that the
American Library Association held its annual meeting this year in
Asheville. A development of sufficient magnitude in the South
brought this deliberative body to the Southern field for the discussion of special problems of the Southern Libraries.

The second is that, at its last annual meeting, the Southern Educational Association created a permanent department of libraries,
thereby insuring the library due consideration in the educational
work of the South.

The third, and equally significant, was the development of Atlanta
as a library center through the philanthropy of Mr. Andrew Carnegie.
He gave, in 1899, $125,000 for the Carnegie Library (formerly the
Young Men's Library), for the central building, and in 1905, $4,000
for three years for the establishment of the first library school in the
South. This marked the beginning of professional training of librarians in the region.

In the last ten years, the Southern library has made a long stride
forward. It has been making for a broader culture and for a larger
view of life. Its success is assured.

The Public Library as an Educator

IN ·AN ASSEMBLAGE OF EDUCATORS such as this, it may seem unnecessary to give an exposition of the nature of education; for it is the daily theme of our life, and whether it be the education of self, or of student, or of community about which we are solicitous, it is the ever shining goal towards which our calm reason, and ardent enthusiasm, impels us. But inasmuch as we are to consider the public library in the capacity of an educator, setting for itself the same high objective to which, as educators, our finer impulses drive us, it is necessary to review briefly the nature of the objective which this the newest recruit to the educational ranks, has set for its task.

Education is the process by means of which the individual is brought through training to an understanding of himself, of the life about him, and of the infinitely numerous relations which connect him with it. It is the process through which he passes in gaining for himself a proper knowledge of the various circumstances of life; from which he acquires the ability to adjust himself properly to them; and by which he learns to know the standards of the true, the good, and the beautiful with which to measure them. It is the highway over which the individual passes in reaching an ultimate point from which he can view with greater clearness than he otherwise could life and the issues of life in their true perspective. To pass this way, is to become educated; to help another on this course, is to be an educator; and to be an educator in this sense, is to be Godlike.

Under whatever conditions the extension of this the great work of life is possible, the lot of the worker will be one of rare privilege. In a democracy such as ours, in which every individual is a sovereign, the opportunity to work this good work cannot be treated merely as a privilege, but as an imperative duty. Whatever may be our con-

Reprinted from *Library Journal*, 37:6–10, January, 1910, by permission of the publisher. This paper was read before the Department of Libraries of the Southern Educational Association at Charlotte, N.C., Dec. 28, 1909.

ception of the duties of our government as to the extent of its pater-
nal relations to our citizenry and to the direction of our individual
affairs, we are unanimously agreed that it is its clear duty to give
security to the persons and property of the members of the government. In order that it may do this without the possibility of dis-
appointment and failure we are also equally unanimously agreed that
the best means our government has to protect these rights is through
the education of every sovereign individual; for if his eye be single
his whole body shall be full of light, but if evil, his whole body shall
be full of darkness.

Accepting education then to be the agency for promoting the kind
of good indicated and recognizing it as the foundation upon which
our form of government must stand or fall, as a people we have
spared no thought or means whereby it might best be promoted
among us and by which its benefits might be more generally conferred on all. Our thinking and planning have resulted in the establishment and maintenance of the school, the museum, and the lecture
platform which, together with the press, the church, and the home,
stand out as the great educational agencies in our American life.
Each has its definite place and each, in the way best suited to the
furtherance of its specific purposes, is working out as a specific, yet
cooperative agency, the salvation of the American people. Each in
the way which has been found the surest and best attempts to contribute its part to the making of the complete man, furnished unto all
good works.

In 1850, or thereabouts, the public library presented itself in
America as a claimant for a place along with these agencies in the
nation's educational work. It asked to be allowed to become an educator, to be permitted to contribute something further to the individual's outlook upon the life around him. By 1876, a date made mem-
orable in America by the founding of the American Library Association as well as by the celebration of the one hundredth anniversary of
American independence, its request for admission had been granted,
and in 1907, when representatives from every section of the country
gathered at Asheville in the twenty-ninth annual meeting of the Association, it was brought home to us of the South as it was to the
entire country that every objection to its admission had been swept

away and it stood accredited as one of the foremost institutions in the dissemination of popular education.

It is in the capacity of an educator, then, a capacity to which it holds an undisputed right, that I wish especially to view it with you. As schoolmen, we have doubtless come to look upon the library, whether for the rural school, high school, college, city or state, as secondary to the school as an aggressive educational agency. Consequently, we may have fallen into the habit of thinking and speaking of the library as supplementary to the school. We insist in driving two of our educational forces tandem fashion with the school in the lead, rather than both abreast, each pulling its proportionate share of the load. As librarians we have possibly insisted more than has been reasonable upon this latter method of pulling, and consequently the load, through misunderstanding and a lack of cooperation on the part of the forces concerned, has not been carried forward as far as it might.

Whatever may have been our theory in the case, we are agreed today that each is indispensable to the other and that each in certain particulars supplements the other and is complemented by the other. The specific functions or missions of both, and the relation which each institution bears to the other I conceive to be as follows: I quote, in part from Mr. W. A. Millis in his paper read before the National Educational Association in 1902, and from Mr. H. E. Legler, in the current number of the *Library Journal:*

"The work of the school is threefold:

1. To awaken aspiration, both general and specific.

2. To give the alphabet of learning and activity—that is, to give the child such introduction to the several lines of learning, art, and enterprise as will reveal to him and nourish his special aptitudes, and at the same time put him into position to live sympathetically with those who follow other activities than his own.

3. To train the powers of thought and expression."

Or, stating the ideas of Mr. Millis in a slightly different way, it is required of the school to awaken in the child an ambition to be well developed, to be a somebody; to quicken his impulse to know what the world has thought and done; to teach him to read, and, to some extent, to develop his taste for proper literature. When the child has been equipped with the rudiments of science, history, language, and mathematics, has been awakened to the possibilities of culture and is ambitious to possess it, when he has learned how to read and think, the school has done the most it can do. Its primary business is to equip him with tools of learning and culture and the impulse for larger attainments. Beyond this point other agencies must take him.

From the viewpoint of social science, the library has a twofold mission. It is the agency specially organized and maintained by the community to serve as an aid to the material progress of the individual and to promote the culture of a community through the individual. "Perhaps," to quote from Mr. Legler, "it may be said more accurately that its first mission is to give scope to its second. For, first of all, man must minister to his physical wants. Before there can be intellectual expansion and cultural development there must be leisure, or at least conditions that free the mind from anxious care for the morrow. So the social structure, after all, must rest, to some extent, upon a bread and butter foundation. Thus it follows, as a logical conclusion, that society as a whole cannot reach a high stage of development until all its industrial members are surrounded with conditions that permit the highest self-development. Until a better agency shall be found it is the public library which must serve this need." In giving skill to the hand of labor, in offering cheer and wider outlook upon life to the home, in rendering acute the thought of the community at large, it lays the true foundation of culture.

And by the culture which it is to promote is meant more than reading and more than information. "It is that compounding of learning, taste, judgment, wisdom, and peculiar mental tone that come of being in sympathetic acquaintance with what has been thought, felt and done in the world, and of companionship, even remote, with the men and women who have thought, felt and accomplished."

Thus both the school and the library have the same objective. Their ways of approach to it are frequently one and the same, and if at times divergent they both bring the individual to the same desired end. The school awakens wholesome personality and social impulses, both general and specific, trains the individual in the elements of the social arts, trains him to think and to study, equips him with the elements of learning. It supplies him with the implements with which he may attain to culture and endeavors to fit him for a larger and more permanent growth to come from activities beyond its doors. The promotion of this larger growth beyond the school; the addition of knowledge, power and culture to the individual's store through the page of the free open book; the development of strong, truth-loving character both in the child and the adult is the special field and the larger opportunity of the library.

However necessary it may be for us as schoolmen and librarians to define clearly for ourselves the theoretical functions of the school and the library as educators in order that we may comprehend the nature of our duties, it is equally necessary for us to direct our attention briefly to the practical methods by which they may best fulfil their missions. As the special problems of the school are being discussed in other departments of this Association, I shall pass at once to the consideration of the particular lines of work to which the library should devote itself. I can only hope to point out certain groups or classes with which the library should especially work without attempting to give any methods in detail.

The library's first duty, obviously, is to aid in the education of the child. Although its part in this special field is necessarily secondary to that of the school, its children's room should always be open; its tables and shelves should be supplied with the best of science, history, biography, literature and story; a trained children's librarian, who is a teacher as well, should be at hand to direct; the mysteries of the catalog should be revealed; and the use of the books should be made clear. If the child is not reached in the library, the central library, provision should be made for reaching it either by school depository or branch library in the school which the child attends or in the branch library in the neighborhood in which it lives. All of good which the library has at its command should be placed at his hand. Furthermore, it should be presented with such knowledge and sympathy as will result in the extension of the instruction imparted by the school and in a definite contribution of culture.

Its second duty is to the adult. It is a fact with which we are painfully conversant that less than 25 per cent of the children between 14 and 20 are in the public schools, including all the grades, and that but one American in a thousand claims a college or university as his foster mother. It is just here that the library finds its chief ground for existence. As soon as the child leaves the school it should enroll him as one of its beneficiaries and it should sustain to him and his father alike the relation of the great university to her sons. Books of knowledge and power, as defined by De Quincey, should be furnished this individual who has passed out of the doors of the school or college to stimulate his aspiration to fit himself for larger, fuller life, the attainment of which is wholly conditioned upon the increase of his intelligence and the improvement of his character.

In a peculiar sense the public library is the logical educator of what I may term special classes. A million or more immigrants, mostly adults, reach our shores annually, the great majority of whom, either because they are over age or because they are not masters of our language, find our schools closed to them. The library is the sole agency which can touch their lives and aid in fitting them for citizenship. It should teach the immigrant through books in his own tongue the principles of our government and a love for the Stars and Stripes which the school teaches the immigrant child. Professor Münsterberg, of Harvard, in speaking of the service rendered by the library to America's middle classes and especially to the foreign laborer, says, "America is the workingman's paradise, and attractive enough for the rich man; but the ordinary man of the middle classes, who in Germany finds his chief comfort in the Bierhalle, would not find comfort in America were it not for the public library which offers him a home."

I have already called attention to the necessity of training the laborer for his work. His head must be trained as well as his hand if he is to win a competence for himself and leisure for the acquisition of a larger culture. Speaking of this point, President Roosevelt sounded a very true note when he said, "Exactly as no other learning is as important for the average man as the learning which will teach him how to make his livelihood, so no other learning is as important for the average woman as the learning which will make her a good housewife and mother." Here then the library has its greatest opportunity, the enlightenment of the workshop and the worker's home.

The last duty of which I shall speak is to the municipality or state which appropriates constantly increasing sums for library maintenance. This service should be a direct one in addition to the indirect one of training individuals for citizenship. I refer to that work of the library or the library commission which has as its special object the collection of laws for the guidance of aldermen and legislators for study and comparison in enacting legislation which will consequently be beneficent and wise. This field has not heretofore been sufficiently well cultivated, but with the more generally prevailing wish on the part of citizens that knowledge shall grow from more to more, that city and state shall rule wisely and well, that laws shall find their basis in equity and justice to all, the demand for its cultivation becomes imperative.

To summarize, it is the duty of the public library to cooperate with the school in its endeavor to awaken in the citizen-to-be an inspiration to make the most of his powers; to give him the alphabet of learning and activity, to train his powers of thought and expression; and to supply him with the implements with which he may attain to culture. Apart from its connection with the school, its chief function is to serve as the lifelong university for the individual, in which he may find freely, without money and without price, an opportunity for the continuous development of all his powers.

This is the task as an educator which the public library has set itself. Although it incurs constantly increasing expense in doing its work, Professor Münsterberg, in speaking of its effectiveness, says: "Admittedly all the technical apparatus of library administration is expensive; the Boston Public Library expends every year a quarter of a million dollars for administrative purposes. But the American taxpayer supports this more gladly than any other burden, knowing that the public library is the best weapon against alcoholism and crime, against corruption and discontent, and that the democratic country can flourish only when the instinct of self-perfection as it exists in every American is thoroughly satisfied."

Such is the work of the public library. Such is its record of achievement. Granting that it has not always met the requirements made of it, the faults by which it has been marred will be eliminated, emotion and sentiment will be aided by reason in promoting its cause, and we of the South, though tardy, will join those of other sections in utilizing it as an institution making strong and permanent the foundation of our democratic American civilization.

The Library in the Advancing South

THE PURPOSE OF THIS PAPER is to set forth in its true perspective the status of the library in this extremely interesting and newly discovered South, to measure the effectiveness of the library in its various forms, and to suggest such measures and agencies as will result in making it the efficient instrument which it can be and must be in the development of a highly complex and enlightened Southern civilization.

I. *Library Perspective*

In considering the perspective of the Southern scene, as it relates to the library, there are certain facts which have influenced, and will continue to influence, Southern library development.

The first of these is that the nine states in this Southeastern Association are predominantly rural. Of the 19,309,643 people residing within them, 77 per cent, approximately 15,000,000 are rural. The average for the United States is 45.6 per cent while the per cents for South Carolina and Alabama, as contrasted with Massachusetts and Rhode Island, are 82.5 and 86.6, respectively, against 2.5 and 5.2. The bearing of this fact upon the library situation is strikingly obvious, when it is considered in relation to the further facts that these nine states comprise one-seventh of the total area of the Nation, and that the development of anything like adequate highway systems within them except in Florida and North Carolina is relatively not far advanced.

A second consideration is that of the 19,309,643 inhabitants 34 per cent, or six and a half million, are negroes, the number living within these nine states being approximately two-thirds of the total 10,463,131 colored population in the United States. The percentages

Reprinted from *Proceedings*, Southeastern Library Association, Fourth Biennial Conference, Signal Mountain, Chattanooga, Tennessee, April 22–24, 1926, pp. 3–11, by permission of the publisher.

of negro population in South Carolina and Mississippi are 51.4 and 52.2 respectively against 1.7 and 1.2 in Rhode Island and Massachusetts. Furthermore, not only is the per cent high, but a two-fold set of institutions has to be maintained to safeguard the separation of the races.

No true perspective can be gained of the library scene in this area which fails to take into account the true wealth of the section, as wealth and leisure seem to be fundamental to the acquisition and reading of books. Overlooking for the moment the land booms in Florida and Western North Carolina, the rapid increase throughout the nine states in wealth accumulations within the past decade, and the amazing annual crop values produced by the South but immediately exchanged for food and manufactured products from other sections of the country, the true wealth per capita of these nine states is outranked by that of thirty-four others. Oregon and California, in which there are relatively large rural populations, and in which library facilities rank very high, have a true per capita wealth of $4,182 and $4,007 respectively. The average for the United States is $2,918. The range in the nine states under consideration is from $2,358 in Florida down to $1,210 in Mississippi. Federal income tax returns for 1923 afford additional evidence on this fact. In California 13.6 of the inhabitants filed federal income tax returns for that year. In Mississippi only 1.56. The average for the United States was 6.94. Florida, with 4.74, stood 33rd and led the other eight.

However, while all these states ranked low in total wealth accumulations, the wealth of their inhabitants increased during the decade 1912–1922 faster than that of any other group of states in the Union. North Carolina led with an increase of 135 per cent. Tennessee followed second, Florida seventh, Mississippi ninth, Virginia and South Carolina eleventh and fifteenth. The bottom places so constantly held in the other instances were relinquished to Illinois, forty-third, Iowa, forty-fourth and California, hitherto always close to the top, forty-sixth. The explanation of this seemingly strange phenomenon is that the curve, which within the decade has swung so sharply towards the top, started from a point far nearer the bottom than it should.

The most important considerations in gaining the perspective desired are those of education, literacy or illiteracy, and the relation of the people to the soil which they cultivate.

In these considerations, the states again revert to the bottom position, although they stand high in the advances made since 1900 in expenditures for education and the reduction of the illiteracy rate.

From a table recently published in North Carolina's *State School Facts*, Vol. 1, No. 24, and showing the educational ranking of the states of the Union as to (1) average length of term, (2) per cent of school enrollment in high school, (3) average value of school property per child enrolled, and (4) current expense per child enrolled, it appears that California led the forty-eight states with an index number of 117.55. Virginia, ranking 39th, led our group of nine states with an index number of 54.56. The lowest number was 40.09, or practically one-third of that of the leader of the field. North Carolina's rank in these four respects was 48th in 1910, 45th in 1918, 43rd in 1920, and 42nd in 1922.

The significant fact here, however, is that while the nine states occupied positions, in 1920, from the standpoint of illiteracy (statistics by races are not given) ranging downward from 36th, in Kentucky, to 48th in South Carolina, the rate of expenditures for education, with the consequent reduction of the illiteracy totals, has been increasingly rapid since 1918. North Carolina spent for total school purposes in 1899–1900, $1,062,304; in 1918–19, $6,768,063; in 1923–24, $29,747,076. Her school property was valued in 1899–1900 at $1,097,564; in 1918–19, at $16,294,859; and in 1923–24, $59,-758,005. And, likewise, her illiteracy rate was cut from 1900 to 1920 from 25.4 to 13.1.

The blight of illiteracy has long been recognized. However, although Arthur Young, the English rural economist, said more than a century ago, "Give a man the secure possession of a bleak rock, and he will turn it into a garden; give him a nine-year lease on a garden and he will convert it into a desert," the blight of farm tenancy in the South has only within recent years become a subject of serious consideration, and, so far, instead of yielding to remedial measures, has steadily increased. Worn out soils, single crops, small annual yield produced without machinery on small farms by small-scale farmers, meager bank savings, represent the economic side of the picture, which Ellen Glasgow has made graphic in *Barren Ground*. The social side is characterized by constant moving from place to place, poor schools and churches, and inability to sustain over a period of years, any program of social or educational improvement. The old adage that a rolling stone gathers no moss may well be replaced by the dictum of the student of society today that no stable, enlightened community organization can be erected upon the shoulders of the roving farm tenant. In Florida and Virginia one farm out of every four is cultivated by a tenant; in Tennessee and North Carolina two out of every five; in Alabama and Mississippi three out of every five; and in South Carolina and Georgia two out of every three.

An equally weighty consideration is the unwillingness of the states to tax themselves for the support of the government. The South generally has resisted the payment of taxes as no other section, and, to a degree hardly realized by representatives of other sections, has limited the functions of government primarily to the provision of courts for the protection of property. Every step taken to provide benefits for all the population through taxation has been persistently and far too successfully resisted. The result is that today when the average inhabitant of the United States pays a per capita tax of $38.90 for state, county, and municipal purposes, eight of the nine pay from $21.50 down to $12.82 or only one-third of the average, while California, Oregon and Nevada pay from $59.86 to $82.09. Wherever you see a stretch of hard surfaced highway or a new school house in the Southeast today, you may rest assured that it has been provided only after a bitter struggle between highway enthusiasts and educational leaders on the one hand and the resistance of taxation on the other.

The considerations presented thus far have not had a direct bearing upon the library. The three which I now present do have.

Reading in the Southeast is less sustained than in any other section of the country. Whether the standard applied be that of the number of books upon the shelves of public and college libraries, or of circulation of national periodicals and daily newspapers, or the prevalence of bookstores, local publishing houses, and pages in the daily press devoted to book reviews—the result is everywhere the same. In these all-important respects, the Southeast stands at the foot, with an achievement equalling a fourth or at best a third of that for the remainder of the country.

It is only since the close of the World War that the Southeast has been economically able to interest itself vitally in the promotion of library activities on anything like an adequate basis. It was not until 1910 that the South regained the economic position it held in 1860, and it was not until 1920 that it reached the economic status held by other states of the nation in 1895 or 1900. The stimulation, therefore, which the donation of Carnegie buildings earlier exercised in other sections has been lost to it. A paragraph from *Publishers' Weekly* for April 3 shows the significance of this stimulation in other sections of the country and the consequent loss in the Southeastern area. From this paragraph it appears that "In the state of Indiana there were, in 1908, 23 public libraries; in 1923, there were 192, of which 155 were Carnegie libraries, while 14 new libraries were built by other types of support. In California, in 1896, there were 28 public libraries; in 1923, there were 169, and of this increase 119 were Carnegie libraries and 22 were from other sources. In the Eastern states, the library movement had been longer under way and the preponderance of Carnegie libraries is not the same, but he presented New York City with a whole system of 66 branch buildings." Statistics from *A Manual of the Public Benefactions of Andrew Carnegie* in 1919 show that, out of a total of 1,520 library buildings given in the United States, at a cost of $38,256,864.71, only 102, or one-fifteenth of the buildings were placed in the Southeast, and that the amount expended upon them was $2,502,461.00, or one-fifteenth of the total expenditure. Consequently, the Southeast has had to launch its drive for library support just at the moment when the stimulation of Carnegie buildings was withdrawn and when the automobile, the movie, the phonograph, the radio, and possibly even more important, the Sunday paper and popular periodical, reached their maximum efficiency in methods of distribution and popular appeal. Libraries in other sections already established and well underway have had their difficulties in meeting these rival interests, but these have been in no sense as great as those of the less well organized communities of the Southeast. Economic surplus rather suddenly acquired has naturally been used in supplying the more obvious types of satisfaction than that provided by the library.

The third special consideration is that of attitude towards the library. A question asked me in 1910 has always stuck in my memory, as it reveals, I think, a fundamental attitude, not of the old South,

but of the South of 1880 to 1920. The question was "do you think a
dollar spent for libraries is as well spent as a dollar spent for the
public schools?" Two college presidents reflected it from a different
angle when in a discussion some ten or fifteen years ago they decided
that the position of librarians should never rank, in the institutions
over which they presided, higher than that of associate professors. Another evidence, so far as the Southern business man is concerned, is that the special library—I do not refer to professional libraries—has not yet made its appearance in this area. Similarly men
of means have only to a very limited degree given or devised money
for library buildings or library purposes. Not having had the use of
college or public libraries that served them effectively, or having had
them only at widely separated points, the Southern public has largely
conceived of the library as an essential only to readers of fiction and
members of women clubs, and not an institution which has a worthwhile contribution to make to every member of a community. For
the college, and, to a less degree for the school, it has been considered something of a necessity, but in no sense has it been considered indispensable to the community at large. And even in the
instances of the schools and colleges, in spite of the fact that standards have been set up by educators and professional bodies, it is possible for a group of 2,000 teachers to meet in annual assembly, as
was done in North Carolina a month ago, and spend three days in
the discussion of school problems without having a single library
topic.

II. *The Present Scene*

The present status and efficiency of the library in this area are
being brought under frequent and serious review. It seems important
to me, however, to sketch in general terms the picture of library
agencies and activities in the South of today.

1. *School libraries.* Standards for secondary school libraries
were set up by the Southern Association of Colleges and Secondary
Schools about twelve years ago. These standards follow lines generally laid down in other sections of the country. Slightly modified,
they have been established by the various state departments of education. Requirements essential to accrediting have been set up as to

numbers of books, but no regulations have been provided concerning training and certification of teacher librarians. Likewise special library funds have not been appropriated for the provision of books. The result in North Carolina is that several hundred high school libraries in state-supported accredited schools have hastily accumulated 200,000 or 300,000 volumes and thereby the requirements have been met. In ten or a dozen instances the collections are admirably administered by technically trained librarians or teacher librarians, but in the main the second step of securing trained personnel and adequate maintenance funds has not been taken. The High School Inspector and other officers of the State Department of Education, and the Organizer of the Library Commission have given such time and thought to these matters as they have been able, but without being able to put the system on the basis desired.

2. *College and University Libraries.* The total resources of Southeastern college and university libraries are very limited. From a detailed study made in 1925 by a graduate student at the University of North Carolina it appears that according to population, the New England colleges and universities contain in their collections one book for each inhabitant, that the average for the colleges of the country as a whole is one book to every three and a half persons, and that the average for Southeastern college libraries is one book to every ten persons. Stated differently, students in the New England area have at their command ten times the number of college library books as Southern students. And not only are the total accumulations ten times greater, but the rate of addition of new volumes is much greater. The University of North Carolina library has been 130 years in building up a collection of 155,000, whereas the University of Michigan, in eighty-nine years, has built up a collection of 594,614 volumes. North Carolina is cited as one of the few libraries in the Southeast spending as much as $30.00 per year per student for library purposes or adding as many as 12,000 or 15,000 volumes.

3. *Public Libraries.* The three most significant facts concerning the resources of the public libraries of the South are: (1) They are available to only one-fifth of the total population; (2) they are available in only one-fourth the quantity that they are available upon the average throughout the United States; and (3) whereas the standard for maintenance per capita as set by the American Library Associa-

tion is $1.00, the actual average in the area is only about thirty cents.

4. *County Libraries.* Statistics for county libraries apart from public libraries, are not available for the Southeastern area. Few, if any county libraries, based upon the taxes for the whole county as a unit, exist in the area. On the other hand, county support, through county boards of commissioners and education, has been given to public libraries for county-wide service. The book truck has been introduced at Durham, Birmingham, and other places and the benefits of county service have been splendidly demonstrated.

5. *Library Schools.* The South has had only one library school for whites, the Library School of the Carnegie Library of Atlanta. In September of last year a school for negroes was opened at Hampton, Virginia. The significant fact, here, is that in these nine states, which now have an area two and a half times as large as that occupied by the nine states of the Northeast, and contain two-thirds as many people, there has been only one school with 16 students and 192 graduates as compared with eight library schools in the Northeastern area with over 300 students and 4,000 graduates. Few library institutes have been held by Southeastern library commissions and few courses on library subjects have been offered in the regular terms or summer sessions, and the enrollments in these courses have been comparatively small. The task, therefore, of supplying trained leaders for effective library development has only just begun.

6. *Library Associations, State Libraries, Commissions, and Extension Service.* Growing out of state library associations, which have been organized in all the states, have come formal library commissions or departments of other state agencies charged with the duty of some sort of library promotion. One of the first of the commissions to receive a separate appropriation and to define its activities was that of North Carolina which was organized in 1909. It set forth its duties as follows: (1) to operate package and traveling libraries, (2) to assist existing libraries, through visitation and advice, in the better performance of their duties, and (3) to stimulate and aid communities and the state in the development and perfection of additional libraries. It began the publication of a quarterly library bulletin, and, more recently, it has extended the scope of its operations by providing a type of reference service through the loan of books not to be found in local libraries, and by putting into the field

a library organizer whose full time is devoted to work in the field with school and public libraries. The state has increased its initial support from $1,500 to $25,000, and has given it the opportunity of demonstrating its effectiveness as a promotion agency. Kentucky and Georgia work through similar organizations and Florida is on the eve of putting one into operation. In Virginia, Tennessee, and Alabama, the state library or archives department assumes in whole or part responsibility for these activities, while in South Carolina and Mississippi the work is supplemented through the extension service of state institutions, and in all the states stimulation of school libraries is attempted by representatives of the departments of education.

7. *Legislative and Municipal Reference Libraries.* Formal legislative reference libraries render valuable assistance to legislators in Virginia and North Carolina as adjuncts to the State Library and the Historical Commission, and the type of material which is ordinarily made available to municipalities and county governments through municipal reference libraries is furnished by the departments of social science and the extension division of the state universities in the same states. In both instances the financial backing and personnel are sufficient to promote the work satisfactorily and its value has been widely recognized.

8. *Library Publications.* The meeting of the need for periodicals in the Southern library field has been attempted only in a few instances. The Virginia State Library has for a number of years published a bulletin devoted to bibliographical and historical uses; the North Carolina Library Commission, since 1909, has published a quarterly bulletin devoted to the promotion of general library interests; and since 1924 the library of the North Carolina College for Women has published monthly an annotated and stimulating monthly record of accessions.

9. *Work with Negroes.* Negroes constitute one-third of the population of the Southeast, but no well co-ordinated plan for the provision of library work for them has been carefully considered. Library training at Hampton has been provided and probably a most effective means for promoting activities in this field would be through the appointment of a field representative working probably in connection with the training school at Hampton. In this way, the field as a

whole, could be studied and instruction could be made to fit the special needs arising within it.

III. *The Future Prospect*

A detailed statement of the progress achieved in the Southeastern library field is not a primary concern at this time. The recital of this story, of the formation of state associations, of the organization of commissions, of the foundation and work of the library school, of the growth in bank resources and budgets, of the development of county service, and of the building up of a personnel of vision and skill, cannot be given now, however moving and inspiring it may be. Our major purpose here is not so much to review in detail existing library facilities or library growth, but rather to discover agencies and means by which a far finer chapter of library achievement may be written in the future than has been in the past. To this end I offer the following suggestions:

1. *Professorships of Books.* That for the building up of a group of citizens throughout the area who will understand the real value of the library as an agent of society and therefore support it adequately and intelligently, there be established in connection with the library certainly at each state university, a professorship in the use of books and bibliography. The incumbent of such a position should give instruction in the use of books to undergraduates in the schools of arts and sciences, education, and journalism. He should train first year law students in legal bibliography, and through him, as a representative of the library and not of the graduate school, should be given the foundational courses in general bibliography required of graduate students. His further duties should be to organize and direct the courses offered school librarians in the summer session, and to contribute to the library and educational journals of his state articles on various phases of library activities in line with his work. His function would not only be to make the library with which he is connected a finer teaching instrument, but he should be the developer of what the psychologists might call an apperceiving group in the state at large, which, later, could intelligently support all phases of the library movement.

2. *Library Schools and Summer Courses.* Facilities for training

more skilled library workers should be multiplied as rapidly as the
demand for their services increase. The Southern field should be
carefully studied from the point of view of the needs of the area and
additional library schools should be established to meet the need.
Likewise, the field should be studied for the purpose of determining
the location of summer school courses particularly for school librarians, the instruction to be provided by the institution concerned,
with the cooperation of the state library commission and the state
department of education. Through the cooperation of these three
groups a teacher-librarian certificate ought to be provided by the
state department of education, whereby the teacher who takes these
courses may have her certificate raised and her salary accordingly
increased just as in the case of professional educational courses at
present.

3. *High School Libraries.* The most strategic point for immediate library advance in the Southeast is offered by the high schools.
Within the past twenty years in North Carolina the high school enrollment has increased from 2,000 to 70,000. The amount expended
for instruction has likewise jumped from a few hundred thousand
dollars into the millions, and no finer buildings are to be found in
the state than the modern high school structures which are the pride
of hundreds of communities. The people have been "sold" the school
idea. Therefore, in spite of the traditional attitude of the library
world towards the separation of school and library, the question of
relationship should be re-examined and the opportunity of serving
the present generation of high school pupils should be seized and
improved. Today the schools have the pupils, the money, and the
public confidence, and criticism of them and the aloofness on the
part of librarians will not take the place of careful study and putting
the library to work through them.

4. *Library Commissions.* The library commissions of the Southeast have rendered valuable service in library promotion. There is a
question, however, whether or not there has been a tendency on the
part of the commissions to shift the emphasis of the function of the
office from library promotion in its large aspects to the provision of
state-wide library service or some other administrative concern. Invaluable as state-wide service may be in this area, library service is
available to only 20 per cent of the population; equal emphasis

should be placed by commissions on making contacts strategic to library advancement, maintaining an intimate advisory relationship with librarians already in the field, and promoting legislation favorable to the best forms of library development.

5. *County Libraries.* The county library, supported by the taxes levied on the total property of the county, unquestionably offers the best means of library development in this area and means should be devised by which the idea can be advanced, in season and out, until its adoption becomes general. In instances where counties are too small to afford adequate support, two counties should be urged to unite. The approach to this whole question of county libraries may have to be made in connection with the schools, as the consolidated school and good roads are the only public institutions which have won anything like a general acceptance among all the people.

5. *Field Representatives and Standing Committees.* As I look back over the story of development in the Southeast during the past twenty-five years, I am impressed with the fact that the great advances made in education, highway construction, sanitation and hygiene, and domestic economy, have been stimulated and directed in large measure by field representatives or associations or national boards who have been able to visualize the particular problems from many points of view, and, while freed from administrative details, have been able to devote their entire thought and energy to the solution of the particular problems before them. It will never be possible to estimate the services of men like J. L. M. Curry and Wallace Buttrick to the cause of general education in the South. The development of Southern schools of education has been wonderfully stimulated by gifts of buildings from the Peabody fund. The rise of Southern high schools—possibly the most notable development witnessed in Southern educational history—has had back of it the assistance of the General Education Board through which salaries for professors of secondary education and high school inspectors were paid over a period of years. The practical wiping out of typhoid fever and hook worm disease and the reduction of malaria have in large measure depended upon the sustained cooperation of the Rockefeller Foundation. The field representatives of these boards have rendered invaluable services, and I believe, something of this nature is particularly desirable at present in the field of library promotion.

Just what form this assistance should take is a matter for the best
thought of this association, of the state associations and commissions, of colleges and state departments of education, of the A.L.A.,
and of groups and foundations interested in this phase of development in the Southeast. Special representatives to promote the work
with white and colored libraries, standing committees, local and national, with financial support, professorships of books as suggested
earlier, additional library schools and summer courses, a closer connection with the high schools—these are some of the instruments
which should be provided in larger measure to insure the Southeast
of the accumulation and use of library resources of which she stands
in need.

A final word about the need. To a group of librarians this may
seem superfluous. Certainly I am not advocating the expenditure of
energy and the time and funds for library purposes simply that we
of the Southeast may stand, statistically on a more equal footing
with representatives of other sections. It is rather that we may perfect an institution which has demonstrated its value as an instrument
in the development of an intelligent and highly complex civilization.
It is that the institution to which we have dedicated our lives may
assist this new advancing South in the discovery and use of those
things which will multiply the more enduring satisfactions of its expanding life.

The Growing Importance of Libraries

THE CELEBRATION OF THE FIFTIETH ANNIVERSARY of the founding of
the American Library Association, October 4–9, participated in by
delegates from a score or more foreign countries and widely noted
throughout America, has contributed greatly to the recognition of

Reprinted from *Proceedings*, Association of Colleges and Secondary Schools of
the Southern States, Jackson, Mississippi, December 3–4, 1926, pp. 225–230,
by permission of the publisher.

the growing importance of the library as one of the principal instruments which America employs for the educational development of its
people. Among the notable developments in the library field brought
to the attention of the nation by that great gathering, and otherwise
during the past twelve months, were the following which should receive consideration by this Association:

Training is Essential for Librarianship

The first of these is that unusual recognition has been given by
American universities of the importance of library training as an
essential part of a university's curriculum. Although library schools
have been in existence in the United States since 1887, it was only in
1926 that training for librarianship on a basis similar to that for the
profession of teaching, or of other professions, was placed on a
satisfactory university basis by American universities. This change
has been effected in two ways. The requirement of an A. B. degree
has been made the foundation on which the library curriculum will
hereafter rest and the character of the degree hitherto awarded
upon the completion of the library course has been altered.

The two-year library school of the University of Illinois, which
hitherto has granted the special degree of B.S. in Library Science,
discontinued the special degree and hereafter will award the regular
master's degree upon the completion of the second year, thereby lifting an inequality from the shoulders of students in the library field
which hitherto has placed them at a disadvantage in comparison
with graduates in education on other allied subjects. The year has
also witnessed the establishment of a new library school, with a two-
year curriculum and leading to the master's degree, at the University
of Michigan, and the combining, at Columbia University, of the
former library schools of the New York City Public Library and the
New York State Library in a school which also confers the master's
degree. In the South, entrance into the library school of the Carnegie
Library of Atlanta has been placed on the basis of an A.B. degree
and the school has been coordinated with Emory University. At the
University of Chicago, through a special grant of $1,385,000, made
by the Carnegie Corporation of New York, provision has been made
for America's first advanced graduate library school, which is to be

organized exactly as other graduate schools of the University. It will receive students in 1927, and offer advanced courses leading to the degrees of A.M. and Ph.D. upon the completion of highly specialized courses and extensive investigations in the field of library theory and practice.

Summer Courses Extended

In this same connection, the summer of 1926 was notable for the number of summer courses offered by universities and library schools in library subjects for the benefit of school and teacher-librarians and librarians for small public libraries, the courses leading to appropriate degrees and, in many instances, being recognized by state departments of education by appropriate credit toward the certification of teachers. Unfortunately such courses were offered in only three Southern universities.

Standards Adopted for Library Schools

A second significant record, paralleling the organization of advanced schools of library science and the offering of instruction through summer schools in library methods for high school and small public librarians, was made by the Board of Education for Librarianship of the American Library Association which completed a survey of all the regular library schools and published a list of those which could be accredited in accord with a system of carefully prepared standards. While no list was published of accredited agencies offering summer courses, many of the agencies were visited during the summer, and standards, both for summer courses and for the preparation of school librarians, were worked out and approved. In this way the whole field of training for librarianship has been subjected to a careful and prolonged study and the standards have, in large measure, been put into operation. A further function of this Board has also been to encourage the establishment of additional library schools, and to seek the establishment of scholarships and fellowships for prospective librarians. The most recent standards to be adopted by the Board are those relating to the preparation of fulltime school librarians for the larger high schools. These standards

were adopted at Atlantic City in October, and are being forwarded
to the respective library schools for incorporation in their curricula.

Notable Library Surveys Completed

Students of education are constantly overwhelmed by the multiplicity of theses and new publications dealing with every phase of their
subjects. The quest for subjects for doctoral theses has gone so far,
I am informed, that recently an aspirant for the Ph.D. in education
at one of our largest institutions wrote his thesis on the subject, "The
School Door Mat." But such has not been the case in the field of librarianship. Until the present year, the literature of library science,
other than that contained in *The Library Journal, Public Libraries,*
and *The Bulletin of the American Library Association,* has been
limited to a comparatively few publications containing the results of
extensive library surveys. The meeting at Atlantic City emphasizes
a third significant development in the library field, namely, the beginning of an era of publication of library investigations and surveys. The achievements of the year in this respect comprised the issuing of the following publications worked out by special boards
and committees which had been carrying on investigations over a
period of years: (1) I mention first the "A.L.A. Catalog, an Annotated Basic List of 10,000 Books," which will be an indispensable
library tool to every public, school, and college library in the country. (2) The second is "Library Extension, A Study of Public Library Conditions and Needs," which covers every phase of public
library endeavor, with the conditions prevailing in each state presented statistically. (3) "Libraries and Adult Education" is a third
publication which treats matters of such fundamental importance as
self-education with Library guidance, library assistance to adult
education agencies, development of reading interests and habits, the
library and rural adult education, coordination of local, state, and
university extension library resources, etc. (4) "A Survey of Libraries in the United States," in two volumes, is the fourth. The first
volume is devoted to the administrative work of public libraries and
of college and university libraries. Both have been long needed and
contain information hitherto uncollected and not accessible except
by piecemeal and through questionnaires. (5) "The Circulation of

Books in Public Libraries," the fifth publication, is one of the first texts dealing with technical library procedure and has been issued in mimeographed form and is now being tested by libraries and library schools before being issued in book form. It covers every phase of work connected with the loaning of books, and is first of a series of notable library texts now in preparation.

County Libraries Developed

The fourth distinctive development of the year has been effected through the county library. Recognition of the fact has gained ground that the county library, like the consolidated school, is the most effective type of library for providing library service for rural areas. The county unit makes for economy and effectiveness without loss of personal touch, and through an adequate system of branches, stations, school deposits, mail service, and book trucks, puts books into the hands of any citizen of the county wherever he may live, the cost of service being met out of taxes levied upon the property of all the county. Laws permitting the establishment of such libraries have been enacted in 31 states, and in a number of others provision has been made permitting county boards of education or county commissioners to contract with existing city libraries for service to the rural population. Among the Southeastern states, North Carolina has twelve counties in which this limited type of service is provided; whereas, in California, the resources of 45 of the 58 counties having county libraries are as follows: Income, $1,617,500; books, 3,588,-895; circulation, 8,887,144, with service to all schools in addition to the library resources of the schools themselves.

School Libraries Improved

To put one's finger on a specific advance in school library work, particularly that of the rural districts, may be difficult, but a summary of the activities engaged in by the supervisors of school libraries of eight of the states having such officers connected with the state departments of education and of other officers connected with other library agencies, reveals the fact that progress of a very gratifying sort has been made in the field. In Wisconsin, every approved high school must have a certified librarian. In New York state, a school library fund of $125,000 is made available to the schools, and in practically every state lists of books for both the elementary and high schools, with manuals for the use of books and library resources, are provided by some state agency. Standards of equipment and book and periodical resources have been generally formulated, and instruction in library methods for the preparation of teacher-librarians has been extensively provided in normal schools and summer schools. A summary of the duties of the library supervisor of the State of New York may serve to indicate the development within this field and prove suggestive to this Association. The duties of this officer involve: (1) The distribution of the state aid fund of $125,000 for books and other library equipment; (2) The handling of librarian certification; (3) Approval of courses for the training of teacher-librarians and school librarians; (4) Recommending librarians for positions in schools; (5) Preparation of manuals on the use of books and library materials; (6) Inspection and organization of school libraries; (7) Correspondence concerning various library activities; (8) Planning library rooms and equipment; (9) Office interviews concerning library matters; (10) Book selection and list-making; (11) Preparation of articles on library subjects for school and library publications and the press; (12) Participation in school and library meetings; (13) Conducting surveys of library conditions prevailing in city and rural school systems and proposing remedies for the existing conditions.

Library Work With Negroes

The year 1925–26 marked the beginning of formal library training for Negroes through the establishment of a library school at Hampton Institute. Provision was made for the establishment of the school by the Carnegie Corporation of New York, in cooperation with the General Education Board and the Board of Education for Librarianship of the American Library Association. The necessary funds were provided by the Carnegie Corporation and scholarships for the students enrolled were provided by the General Education Board. The purpose of the school is to train librarians for the schools and colleges and branch libraries for Negroes in the south. The establishment of the school marks a new step in Southern education,

and calls for the thoughtful cooperation of the Southern state departments of education and Southern library commissions in the direction of their work with Negroes. The establishment of the school
brings up for consideration a question which hitherto has been generally overlooked, namely, the relation which should exist between
the existing school and library agencies and the Negro libraries. Inasmuch as little attention has been given to the development of library resources for Negroes in some of the states, a number of Negro
libraries have sprung up in cities entirely independent of the general
library system of the cities in which they are located. Cooperation
with the school and the proper absorption of its graduates by the
school and city library systems would seem to be highly desirable at
this particular time.

New Library Buildings Provided

A final development worthy of mention is that within the year
several notable library buildings have been opened for the use of
city and college and university constituencies. In the future it is
highly probable that all new municipal library buildings will be influenced by the plans of the new central library building of the city
of Cleveland. At no place in the country, certainly, has a finer instrument for the education and enlightenment of a whole city been
worked out and placed in such satisfactory operation. Organized
somewhat on the plan of a great university with various departments,
but, in this instance, united under one roof and tied in closely with
appropriate book collections, the building affords the entire city a
superb continuation school for all of its citizens. In it, more than in
any city library in the country, have been found the means of promoting effectively the best sort of adult education.

The year has also witnessed, within the collegiate and university
fields, the planning or completion of some notable college and university library buildings. At Yale the great collections of the University are to be brought together in the Sterling Library now being
erected, which is to cost between four and six million. At Dartmouth, with a student body limited to 2,000, a building to cost
twelve hundred thousand is being erected which will make possible
the utilization of the best in library practice for the instruction and

inspiration of the student group. In our Southern field, among the most notable buildings completed are those of North Carolina State, Louisiana State University, Duke, and Emory. In the planning of these buildings and in the planning of others now under construction or in contemplation, there has been evidenced the deepening conviction on the part of Southern educational institutions that the library, next to the group of skilled teachers and investigators gathered together into a well organized faculty, is the most effective instrument of instruction that the modern college or university possesses. Its functions have been subjected to an unusually critical review in the light of its development and use in other sections of the country, with the result that there is general agreement that the present generation of college students cannot be adequately trained to meet the rapidly increasing complexities of Southern life unless, in general and special reading rooms, in seminars, in stalls within the stack, they are surrounded with an abundance of materials on every subject embraced within the curriculum and are given the training in the expert handling of these materials essential to the furthering of the study or investigation in hand. The realization has become more and more general that the lecture and the textbook, even in the high school, may have to yield place somewhat to the library. The South, which, unfortunately, has not had available for the use of its students such library resources as other sections of the country possess and utilize in every phase of their work, has begun to realize what this lack is costing it in educational efficiency. It has begun to understand that the library, while it may not be able to equal such tools as direct thinking, observation, or intercourse by word of mouth in the classroom, may well arouse the mind to the employment of these other tools, supplement them with a knowledge of what diverse and perhaps clearer minds have thought, and furnish that quieter, richer background of accumulated fact and wisdom which is often the sharpest spur to right valuation and creative accomplishment in human life.

Application to Southern Conditions

It would doubtless be too much to expect me to conclude this recital without pointing out a moral insofar as the story has significance for the South. I shall content myself, however, with the briefest sort of moralizing. Today the South no longer has as its chief concern the driving of the wolf from the door. Today, on the contrary, it has the opportunity to evaluate those standards and agencies which can best assist it in the fashioning of a finer intellectual and cultural as well as economic and social life. If, in addition to consolidating the ground won in its economic rehabilitation, it is to fashion a finer social, intellectual, and cultural order, it will have to multiply many fold from the elementary school all the way up and out into its expanding, advancing life, its library resources.

New Objectives for Southern Libraries

THE PURPOSES OF THIS PAPER are three. I wish to review the background of two meetings dealing with libraries in the south in 1911 and 1926 respectively; to summarize conditions and ideas relating to libraries which exist in the south today; and to propose objectives for the united action of southern librarians and others interested in the future library development of the south.

Platform for School Libraries

In 1911, I served as chairman of the department of libraries of what was then known as the Southern Educational Association. In that capacity I presented a paper before the association entitled "A Constructive Library Platform for Southern Schools."[1] The library department of the association was the only interstate body of librarians in the south at that time, and its members numbered less than fifty. The meeting of the association was held at Houston, Texas.

Reprinted from *Bulletin*, American Library Association, 28:845–858, December, 1934, by permission of the publisher. Presidential address before the ALA Regional Conference of the Southeastern and Southwestern Library Associations at Memphis, Tennessee, 1934.

[1]For notes, see page 51.

Modeled after the National Education Association, but limited in its field to problems concerning education in the south, the association was less concerned with colleges and secondary schools than its younger sister, the Association of Colleges and Secondary Schools of the Southern States, and its sessions were participated in less extensively by educators and civic leaders from the north and east than the Conference for Education in the South whose interest was centered largely upon a better type of economic and industrial education for the section.

A number of the papers presented at the meeting dealt with the education of the mountain girl, the farm boy, the southern Negro. Several of the speakers, veterans of the Civil War, so extended their reminiscences and so overspoke their time that the one paper on libraries had to be presented by title only and discovered, if discovered at all, in the proceedings published six months later.

My paper dealt with the status of libraries, particularly school libraries, then existing in the south. Each of the states represented had developed between 1900 and 1911 a system of what were known as "$30 elementary school libraries." These contained over 2,000,000 volumes. Limited instruction in the use of libraries was given at only a half dozen institutions in the south, teachers' institutes devoted little consideration to the subject, no plans had been perfected for the exchange of book collections among schools within counties, and state teachers' associations rarely scheduled papers on school or other kinds of libraries in their annual programs. In my "constructive platform" I described this situation and urged: (a) the training of school librarians, (b) the provisions of means of circulating collections within counties, (c) the development of systems of public and traveling libraries, (d) the training of teachers in the use of libraries, (e) and the appointment of school library supervisors.

Progress Prior to 1926

The second meeting was held in 1926. Signal Mountain was the place and the Southeastern Library Association was the organization in session. The library setting of that meeting and the participants in the conference were very different from those of 1911. The Southern Educational Association and the Conference for Education in the South had both expired in 1915. They had been unable to survive the first year of the World War. Their younger members had become in large measure members of the Association of Colleges and Secondary Schools of the Southern States and the N.E.A. The librarians who constituted the membership of the Southeastern Library Association, organized in 1920, had been drawn together through an impelling interest in and enthusiasm for effective library development. They were seeking assistance from every quarter. To that end they extended invitations to participate in their conference to three of the principal boards of the A.L.A., to representatives of national educational foundations, and to representative educational leaders and high school inspectors throughout the south. The best library experience, whatever its origin, was carefully sought, and the objectives for which the association was urged to work in a paper entitled "The Library in the Advancing South"[2] were: (a) provision of library extension agencies for all the states, (b) establishment of more library schools, (c) adoption of an effective system of high school libraries, (d) development of county libraries, (e) appointment of school library supervisors, (f) provision of a library field representative for the south, and (g) participation in library development by educational foundations.

Present Library Conditions

Today, eight years after the Signal Mountain meeting, we are holding in Memphis a regional conference which embraces the Southeastern and Southwestern Library Associations under conditions that are in many respects significantly new. If I may, I wish to consider what it is that is new in this setting.

Organization. The first new fact I should note in the situation is that of library organization. In this respect the southern library field exhibits much that it did not in 1926. It is more definitely and adequately organized than it has ever been. Every state within the two associations has a statewide library association and all of the states have library commissions or other library extension agencies except Arizona and Alabama. The number of these agencies has increased from six in 1926 to fourteen in 1934. (Three of them, however, are still without appropriation.) Six of the states in the area have full-time school library supervisors. All of these offices have been established since the Signal Mountain meeting. In 1926 only two library schools existed in the south. They were located at Atlanta and at Hampton and served whites and Negroes respectively. The list today includes additional library schools at William and Mary, North Carolina, Peabody, Alabama, Kentucky, Louisiana, Oklahoma, Our Lady of the Lake, Texas State College for Women, and briefer courses and summer courses for the training of teacher-librarians and school librarians are offered by various institutions in every state in the area with the exception of Arizona, Arkansas, and New Mexico. To me, the most significant aspect of this conference is the number of organized groups—county librarians, school library supervisors, directors of library schools, policy committees, et al.—gathered here that have been brought into existence since 1926 and whose experience and vision are available for future library development .

Cooperation with Other Agencies. The second of these new conditions is that of effective collaboration with other organizations and agencies. Today the Southeastern and Southwestern Associations enjoy the support of a greatly extended and influential group of collaborators. In 1926 both associations consciously sought the assistance of the Association of Colleges and Secondary Schools of the Southern States in establishing standards for school and college libraries. They successfully gained it and cooperation with that association has steadily increased and standing committees of librarians and schoolmen are harmoniously at work on the common problem of perfecting a more adequate program of school library service. Reports from these committees biennially record distinctive progress. Similar cooperation with educational bodies has also carried over into individual states, particularly into those in which school library supervisors have been appointed. As a result state departments of education have added school and children's librarians to educational committees charged with curriculum revision, the preparation of book lists for state school systems, and the conduct of state school surveys. These departments have generally recognized the educational importance of the library to the school and have increasingly sought the assistance of librarians in planning courses for school and teacher-librarians and in perfecting plans of library organization and service to schools.

Effective collaboration has also been established with civic bodies. Notable examples of this nature have been demonstrated in the organization of the Citizens' Library Movement in North Carolina,[3] in the support given various library extension agencies in their effort to maintain their appropriations during recent sessions of legislatures, in the establishment of the Rosenwald-aided and other county and city libraries, and particularly in such state-wide and sectional conferences as those held at the University of North Carolina[4] and Clemson College,[5] at which the promotion and support of library service was accepted not merely as a concern of librarians, but of editors, churchmen, schoolmen, public health and social workers, and of people and organizations engaged in every kind of civic enterprise.

Collaboration with the A. L. A. has taken the very important form of the provision of a southern field representative. This office is entirely new in American library development and it has served the library interests of the south in much the same way that representatives of foundations have served the south since 1900 in promoting public health, in stimulating research and investigation in the social sciences, and in cooperating with southern leaders in the development of a more adequate program of elementary, secondary, and higher education for the whole area. This office, established by the A.L.A. in 1930 and supported by the Carnegie Corporation, has not only been in constant contact with librarians in the section but has served as a valuable consultant to educational and civic leaders and foundations in all matters relating to library development in the area. Cooperation with the officers of these associations in the organization and direction of this unusually successful conference is the latest instance of its value as an important collaborating agency.

The collaboration of the Carnegie Corporation, the General Education Board, and the Rosenwald Fund has likewise been notable. These foundations, long interested in the south, have contributed in different ways to the establishment of library schools, the provision of library school scholarships and fellowships, the holding of library institutes, the survey of library conditions, the stimulation of county libraries, the provision of a state-wide library demonstration, the strengthening of college and university library resources, and in the constant study of means of increasing the efficiency of library service in the area.

The most recent addition to these groups and organizations is the Tennessee Valley Authority. Its unprecedented experiment in the social, economic, and industrial fields, so boldly conceived and based upon the support of the federal government, has stirred the imagination of the nation, and its recent appointment of a library consultant concerning library development within its bounds has been welcomed with high expectancy in all the south.

Conditions Being Studied. A third new characteristic of the development of the southern library situation since 1926 is that a far greater body of information concerning the south's economic and social status is available than formerly. Furthermore, it is in such form that it can be readily used in the study of library conditions. From studies by Vance[6] and Odum,[7] at the University of North Carolina, the south is shown to be rich in human resources, but poor in financial resources to insure their adequate development. The per capita wealth of the south is lower than that of any other section, while the per cent of its population of school age is greater than that of any other. Conversely, the per cent of the adult population, which may be thought of as having to provide support for the school age group, is lower. North Carolina, for example, with a population of three million and a quarter, has over 900,000 children of school age. Chicago, with the same population, has only 700,000 children of school age. And in addition, North Carolina has to provide a dual set of schools for two races. In California, where libraries are particularly well supported, the ratio of children to adults is even lower than in Chicago, and, to that extent, the problem of school and library support is simpler. From studies by the Graduate Library School of the University of Chicago[8] it is also apparent that although school children and students constitute a comparatively small per cent of the population, they constitute a larger per cent of the library registrants of the nation, and borrow a still larger per cent of the books lent by public libraries. The study of the Rosenwald-aided libraries[9] shows an even higher per cent of books borrowed by students than by any other element of the population in the south. From other studies, by Cheney[10] and Gray,[11] it is known that the south has relatively fewer libraries, bookstores, news stands, and other agencies for the distribution of reading material than the west or north, while its ratio of illiteracy, farm tenancy, rural population, and dependence upon agriculture rather than upon industry, is high.

New Social Concepts

New organizations, new collaborators, new information have likewise been attended by the emergence of a host of new ideas since the meeting at Signal Mountain in 1926. An unprecedented depression has stirred the nation to thought. The terms New Deal, social trends, planned society, have become as familiar to everyone as square deal and normalcy were a decade or so ago. A half dozen of these new conceptions have great importance for southern library development.

School Libraries. First among them I should place the conviction now shared by southern schoolmen generally that school libraries are educational necessities. Time was when many people considered them frills. The widely advertised taxpayers' league in many quarters still do. But modern methods of teaching have demonstrated their indispensability and progressive southern schoolmen know that the school cannot prepare the oncoming generation for its social and cultural responsibilities without them. They know that the school which depends upon the single textbook is as outmoded as the Model T. They know that if books, magazines, pamphlets, and pictures to be used under expert supervision are absent, good teaching and adequate preparation for citizenship are impossible.

The New Leisure. In the second place, we have been rudely confronted with the idea of leisure. Thousands of young people who have gone out from the high schools of the nation since 1930 have not been able to find work. The Civilian Conservation Corps has absorbed some, and the National Recovery Act has attempted to distribute the opportunity to earn a living among the millions of the unemployed by reducing the hours of labor per week. But the ranks of the unemployed still run into the millions and leisure, whether for the young or the old, and however occasioned, is here to stay.

Adult Education: A Challenge. Closely joined to this idea is another. If leisure is to be used profitably, much of it must be spent in continuing education. Adult education as a means of learning new vocations and making new adjustments to life, of preserving metal health and morale, of increasing intellectual and spiritual capacity, is a concept with which we have become familiar and about which society is doing and must do something. In 1932 we saw 4,000,000 new borrowers crowd into our libraries. In February, 1934, in great centers like New York and Chicago, in rural areas, in Civilian Conservation Corps camps, we saw almost over night 925,000[12] men and women enrolled in vocational and adult classes taught by a new corps of 30,000 Federal Emergency Relief Administration teachers. In addition to this new body of students,—an enrollment almost equal to that of all American colleges and universities—thousands of other adults were engaged in more or less formal study under other longer established adult educational agencies. Even if there were no unemployment, the complexity of modern life is such as to require constant study after the period of formal education is ended to keep abreast with the changes which science and invention produce.

Fewer Political Units. A fourth idea which has recently gained wide acceptance is that the number of political units of government should be greatly reduced in behalf of more effective service. Larger units of government and quicker methods of transportation, which increase the adequacy of support and extend the range of unified service, are recognized as desiderata that now have a place in most social planning. They are particularly applicable in library promotion in the southern area where individual communities and even single counties are frequently not large enough or wealthy enough to provide adequate library support. Library laws embodying these ideas have recently been passed in Michigan and South Carolina and librarians everywhere in America are considering similar measures. Helen Gordon Stewart, pioneering in library development in Fraser Valley, has said that a regional library cannot be operated effectively which does not serve from 20,000 to 40,000 people and does not have an income of at least $20,000.[13]

Government Aid for Libraries. A final set of new ideas about which librarians have previously been excessively timid but are now becoming bold are those of state and federal aid and careful planning for libraries. There is nothing timid about the proposals by Commissioner Cocking,[14] of Tennessee, Mr. Modisette,[15] of Louisiana, and Miss Robinson,[16] of Mississippi. Their proposals to put the full power of the state department of education behind library development, to appropriate $2,000,000 for library service, and to utilize Federal Emergency Relief Administration workers in developing county library service in their respective states no longer frighten us. We know that formal and informal education are dependent upon books and libraries. We also know that if both types of educational opportunity are to be provided equally for all the population, both state and federal aid will be required. We know that planning that looks to the educational and cultural advancement of our civilization as a whole will have to receive from us the profoundest consideration we can give it. We know that while the Tennessee Valley Authority is putting rivers to work to electrify farms in the Tennessee Valley and to elevate the economic status of a great area, we must put books to work to electrify and illumine the hands and minds of the south as a whole and lift it to a higher social and cultural level.

A Ten Plank Library Platform

So far, I have considered the background and the new organization, information, collaboration, and ideas associated with the library movement in the south. I now wish to propose objectives which, if achieved, will result in a marked advance in southern library service.

The Library a Social Agency. The first objective I shall set up is a redefinition of library service in terms of the needs of the south. I believe and have believed for years that many of us in the south think of the library as a literary rather than as a social institution. We think of it as an institution through which we gain acquaintance with authors of literary forms rather than as an institution that can convey to us ideas to be utilized in daily living or in acquiring and broadening our general education. We have not thought of it as a symbol of democracy and as an equalizer of educational opportunity as the north and west thought of it during the rising tide of immigration and the building up of the west. We have largely failed to think of it as vocational or utilitarian. We have invested it too much with the aristocratic tradition of the Old South and have draped it as it were with a kind of literary or cultural Spanish moss. We have too narrowly limited its usefulness in adjusting the individual to his future economic and social environment. What is desired in library service in the south is a nice adjustment to both the practical and cultural needs of the people. The willingness of the Californian to tax himself $1 per capita for rural library service to adults and from $25 to $50 per teacher for school library service may be explained in part by the fact that the function of libraries in that state is more adequately conceived in these respects than it is in the south. It may also account in part for the greater per cent of books dealing with home economics, agriculture, and other practical arts and the closer integration of library service in California with agricultural and health and other services than in the south. The south has specific needs to which library service can and should minister. Our first task, then, is to define them and to adjust library service to them.

Facilities for Professional Research. The second objective I propose is a more intensive and more objective study of southern library conditions. Recently I have been comparing the means which librarians and schoolmen employ in reaching a fuller understanding of their respective fields. As a result I have come to the conclusion that by and large librarians depend far more upon attendance at library meetings and the reading of library literature for their professional advancement and the solution of library problems than upon advanced study and investigation. In this respect they differ sharply from schoolmen. The reasons for this, of course, may be altogether convincing. Vacations are not so available. Library schools have not been staffed and equipped for the effective study of problems under laboratory or experimental conditions. Reduced staffs and budgets, with increased service, have made absence for study impossible. However this may be, during the summer of 1934 only 121 of the 20,000 or 30,000 librarians in service pursued advanced work in American library schools.

Of the 121 students who were enrolled, 64 were from college, teachers college, and university libraries; 29 were school librarians, including 2 children's librarians employed by two public libraries; 12 were faculty members of other library schools; 9 came from public libraries; 5 were unemployed; 1 had been employed at A. L. A.

Headquarters; and 1 was librarian of a commercial chemical company. The fact remains, however, that the library is a public, social institution. Inasmuch as society is constantly undergoing significant change, the library must strive to fit itself to meet such new requirements as this change makes necessary—a task which it will be able to perform satisfactorily only through study, investigation, and experimentation. In view of this situation it is imperative that the A. L. A. Advisory Board for the Study of Special Projects, library school faculties, and advanced students undertake special studies in the library field and utilize members of social science research institutes and investigators in various university departments to assist in the careful study of library problems. Southern librarians share this responsibility with librarians in general and should organize their resources of investigation accordingly. Studies by the Tennessee State Department of Education,[14] theses and reports prepared by Peabody[17] and Emory[18] library schools, and the study by Wilson and Wight[9] indicate some of the directions which investigation in the southern area should take.

Extension of Training Agencies. The third objective which the south should strive for is more extended and effective library training. This training should take three directions. It should place emphasis upon nice adjustment of library service to practical and social ends as well as upon technical procedures; it should make possible greater specialization in different library fields; it should foster the spirit of scientific investigation in the solution of library problems. Through such training, the college librarian should know how to organize and administer his library in accord with the curricula of 1934—not of 1929. He should know the fashion in curricula in socially minded colleges as well as in classification and cataloging. When his faculty changes the curriculum, he should help change it, because the library must provide many of the materials through which the change is effected. The public librarian should have a definite understanding of the general objectives of society and the way in which the library may cooperate with other public agencies in achieving them. This may involve knowledge of the groups into which the population is divided, their educational attainments, the nature of the demands which they may legitimately make upon the library, and the standards by which effective service to all patrons may be appropriately measured. Competent diagnosis of these situations is essential to correct prescription of service and the southern librarian, whether in college or public library, cannot attain the highest degree of professional skill until his training embraces these essentials.

In similar fashion the training of school librarians, and of teachers, supervisors, principals, and superintendents of schools should be definitely shaped to meet the needs of these respective individuals in so far as they are involved in school library service. For supervisors, principals, and superintendents, a unit of instruction concerning the library should be provided in the courses in school administration which will give them an adequate understanding of the function of the library in the general organization of the school and how to secure the most effective use of the librarian, teachers, and library materials in carrying out the purposes of the curriculum. However competent the school librarian may be the school library cannot render maximum service unless these key people in the school know what the library is for and how to center the work of the school around it. Training in book selection, children's and adolescent literature, and the use of libraries should be provided for all teachers. For teacher-librarians and full-time school librarians, training in these subjects as well as in school library methods should be based upon a broad general education in which methods of curriculum construction, child and educational psychology, and the best methods of supervised study have been adequately represented. Effective library service to schools in the south can never be provided until some such general program of training has been put into effect.

Expansion of Service to Schools. The development of a plan which will insure adequate library service for elementary schools is the next objective—an objective at which the south has been unsuccessfully fumbling since 1900. Fortunately California has provided an excellent example in two respects. Through the schools it has made mandatory the expenditure of from $25 to $50 per teacher for library purposes. Through the county libraries it has provided a purchasing agent for these materials on a contractual basis. But even California has failed to provide a thoroughly coordinated program of curriculum making, book selection, and training and supervision for school library work which are essential to maximum efficiency in this field. The south must provide all of these elements in a carefully integrated program. It has done this in part for the high schools. It must also do it for the elementary schools.

Service to Adult Education. As the fifth objective, I propose a frontal attack upon the problem of the proper organization of library resources for adult education. In the paper I read by title at Houston in 1911, I defined the library as an educational institution, and during the thirty-one years in which I served as librarian at the University of North Carolina I considered myself as much a teacher as I do today. There has never been a day since I became a librarian that I have not considered it the function of the library to teach— to teach through the means which are available to it, but which may be different from those of the teacher engaged in formal education. That the library is merely a passive servant of the individuals and groups that make up the public has never been a part of my creed. Of course, it should serve the individual when he comes to it. It should also concern itself with the individual who does not come to it, to the extent of knowing that he does not come, who he is, and, if possible, why he does not come. But beyond that I hold it to be the duty of the library to know the groups in the community which can be served in an organized way through formal and informal contacts and by means which are yet to be discovered. The FERA experiment in adult education last winter resulted in the discovery of many new ways of teaching adults not previously employed in formal education, and the libraries of Evanston, Chattanooga, and Cincinnati, to mention three which advised adult groups, conducted special classes, and participated generally in that program, gained experience in what may in the future become a normal function of the public library. Children's librarians in the nineties discovered before teachers the ministry of the book to the child. Public librarians led in the Americanization of immigrants. Readers' advisers became concerned with the guidance of adult reading a full decade ago and as far back as 1926 advocated the preparation of readable books for adults of limited reading ability. On this record, and in view of the fact that the library is publicly supported, I see no convincing reason why the public library should hesitate to become an active, creative force in any major program of both formal and informal instruction of adults.

The minimum that a library can do in adjusting itself to this situation is to make available through its own resources or in cooperation with other organizations: (a) a list of all the agencies in the community which offer educational programs for adults; (b) a subject catalog, on cards or in printed form,[19] of the subjects offered (with cost and hours of meeting) by the agencies concerned; (c) the use of consultation and classrooms; (d) readers' advisers' service; (e) lecturers and class leaders for the discussion of books; and (f) active participation in the organization and administration of the formal adult education council of the community. I do not know where the money is to come from for such service, but I believe it will be provided more willingly, and with more justification than a service predominantly characterized by light fiction for isolated individuals. I commend the study of the *Handbook* of the American Association for Adult Education[20] and the community organizations of Radburn, New Jersey,[21] to us all for an understanding of the number of these organizations and the way in which libraries may serve them. A check-list of these organizations in the south, how they differ in range between the two races and between urban and rural areas, will be exceedingly illuminating and suggestive in planning future service.

Regional Subject Repositories. The sixth objective I propose is the building up of library resources for research in the south. The facts about these are generally known by us. We know too well that they are distressingly limited. Texas has the only university library in the south that has a half million volumes. Only North Carolina, Duke, and Texas have bibliographical materials which approximate the holdings of a dozen or more university libraries in other sections. And only Peabody undertakes to give more than one year of training in library science, that being limited to school libraries. We have been aware of this situation for a long time, but its seriousness has only recently been strikingly emphasized by the report of the Committee on Graduate Instruction of the American Council on Education[22] which lists departments in American universities which are adequately staffed and equipped with library and laboratory materials to carry on effective work for the Ph. D. In comparison with institutions in other sections of the country, only eight institutions in the states having membership in the Southeastern and Southwestern associations were adjudged adequately staffed and equipped to offer instruction in from one to twelve departments out of a total of thirty-five departments listed in sixty-one institutions. The institutions in the south which qualified were Texas with twelve departments; North Carolina with eleven; Duke with eight; Virginia with four; Rice Institute with three; Oklahoma and Peabody with two each; and West Virginia with one.

The steps which should be taken to remedy this situation are plain. Universities must cooperate in defining fields of specialization, and, once the fields have been determined, effort must be concentrated upon building up bibliographical aids and materials for research. The appointment of faculty committees on intellectual cooperation and the exchange of author cards by the libraries of the universities of North Carolina and Duke; the conference of southern librarians in Chapel Hill, North Carolina, in April on the location of document centers and the distribution of responsibility for the collection of documents; the general utilization by libraries throughout the south of FERA workers in compiling check-lists of documents, newspapers, and manuscript holdings; the concentration of Hispanic-American documents and records of exploration at Texas and Tulane; the broadly planned collection of source materials for the study of social and economic problems at North Carolina—these are examples of the kind of activity southern librarians must engage in if southern library resources are to become sufficiently extensive to meet the requirements of a highly complex civilization. Use and mastery of extensive and complex materials promote intellectual alertness and skill, without which southern students will have difficulty in solving the social and economic problems which confront them.

Side by side with this program of up-building should go the perfection of the south's program for training librarians. As already indicated, no library school, except Peabody, and that in a limited field, offers advanced work or training in investigation in library subjects. A strong school at the University of Texas should be provided to take care of the needs of the extreme southwest, and at one or two centers where resources are adequate, provision should be made for advanced study and investigation. The southern library field presents problems that are far too complex to be effectively solved by a library personnel whose training has been limited to the usual technical processes embraced within a one-year library school curriculum.

More Readable Books Needed. The south needs reading materials which can be used by individuals whose level of reading ability is low. This is the seventh objective I propose. Recent studies by Gray[23] show that fully 50 per cent of adults in America have only seventh grade reading ability. This is the average for the nation at large. In the south, where illiteracy is high, where school terms are short, where high school systems are comparatively young and enroll only approximately 50 per cent of the high school population, the number of adults who find present reading materials too difficult to serve as sources of ideas is even higher. In view of the fact that these conditions exist, it is the duty of librarians to join students of reading difficulty, authors, and publishers in providing less difficult yet enlightening reading materials. The ideas presented must be suitable for adults, but the number of unfamiliar words and complex sentences, which make the ordinary book difficult for the reader of limited reading attainment, must be materially lessened. Ideas concerning health, agriculture, and the problems of society in general will never be widely derived from the printed page in the south until the present difficulties experienced by adults in reading are minimized. This is as much the duty of the librarian as of the author or the publisher, and many of the library's potential patrons will never become actual patrons until this duty is performed.

School and College Library Standards. In 1926 these two associations started a movement for the revision of library standards for high schools and colleges in the south. Their continued study of this subject constitutes the eighth objective. In April and May of this year I spent a month or more visiting southern libraries from North Carolina to Texas. In every state I visited I saw evidences of the value of these standards at work. In one day a library school which did not exist in 1926 when standards were first proposed was preparing school librarians for expert school library service; in another, two new high school buildings included complete units of library, work room, and consultation room for library purposes; in still another, the library collection was carefully selected (with periodicals, pamphlets, maps, and pictures to supplement it) to support every course in the curriculum and to provide for recreational reading as well; and in still others trained librarians were teaching the use of the library to every student enrolled. In certain respects, these standards may seem too rigid. Too much emphasis may be placed on quantitative rather than qualitative measures. But revision in the latter direction and maintenance of standards for all classes of schools should continue one of the southern association's major aims, because through standards the schools are kept library conscious. A large part of the program of library training in the south has been built up in response to them, and the extension of supervised study based on library materials has been stimulated by them.

Library Legislation. A ninth objective is new legislation which will implement this library program. This subject has been thoroughly covered by other speakers. I merely wish to urge that in such legislation the following goals be kept in mind. First of all, such legislation should be as uniform as possible and free from special, as contrasted with general, provisions. Freedom from specific requirements which characterizes the library laws of England and California is in part responsible for the splendid library development which they have experienced during the past twenty years. In the second place, standards of professional efficiency should be embodied in a scheme of certification which will insure the employment of a group of library administrators thoroughly equipped to carry an adequate library program into effect. This has constituted the second point in California's smoothly functioning scheme of county library service. Again, larger units should be provided for which will eliminate unnecessary duplication of overhead expenses and will insure a more satisfactory base of support.

And finally, state aid to insure a minimum service in all units, with provision for additional revenues secured through local taxation, should be striven for. This aid should be sought on the basis of the service of the library to the elementary and secondary schools as well as to informal adult education. California's third guarantee of excellent library service is to be found in the mandatory statute that every school shall spend from $25 to $50 per teacher for library purposes, the books to be provided directly for the school, but preferably by the county library. Here there is clear recognition that the state has a stake in the education of every child and that it realizes this interest can best be promoted by insisting that teachers shall have essential materials at hand. This mandatory support of from a minimum of sixty cents per pupil for a class of forty pupils to a maximum of two dollars per pupil for a class of twenty-five is a far cry from the dependence upon parent-teacher associations and other organizations rather than upon state appropriations for school library materials which is characteristic of most southern states today. State aid for use as a library stimulating fund and for the equalization of educational opportunity, and federal aid for the building up of special collections, particularly bibliographical apparatus and materials for research, and for the investigation of library problems and the recording of library statistics on a nationwide basis, may well constitute the fighting front of any southern state library program. The proposals by Joeckel,[24] Cocking,[14] and Modisette[15] point the way.

Planning for Future Needs. The tenth and final objective I propose is that these associations shall continue to imagine vividly, to plan constructively for future library development. The new times demand a new library outlook. They demand the pooled judgment and experience of such groups as have been here for the past three days. From their establishment these associations have met to plan, to confer, rather than to read papers. They have had planning or policy committees for years. Much of their achievement has been due to the way in which these and other standing committees have carried on their work. Librarians will have difficulty in finding anywhere else in America a better example of what library planning can accomplish than in the record of these associations in recent years. I refer to this evidence again, to the plans summarized by Miss Tommie Dora Barker yesterday, to the imaginative and constructive ideas which have characterized this significant conference, because ideas are powerful. Once clearly conceived and wrought into workable measures they contribute more than anything else to the elevation of a section or nation.

NOTES:

[1] L. R. Wilson, "A Constructive Library Platform for Southern Schools." *Library Journal*, vol. 37, no. 4, April, 1912.

[2] L. R. Wilson, "The Library in the Advancing South." *Proceedings*, Southeastern Library Association, Fourth Biennial Conference, Signal Mountain, Chattanooga, Tennessee, April 22–24, 1926.

[3]*The Handbook of the Citizens' Library Movement*. Edited by the North Carolina Library Commission. Charlotte, N. C. North Carolina Library Association, 1928.

[4]*Library Extension News* No. 15, May, 1933. Report of Conference of Southern Leaders, A. L. A., Chicago. (mimeographed)

[5]Citizens' Conference on Library Needs of South Carolina, *Proceedings*. Clemson College, January 4–5, 1934. (mimeographed)

[6]R. B. Vance, *Human Geography of the South*. University of North Carolina Press, Chapel Hill. 1932.

[7]H. W. Odum, Southern Regional Study Tables in Cooperation with the Southern Social Science Research Committee. University of North Carolina, Chapel Hill. (typewritten manuscript)

[8]Unpublished data collected by Lee Wachtel in study of Du Page County (Ill.) libraries. Also report made on study of Fordham Branch of the New York Public Library by Dr. R. W. Tyler for the Seminars on Adult Reading and Adult Education held at the University of Chicago, October 13, 1933, pp. 95–128 of typewritten proceedings.

[9]L. R. Wilson and E. A. Wight, Current study of Rosenwald county libraries in the south.

[10]O. H. Cheney, *Economic Survey of the Book Industry, 1930–31*. New York, National Association of Book Publishers, 1931.

[11]W. S. Gray, and Ruth Monroe, *The Reading Interests and Habits of Adults; A Preliminary Report*. New York, The Macmillan Company, 1929.

[12]Federal Emergency Relief Administration. Emergency Educational Program. Notes for February, 1934. (mimeographed)

[13]Helen Gordon Stewart, "Advantages and Difficulties in the Administration of a Regional Library Unit." A. L. A. *Bulletin*, vol. 28, no. 9. September, 1934.

[14]W. D. Cocking, Proposal made by Dr. Walter D. Cocking, commissioner of education of Tennessee.

[15]J. O. Modisette, Proposal to the Louisiana Tax Reform Commission, May 15, 1933. (mimeographed)

[16]Letter from Elizabeth Robinson, Mississippi Library Commission, October 9, 1934.

[17]Margaret I. Rufsvold, "History of School Libraries in the South." *Peabody Journal of Education*, vol. 12, no. 1, July, 1934; J. I. Copeland, "Periodical Checklist for a Teachers College Library." *Peabody Journal of Education*, vol. 12, no. 1, July, 1934.

[18]Lydia M. Gooding, "Students' Reading Interests and the Library." Paper read before the College and Reference Section of the Joint Meeting of the Southwestern and Southeastern Library Association, October 18, 1934.

[19]*Educational Opportunities of Greater Boston, 1933–34*. Prospect Union Educational Exchange, Cambridge, Massachusetts.

[20]*Handbook of Adult Education in the United States, 1934*. New York, American Association for Adult Education, 1934. 384p.

[21]R. B. Hudson, *Radburn; a Plan of Living*. New York, American Association for Adult Education, 1934.

[22]Report of Committee on Graduate Instruction of the American Council on Education. Washington, D. C. American Council on Education, April, 1934.

[23]W. S. Gray, and Bernice Leary, What Makes a Book Readable, with Special Reference to Adults of Limited Reading Ability. (manuscript)

[24]C. B. Joeckel, The Government of the American Public Library. (unpublished doctor's thesis) August, 1934.

Restudying the Library Chart

TEN YEARS AGO the American Library Association celebrated its fiftieth anniversary at Atlantic City. Representatives from libraries from many parts of the world met with us, participated in our deliberations, felicitated us upon the accomplishments of the fifty years and wished us greater success in the years to come. We, in turn, reviewed our past, and, to document it appropriately, we submitted in the form of four notable publications our record of activities and our platform for future development in the fields of library extension, adult education and service to the public through the library.

Though we are not formally considering it as such, this meeting marks our sixtieth anniversary. Since our celebration in 1926, ten years have sped by with such swiftness and with such confusion that we have had little opportunity to take account of our bearings. From the Atlantic City meeting until 1929, all our energies were absorbed in the expansion of library activities incident to the rise of library income. Then, with a suddenness that was breath-taking, we were plunged into the most profound depression America has known. Banks collapsed, factories stopped, millions of men went out of employment onto relief, and millions of youth faced the world without prospect of profitable employment. In this maelstrom, library reve-

Reprinted from *Library Journal* 61:391–397, May 15, 1936, by permission of the publisher. Presidential address, First General Session, Fifty-eighth Conference, American Library Association, May 11, 1936. Also published in A.L.A. *Bulletin*, 30:480–490, June, 1936, and *School and Society*, 43:793–802, June 13, 1936.

nues dropped to unprecedented depths, circulation mounted to unprecedented heights, and almost overnight a million adults were organized in adult educational groups through federal subsidies, and planning and legislation affecting the social order were participated in by the Federal Government to a degree never equalled in the history of America.

As we meet here on the banks of the James, where the first permanent American colony began three centuries and a quarter ago to convert the wilderness into our present habitation and where the early leaders of the nation began to formulate the structure of our government and to lay the foundations of the social institutions which minister to us, we meet in an atmosphere that is less tense than that in which we have moved for the past ten years. We meet amid surroundings that should stimulate us to view our achievements of the past decade in perspective, and should enable us to discern more clearly the pattern which our thinking and our activities as a great national association should take concerning the perpetuation and improvement of the educational, social and cultural wellbeing of America.

Against this background of our recent activities and the historic past, I wish (1) to point out four major tasks which confront American librarians, (2) to indicate their general nature, and (3) to propose means by which they may be performed.

The first task which confronts the American Library Association to-day is to provide library service for the 45,000,000 people who are now without it. In spite of the fact that the number with service has increased since 1926 from 60,000,000 to 76,000,000 and the per cent without service has fallen from 43 to 37, the increase has not quite kept pace with the increase of population. This unserved group, therefore, constitutes the first challenge to the association as an official organization and, until this challenge is met, the association can not relinquish its efforts in this field.

In undertaking to meet this challenge, however, the association is better equipped than it was in 1926 because it better understands the nature of the problem than it did then. To-day this problem is recognized as largely a rural problem. Eighty-eight per cent of those who lack library service live in rural areas. Only 12 per cent live in towns or cities. It is also known that this lack is not evenly distrib-

uted throughout the nation, but is localized in certain well-defined regions, such as the Appalachian-Ozark region, the cut-over lands of
Michigan and Wisconsin, the spring and winter wheat regions and
the eastern and western cotton belts. One half of the 45,000,000 live
in thirteen Southern states, although the population of these states
constitutes only one fourth of the population of the country as a
whole. The percentage of the population in the South without service
is 66, whereas for the nation it is 37.

The problem has been clarified in another way. It is known that
wealth contributes to the development of library resources even
more than urbanization, and wealth is very unevenly distributed
throughout the various regions of America. The average per capita
incomes for the six major regions of the United States in 1929 were:
the Southeast $252, the Southwest $377, the Northwest $521, the
Middle West $610, the Far West $681, and the Northeast $687. The
maximum in Connecticut and the minimum in Mississippi were $749
and $160, respectively. It is also known that the states with lowest
per capita incomes could not support what other states consider adequate school systems, even if they devoted their entire income to
educational purposes alone. The basic economic resources are not
sufficient to provide this fundamental service. Consequently, in such
states it is obvious that library service can be secured, if secured at
all, only by means of tax rates that would seem confiscatory, or that
the service furnished would have to be exceedingly poor.

Other significant facts concerning the problem have been discovered. The percentage of population that is adult is closely associated
with its ability to support public services. In this respect states and
communities also differ widely. Rural populations invariably contain
larger percentages of persons nineteen years of age or under than
urban populations. In some states this ratio of adults to children is
very low. In each hundred of population there are only fifty adults
to fifty children. In others, there are sixty adults to forty children.
And in some very wealthy cities and suburban communities the
number of adults rises to seventy-five to twenty-five children, or three
to one. When this three to one difference is combined with such differences as exist in the per capita incomes of Connecticut and Mississippi, the differences in ability to support such public services as
the library increase in a geometrical rather than an arithmetical

ratio, and where this inability to provide public service exists, it is attended by a corresponding inability on the part of individuals to purchase books, magazines, newspapers, radios and other media of communication through which ideas may be effectively conveyed.

The second task to which the association must devote itself is the improvement of the service to the 40,000,000 people who live in areas served by libraries whose service is distinctly poor. Information concerning the nature of this problem is more illuminating and positive than it has been formerly. Through studies of the libraries in the metropolitan area of Chicago and Illinois, in the Southern states and Westchester County, New York, it is clear to-day that service in many libraries is inadequate in four fundamental respects. Book collections are too limited; qualified personnel is largely lacking; per capita support falls far below the recognized minimum standard; and methods of cooperation with other libraries have not been perfected by means of which inadequacies could be reduced or eliminated. Extensive data on all these points show conclusively that by no stretch of the imagination can the service provided be considered other than poor.

The third task which the association faces is that of making the library a significant adult educational force in the life of the nation —a task to which the association seemed to devote itself specifically in 1926 in the published report prepared by the Board on the Library and Adult Education.

In the interval between 1926 and to-day the work of the readers' adviser has developed in two score or more libraries according to a well-defined pattern, and an extensive body of information concerning individual patrons and of methods of meeting their needs effectively has been built up and is available for application under present or modified conditions. In other libraries this office has established contacts with formal and informal study groups. In still others, the various departments of the library have been organized on this basis, and in a number of communities the library, through membership in the organized adult education council of the community, has taken general leadership in this field. The work begun by the committee on readable books has likewise been attended by significant results. Not only have lists been prepared for readers whose reading attainment is not high, but the problems of such readers have been studied by students of reading and psychology and are now being considered in a practical way by publishers as well.

But by and large, other organizations than the library have assumed principal leadership in this field. The American Association for Adult Education, which will celebrate its tenth anniversary in New York immediately following this meeting, has assumed the principal directive rôle in the field of informal education, and under the emergency relief program of the federal government, the public school has become the organizer and conductor of certain types of organized formal instruction for adults. The public forum, connected with the public school or organized through funds provided by the Emergency Relief Administration, has been extensively developed, and, regardless of the effectiveness of the results achieved through the efforts of these emergency educational agencies, the idea of adult education as a function of the school and the community forum, as contrasted with the library, has been widely established. Departments of education in the major universities rather than library schools have begun to develop courses dealing with methods of presenting subjects of adult interest, and the library, which at the beginning of the decade gave promise of becoming the leader and coordinator of the various agencies which are dependent upon it for reading materials, has, with a few notable exceptions, largely failed to meet the expectations held out for it ten years ago. The main objectives of the library in this field have not been broken down into concrete programs, methods and procedures for implementing these programs have not been specifically detailed, and the movement as a whole, so far as the library is concerned, has had to place its principal dependence for instrumentation upon the thinking and activity of other organizations.

The fourth task to which the association should address itself is the conscious, united effort of increasing the resources of the great scholarly libraries of America for the purposes of scholarship and research through the development of regional centers for bibliographical materials, the multiplication of union catalogues, the provision of means of exchange of duplicate materials, the description of the holdings of special and scholarly libraries and the reproduction of materials for research through mechanical processes. Committees on documents, on bibliography, on cooperative cataloguing, with the committee on resources and other committees of related character, have long been concerned with aspects of this general subject. The various union lists of serials and foreign documents, the development of the union catalogue at the Library of Congress, interest in the publication of the Gesamtkatalog and the Catalogue of the Bibliothèque Nationale and the republication of the British Museum Catalogue—all these have been matters of vital concern to the American Library Association. But they have been matters of concern to other organizations as well, and have not been kept as steadily and unitedly in mind as have the objectives of the association in the fields of library extension and training for librarianship. In order that this interest of the association may be coordinated and more extensively developed, it is proposed that at this conference the Committee on Resources of American Libraries shall be changed into a board which, with other committees and affiliated organizations, shall devote itself to the cultivation of this general field.

The extension of library service to the 45,000,000 people without it; the enrichment of service to the 40,000,000 with inadequate service; the organization, administration and development of libraries in such way that they can serve the nation as effective agencies for adult education; and the building up of bibliographical centers and resources for the use of the scholar and investigator—these are phases of librarianship which challenge to-day, as they never have before, the best thought and effort of American librarians. The one justification for the library in a democracy is that it shall be a medium through which ideas may be transmitted from which society may profit. This is the fundamental reason for the library's existence and support. It is, therefore, of ways and means of enabling the library to perform this service that I shall now speak.

Rethinking these problems realistically in the light of present conditions is the first means I propose for the achievement of these objectives. It is fundamental that we realize that the forces which have been playing upon American life for the past decade, and which therefore involve librarianship, while unusual, are still operative and will continue to be operative in American life. Glacier like, they have plowed their way into the life of the nation and, even though they have receded somewhat, changes have been wrought by them, the effects of which will still remain. A librarianship concerned largely with technical and bibliographical matters, as much of our earlier librarianship has been, is not sufficient to cope with the present situation which the great war and an equally great depression have created. As a profession we are confronted with the inescapable duty of meeting the present and the future realistically, of restudying our functions, reshaping our methods and procedures and readjusting our thinking in such ways that our libraries will serve society to-day and to-morrow in fundamentally desirable ways. The facts that national income was greater by several billion dollars in 1935 than it was in 1934, that support for library service has been somewhat restored and that great effort has been made through planning and legislation to remedy existing conditions should not blind us to our true situation and the necessity of meeting it realistically. Our march is forward to a challenging future, not backward to a familiar past.

The second measure I suggest is the study and formulation of legislation applicable to present library situations. I have no specific formula to propose. There is no specific formula that will be universally applicable to the varied conditions which promote or retard American library development. But I propose the consideration of legislation by librarians as a means of effecting social ends. For two years the whole American library profession has been studying library plans. I urge now that we become legally-minded in order that we may express these plans in effective legal form. Carefully conceived legislation based upon knowledge of present conditions and trends in government is necessary if some of the difficulties now met with in extending library service and providing for effective cooperation among libraries are to be sucessfully met. The kind of legislative thinking which is embodied in the California county and school library laws illustrates the idea of simple, effective legislative formulation I have in mind. The law provides that the county governing board can organize a library and provide, through income from taxes, for its support. Each county school outside incorporated cities must provide a fund of not less than $25 per teacher for the purchase of library materials. School boards are permitted to join with county commissioners and library boards to furnish library service to the schools. Through these three simple provisions library organization, support and means of cooperation have been insured and a state-wide service of distinction has been built up. Legislation like this (or the simple legislation under which the English county library system has been developed) which will provide for the organization of library service in areas that may exceed the limits of traditional political units and which will coordinate support that now goes to schools, libraries, agricultural organizations and public health agencies, all of which utilize print as a medium for the transmission of ideas, will be of the greatest assistance in bringing books to the 45,000,000 rural dwellers who are now without them.

The third means which I propose is the provision of wider bases of financial support for libraries from local and other sources. In making this proposal, I am not advocating a raid upon the treasuries of the counties, states and the nation in which local communities find themselves. I am not proposing libraries at the expense of those who have them for those who do not have them and can not provide them merely that a program of the American Library Association may be carried out. I make the proposal because I am aware that fundamental changes have taken place in the taxing systems of towns, counties, states and the nation; that communities vary greatly in their ability to support public services; and that in recognition of these facts means must be devised for dealing effectively with these conditions. I make the proposal because I am aware that twenty odd million people in the United States, many of them between the ages of sixteen and twenty-five, are on relief, and many others who live in well-recognized problem areas of the country are without library resources and can not provide them. These facts are realities, just as the drought of 1934, the recent floods and the still more recent tornadoes were realities. In a democracy, which depends upon an educated electorate for its perpetuation and in which the thinking of one state or region affects for good or ill the well-being of other regions or the nation as a whole, I am convinced that the continuing education of all electors is a matter that has serious implications not merely for the localities in which the situations described exist, but for the nation generally, and should become a charge against society in the event local support is inadequate or lacking. I make the proposal because I believe that libraries can be and should be educational agencies that influence situations of this character for good and that their provision up to a given level is fundamentally essential to the maintenance of democratic institutions and governments.

The fourth means which American librarians have at their command in achieving the objectives mentioned is that of cooperation. It is unnecessary for me to develop this idea at length, as we are honored at this conference by the presence of Mr. Lionel R. McColvin, librarian of the Hampstead Public Library and honorary secretary of the Library Association of Great Britain, who is to discuss at a later general session the methods of cooperation employed by libraries in Great Britain in making their resources as available to the student in the remotest village as to the scholar in the major centers. The committee on resources of American libraries, under the chairmanship of Dr. Bishop, the various groups associated with Dr. Raney which are sponsoring the demonstration of methods of reproducing materials for research, and Dr. Connor, national archivist, also deal with significant phases of this subject.

There are certain aspects of the subject, however, about which I do wish to speak. The first thing I wish to say is that although there is no central authority in America charged with the direction of libraries, as there usually is in European countries, a very great degree of voluntary cooperation among libraries can be achieved in individual American states. California, with its highly developed state and county libraries, offers a notable example of what I mean. A union catalogue of the county libraries, supplemented by cards from several university and other libraries, is maintained by the state library. The strong central collection of the state library materials is placed at the service of the libraries of the state to supplement their local resources. The libraries, while maintaining an independent existence individually, operate as a system and by doing so increase their effectiveness tremendously. What I wish to urge is that individual community libraries learn the art of borrowing from and loaning to each other on an extensive scale, of placing little used books in one center where they can be drawn upon by all and of making available materials from special collections to others, thereby greatly increasing the resources of the whole group many fold. What I propose is not merely an extension of interlibrary loan service involving an occasional book. It is rather the unlearning of the art of splendid isolation which many small libraries steadfastly practice, and learning how to supplement their resources and those of neighboring libraries by a positive, well-conceived policy of renting, loaning and exchanging considerable portions of their book stocks. I am urging, within bounds, the *use* of books as against the *ownership* of books, the practice of which keeps books moving where they are needed, rather than the opposite procedure usually followed, as indicated in a recent study of a county which contains thirty-one libraries, eighteen of which borrowed 1,465 volumes in one year from the state library and a large public library outside the county, but only ninety from each other, although four of the libraries contained more than 50,000 volumes each. All thirty-one were located within an area of approximately 400 square miles, and all together loan more than 3,000,000 volumes annually. The lack of cooperation in this instance is further evidenced by the fact that one small village in the county is located within two miles of six independent libraries but is without service except upon payment of library fee!

The second thing I wish to say is that as yet there has not been the close integration of university extension divisions, workers educational groups, governmental educational authorities and libraries in the common enterprise of adult education in America that there has been in England. The American public library has seldom made books available in extensive duplication to study groups, and the custom of making loans to such groups for from two to six months for sustained study, as contrasted with two-week loans to the individuals who constitute the groups, is comparatively rare.

The third observation I wish to make is that far greater cooperation is desirable between state library extension agencies and the libraries and library schools of state universities and land-grant colleges, on the one hand, and state agricultural agencies and departments of agriculture of state universities and land-grant colleges on the other. Local farm and home demonstration agents constitute the largest single group of trained adult education workers in America and their field of operation is exactly that field—rural America—in which library resources are inadequate or do not exist at all. Altogether there are 7,800 of them, and one half of them are in Southern rural areas where library needs are most acute. I suggest, therefore, that the American Library Association and the various state library associations consciously seek the cooperation of the United

States Department of Agriculture and all the institutions and workers mentioned above in changing this situation. There was a time when these workers were more concerned with increased crop yields and better breeds of cattle than with the enrichment of rural life. But that day has passed. Through purposeful cooperation these organizations, found on the same campuses or in the same state and county offices and now interested in the cultural aspects of rural life, should break down the departmental walls that separate them and assist in bringing books to rural America.

In the university and reference library fields the same principle can operate, but differently. Here again it is obvious that though income has been partly restored, it has not been and probably will not be completely restored for some time. And the devaluation of the dollar has reduced purchasing power abroad. As the committee on resources has indicated, the extension of the Union Catalogue of the Library of Congress and the development of regional union catalogues and bibliographical centers, as at Philadelphia, Chapel Hill-Durham and Denver, the descriptions of the holdings of major collections, such as is provided by the Handbook of the Harvard Library, and cooperation among libraries and other national organizations interested in the reproduction of materials by photostat and film for the use of scholars are means which can be used in overcoming the serious limitation of income and hold out a prospect of the increase of materials for research and scholarship of the greatest significance. Resources, such as these, developed nationally and regionally and coordinated through voluntary cooperation with the resources of the Library of Congress and the National Archives, can be made to insure America a service to the scholar of the highest order.

The fifth measure which I propose is that we revise and refine the standards by which at present we measure library service. The best books for the most people at the least cost may have been and may still be the best possible motto for American librarians. A dollar per capita, 25 to 40 per cent of the population registered, and 5 to 9 books circulated per inhabitant, depending upon the size of the city, may have served and may still serve as excellent standards of service. Certainly they have been attained in only a small per cent of the cities of the nation. But for whom the best books are best, what groups of the population make up the body of the most people and what constitutes socially significant cost remain to be more exactly determined. The fact that the library in a given city has spent a dollar per capita for library service will not answer the question as to whether the service has gone largely to students or to housewives or to factory workers. Nor will it show whether the best books —that is, the books that might be best from the point of view of how they influence social behavior—have been supplied to these and other groups in the total population. Nor will it answer the questions with which all of us are met today when we undertake the extension of library service into rural areas, because it is a standard devised to measure urban situations rather than rural. It will not tell us exactly as we desire what service to schools, to the different elements of the population, to rural areas and to other county offices and institutions costs. And it will furnish us little that will be of practical value in determining the part that wealth or size of political units or educational status or racial background plays in making for or against the provision of adequate library service in areas now without it. Step by step exact information concerning these and other matters which influence the provision of such service will have to be painstakingly discovered; new formulas that more exactly fit the circumstances will have to be evolved upon the basis of these data; and practical applications to the present situations which have not yielded to present formulas will have to be made if library service is to be extended and improved and the taxpayer is to be convinced that his expenditure for the library is soundly based.

The sixth means of attaining the proposed ends is concerned with the training of future librarians rather than with the readjustment of the thinking of librarians in service to present conditions.

In a paper which I presented at Memphis, in 1934, I said that in my opinion the librarian of the Southern public library was too much engrossed with the idea of the library as a literary institution —an institution whose principal function was to make fiction and drama, and poetry and essays, and other literary forms available. I also said that the Southern university librarian had been seemingly less concerned with building up fundamental collections in the social, physical and biological sciences than he had been in the preservation of local and Southern history. I myself emphasized this latter aspect of librarianship for three decades at the University of North Carolina. These attitudes might, in a sense, be attributed to a carry over from the literary and historical tradition of the Old South. They might also be attributed in part to a library training which emphasized technical processes and knowledge of bibliographical subjects rather than a knowledge of the purposes of the library and of the significance of the library as a social agency. Recently, I developed this idea more extensively in a paper before the New York Library Club and shall only refer here to the conclusions reached in that paper. Certainly, the extension of library service into areas now without it, the improvement of service where it is notably inadequate and the development of a coordinated system of libraries, popular and scholarly, which will meet the educational requirements of general and scholarly publics, call for training on the part of the librarian which will transcend these restricted views. They call for training which will make clear to the librarian what the purposes of the library are; which will acquaint him with what the various groups that constitute the library's clientele read and what the effect of reading upon these groups is; which will familiarize him with the methods of investigation and experimentation essential in attacking difficult problems in his work; and which will supplement and reenforce his technical training with a body of supporting information drawn from related fields that will make him, as nearly as training can do, adequate to the task to which he puts his hand. The present training provided by the library school dealing with technical processes and bibliographical procedures, or such of it as is requisite to the skilful and economical handling of books and other library materials as such, will, of course, be retained. It will serve as the spearhead of the librarian's professional equipment, but it will be a spearhead backed by a total knowledge comparable to that which the engineer or physician or scholar in other fields brings to the support of his professional undertaking. This total training will enable the librarian not only to know books and how to process them, but how to know communities and adult educational processes and how to cooperate with other agencies in their endeavor to make books significant in the lives of men.

The final measure which I propose is the development of an adequate philosophy of librarianship. President Isaiah Bowman, of the

Johns Hopkins University, in an address at the sixtieth anniversary of the university, recently pointed out the necessity of a design or frame of reference or philosophy in the life of an individual or university or national association, if the individual or institution or association is to achieve optimum results. As a librarian looking at the objectives which I have suggested for our consideration, I wish to emphasize the necessity of our possession of such a design or frame of reference or philosophy of librarianship by which we may test the value of these proposals and in the clear light of which we may devote ourselves unreservedly to their accomplishment. Much of the confusion and sense of futility which we have experienced during the past decade has been due to the lack of such a frame of reference which place first things first in the field of librarianship. Certainly the younger members of the profession who have taken up their work during these years of dislocation and upheaval have felt the lack of such guiding principles as they have sought for them in the records which constitute the history of library development in America.

Today we should stop and ask ourselves—what are these guiding principles, what is this fundamental philosophy in the light of which we propose to rethink and reshape our activities in the effort to make our libraries more signicant to the society which they are established to serve? Is the American Library Asociation spending the income from its endowment and from membership dues on those things which mean most to the advancement of American society? Are the library schools emphasizing those aspects of librarianship which future librarians can be sure will enable them to accomplish the greatest social good? Are individual librarians throughout America guided by purposes and principles in the organization and direction of libraries, in the building up of book collections and staffs and in the nice adjustment of library service to the needs of the communities that are sure of effecting results by which men's lives assume new and richer meaning?

If the four major tasks about which I have spoken are to be accomplished in such a way as to yield increasingly significant results, these are some of the measures we shall have to employ. Our look will have to be forward to the new and unfamiliar. Legislation will have to be formulated to meet new needs. Financial support will require broader bases. Cooperation will have to assume varied forms.

Measurement of library service and training for librarianship will have to be adjusted to new conditions and related to a frame of reference which will illuminate, which will justify and which will vitalize the work of the library as an American social institution of fundamental importance and worth.

Here, in this setting which so vividly brings back to our minds the high aims of those who laid the foundations of our liberties, I place these objectives before us and urge the united effort of us all in their successful accomplishment.

Library Readjustment for Effective Adult Education

IN FEBRUARY 1936 in an address before the New York Library Club entitled "The Next Fifty Years," I took the position that the public library would revise its objectives, go consciously educational, and take those steps in the readjustment of its organization, resources, equipment, and personnel which would enable it to meet the adult educational needs of the individuals and groups who had a right to make use of its services.

In this paper, two and a half years later, I wish to follow up this general theme. I wish, specifically, to do two things: (1) to show that the objectives of adult education have been greatly clarified recently, and (2) to suggest means by which the library may effectively promote a significant program of adult education.

The clarification of library objectives concerning adult education may be attributed to the activities and thinking of several groups, organizations, and individuals outside the library field as well as within it. The organization outside the library field which has contributed most to it has been the American Association of Adult Edu-

Reprinted from *Michigan Librarian*, 4:3–8, December, 1938, by permission of the publisher. The paper was read before the Michigan Library Association, Lansing, Michigan, November 3, 1938.

cation. In 1937 it began a study of various organizations engaged in adult educational activities. *Listen and Learn,* for example, by Frank Ernest Hill, published by the Association as the first in this series of studies, dealt specifically with the educational significance of the radio for adults. Mr. Hill shows clearly what adults who use the radio for self educational purposes try to gain from it. They seek recreational entertainment, knowledge of what is going on in the world about them, particularly in the fields of local, state, national, and international relationships, and self-realization through the cultivation of their intellectual, esthetic, and ethical interests. This study, of course, does not undertake to show how the library may use the radio or supplement it in achieving the aims of individuals and groups who make use of it for these purposes. It does suggest, however, what the educational significance of the radio is, and leaves it to the imagination and experimental genius of the library to devise means by which it may utilize its resources, personnel, and equipment in increasing the effectiveness of the radio in this work.

I shall not undertake to set down the kinds of educational assistance sought by adults and the corresponding success achieved by them which are presented in *Why Forums?*, by Mary Ely; *The Civic Value of Museums,* by T. R. Adam; *The Music of the People,* by Willem van de Wall; *Outposts of the Public School,* by Watson Dickerman, and in the other titles which have appeared in the series. These volumes summarize the objectives of millions of the library's clientele who carry on adult educational activities in these fields, and should be studied by the library in order to determine how to relate effectively its activities to the achievement of the objectives revealed. This should be a required exercise not only for students in advanced courses in library schools and students of the organization and administration of adult education, but for the staff of every library that is undertaking to carry on a significant program in any one of these fields.

A group of library organizations which have contributed to the sharpening of these objectives includes the American Library Association, various state library associations and clubs, individual libraries here and there, the Graduate Library School of the University of Chicago, and the Library School of Simmons College. Both of the latter institutions have held institutes for librarians on this subject. Both institutes used speakers from various adult educational fields who stated their general and specific objectives, and showed what are the most effective ways in which the library can assist in carrying them into effect.

Individuals have likewise contributed to this clarification. Lyman Bryson, Professor of Education at Teachers College of Columbia University, 'through his "Philosophy of Adult Education and its Implications for Librarianship," in *The Role of the Library in Adult Education*, and in his *Adult Education*, has clearly defined these objectives under five headings. They are remedial, occupational, relational, liberal, and political, and are defined as follows:

> Remedial adult training is more or less formal study undertaken to give a person of adult years whatever he needs to bring his educational equipment up to the minimum that is necessary for life in an American community. . . .
>
> Occupational training may be: (a) for advancement on the job; (b) for advancement to another job of a different sort; (c) for the industrial rehabilitation of the victim of machine unemployment; (d) for guidance in choosing or adjusting to an occupation.
>
> Relational education includes "parent education" and also the studies of emotions, attitudes, and psychological habits which are designed to help us better to understand ourselves and our relations with other persons.
>
> "Liberal education" is the best term available to describe activities which are undertaken chiefly for their own sake, for the pleasure that is in them. . . .
>
> Political education includes all those studies, practices, and experiences which men deliberately undertake to make themselves better members of the commonwealth. . . .

Malcolm S. MacLean, in his article "The College and Adult Education," in *The Role of the Library in Adult Education*, presents the results of an analysis of the educational interests of 5,000 university extension students, several hundred students in the General College of the University of Minnesota. and their parents. Barring approximately 40 per cent of the university extension students who were working for credits or for degrees, he found that the other 60 per cent pursued adult studies for four main purposes. They wanted to learn (1) how to fit themselves for their vocations; (2) how to interpret what is going on in the world about them; (3) how to understand themselves; and (4) how to feed their inner lives.

In *The Public Library—A People's University*, Alvin Johnson has carried the clarification a step farther. He has dealt not only with the interests which lead adults to seek additional education, but has also suggested ways in which the library should readjust itself in its effort to aid adults in the realization of these desires. On the basis of a careful analysis of the activities of the library he concludes that the "mere supplying of books without any regard to any influence they may exert," the work done by persons interested in establishing their family trees, by cross-word puzzle "researchers," and by the many individuals who make use of the library's extensive informational service for the determination of some specific fact are not significantly educational. He likewise discards as of no educational significance "giving the public what it wants," the preparation of booklists that merely bring titles together that bear on the same subject without exhibiting or developing a definite educational purpose, and the extension of library service for the purpose of "coverage." He discards them because they do not contribute the element of direction and sustained interest which enable the individual (1) to keep himself fit as a technician by constant occupational reconditioning, and (2) to maintain a clear understanding of sound political, social, and cultural ideas upon which American democracy must rest. To aid the individual in successfully achieving these two ends, is, Dr. Johnson insists, the library's principal justification for existence.

Through the studies of these organizations and individuals, the haze which has obscured the objectives of the library in the field of adult education has been largely removed. If the library is to serve the individual in a way that is educationally significant, it must do something more than hand him book lists, answer his inquiries, and loan him certain books. It must furnish him materials and personal guidance adjusted to his special needs which will be of value to him with respect to (1) limitations in his early training; (2) his occupation; (3) his understanding of the current scene in the world around him; (4) his ability to adjust himself properly to the social and political life of which he must be a part; (5) his understanding of himself; and (6) his effort to develop an inner life of deep and permanent satisfactions.

If this statement of the library's functions in adult education can be accepted as satisfactory, I shall now suggest several practical steps which libraries must take to make their work successful.

1. The first step I propose is to analyze the total adult population which the library is to serve and to determine, on the basis of the analysis, what the specific adult educational objectives of the community are and how the library can most effectively promote their achievement. These objectives will vary from community to community and from state to state. In Michigan the library will think first of individuals; then of groups in which individuals have organized themselves to carry on some program of study. Of the 5,000,000 inhabitants of Michigan approximately 3,500,000 are 18 years of age or over. These 3,500,000 constitute the ligitimate adult clientele of the public library. Recent studies of library patrons[1] will suggest how this total can be broken down into categories such as skilled and unskilled workmen, students, housewives, professional men and women, etc., what percentage of the total population each category constitutes, what kinds of educational demands each category makes upon the library, and how effectively the library is meeting these demands. Other studies[2] will indicate the number and character of the groups into which these individuals will organize themselves and what services they will require of the library.

The Geography of Reading, for example, will show that in Michigan at varying times between 1930 and 1937: 38,000 individuals were members of adult education classes organized under the public school system; 26,742 were enrolled in Federal Emergency Relief classes; 140 United States Agricultural Extension workers and county and home demonstration agents were in charge of the educational programs of the U. S. Department of Agriculture in which approximately 200,000 farmers, farm women, and farm boys and girls were engaged; 18,700 women were members of the National Federation of Women's Clubs; 43,084 persons were members of Parent-Teacher Associations; 43,779 boys and girls were members of boy and girl scout groups; 919,946 families were owners of radios; 526,411 subscribers were readers of farm papers; 691,407 persons subscribed

[1]For notes, see page 77.

for or purchased from newsstands copies of 47 national magazines; and 7,621 persons were members of the Book-of-the-Month Club and the Literary Guild. The list could be extended by reference to other compilations. But it is sufficient to indicate what kind of organizations are to be found in Michigan and what the objectives of these organizations are. Every library in the state should determine what part of this clientele is included within its area of service, and plan a definite program of service for it. A census of library patrons should be as essential to successful adult educational service through the library as a school census is to sucessful school work with children.

2. The second step which the library should take follows naturally. Once the library knows the nature of its clientele, it should find its place in the total group of adult agencies in the community which undertake to meet its adult educational needs. This place should be one of purposeful, intelligent cooperation and leadership. I share the opinion of Alvin Johnson that the library has in general been too timid in claiming its place, and that it should assume an attitude of positive, aggressive leadership among the adult educational agencies of the community. "The Adult Educational Council—An Arm of the Library,"[3] by R. B. Hudson, and the forthcoming A.L.A. publication by Chancellor on *The Library as a Community Intelligence Center* deal with examples in which such a claim has been made successfully.

3. The third step which the library must take in fitting itself for its work in adult education is to overhaul its internal organizations and administration for educational purposes. This calls for something more than the designation of some member of the staff as a readers' adviser. It should involve the policy of book selection and book duplication, the utilization of rooms and equipment, the adjustment of hours to the needs of adults who otherwise cannot make use of library materials, and the pointing of all the work of the library toward an educational goal. In the larger libraries departmental organization, provision of readers' advisers and subject specialists, preparation of sustained reading lists, assistance in vocational guidance, provision of rooms for radio and films, and participation in forums and other group activities should become matters of regular procedure. Provision of staff members to establish outside contacts and the involvement of community specialists who would not disturb

professional performance should likewise become routine practice and would undoubtedly contribute greatly to the library's educational effectiveness.

Articles by Flexner, Farquhar, Rutzen, and Freeman have dealt with these phases of organization and administration and the A.L.A. is soon to issue a volume of case studies on the subject under the title *Types of Library Adult Service*. The volume, *Printed Page and the Public Platform* by Chancellor and Williams, and *The Library and the Radio,* by Faith Holmes Hyers, to be issued by the University of Chicago Press this month, should become library staff texts for these phases of adult education and a similar text, with examples of best practice, should be prepared on the use of documentary and educational films. Reorganization along these lines and the maintenance of an alert, experimental attitude toward educational objectives will help transform the library from an ordinary, successful administrative library organization into a significantly effective educational institution.

4. The fourth step which the library should take in making itself an effective educational instrument is to provide a staff which understands what educational aid the library's patrons normally seek and the best educational methods of supplying it. The general and professional education of the library school graduate in the past has not furnished this background. Approximately 65 per cent of such graduates have devoted most of their educational preparation to the subjects of English and history. The other 35 per cent have "majored" in the other 25 or more subjects embraced within the usual undergraduate curriculum. Library staffs composed of individuals trained in this disproportionate fashion have had to cover the other vast fields of the social, biological, and physical sciences and the general fields of art and technology with which great numbers of the library's clientele are vitally concerned. Such training has likewise failed to provide essential understanding of how adults learn, of the methods by which such learning can best be promoted, and of the organization of staff and library resources that will enable the library to point its activities toward a well-devised, well-sustained educational goal.

To provide this background properly calls not only for the selection of new staff members with training in the fields of government,

technology, and science, but for the reorientation of the thinking of
staff members already in service. Knowledge of student motives, appropriate curricula, well-devised outlines and syllabuses, and experience and skill in interviewing and advising, are fundamental to successful educational performance. In-service training, staff instruction,
attendance at short term institutes, specialization in varied subject
fields should be insisted upon by library boards and provision for
the financial support of such a program made accordingly.

This situation calls for the serious consideration of state library
agencies, boards of trustees, head librarians, library schools, and
the Boards of Education for Librarianship and Adult Education of
the A.L.A., because public libraries, as contrasted with school, college, and university libraries, have made little provision for in-service
training for their staffs. These organizations should likewise cooperate in issuing a series of volumes containing case studies and
the results of successful experiments and demonstrations in adult
education. The volume, *Helping The Reader Toward Self-Education,*
which attempts to introduce the library staff to effective educational
procedure, is an excellent example of what is proposed and should
be widely read by public library staff members.

5.   The fifth step which libraries should take is that of providing
books which may be used successfully in meeting the educational
needs of their adult patrons. This is a step which librarians will find
it difficult to take, but it must be taken by them or they must find
others who will take it for them. They can at least increase their insistence upon the production of such materials, and, as they gain experience in adjusting library resources to specifically educational
ends, they can greatly increase the value of their suggestions to
authors and publishers. The work of the Committee on Readable
Books and the lists of books by Chancellor, Felsenthal, Hoyt, and
Edge, have been extremely valuable in this respect. They have been
based upon the assumption that self education and understanding
result ultimately, not from information which individuals may gain
from the study of books, however important they may be, but rather
from the discovery of how an author's mind works in the presentation of his subject and the ability which such discovery gives the individual to analyze, evaluate, and modify his own mental processes.
This is the supreme function of the book, and if books are not avail-

able to thousands of individuals who are striving to discover themselves in this way, it is one of the major responsibilities of the librarian to seek their production.

Dr. Johnson, in summarizing his suggestions for improving the library's performance in adult education, offers seven recommendations, which I repeat here because they supplement and complement the suggestions made above. He urges (1) greater use of rooms for lectures, forums, etc., the exhibition of documentary films, and actual leadership of classes; (2) the development of a body of quantitative data through case studies of readers and the experience of readers' advisers; (3) the enlistment of the services of community specialists who can participate effectively as educational leaders; (4) the abandonment of "pure librarianship" and "coverage" as principal library objectives; (5) the preparation by the A.L.A. for use by libraries of educationally developed book lists which individual libraries could not provide on account of lack of personnel or excessive cost; (6) the development of publicity which will sell the library; and (7) the inclusion in library school training of those subjects which will equip the library personnel for effective educational work.

6. The steps which have been proposed so far have principally concerned the individual library. The sixth step which I am convinced the library must take is that of cooperation among libraries on a large scale basis, preferably that of a whole state, through which the total library resources of a state may be drawn upon for educational purposes. Recent surveys of the resources and personnel of a large number of individual libraries have shown the utter inadequacy of many of them, particularly of the very small libraries, for effective educational performance. They have likewise deepened my conviction that the failure of such libraries to provide excellent service has affected adversely library support in general. On the other hand, examples of libraries in states such as California and New Jersey, in which excellent systems of cooperation and coordination have been affected, show how small and large libraries alike have provided union catalogs for all their resources, have supplemented their holdings from large state library collections and, like the local and regional libraries in England and the National Central Lending Library in London, have perfected state systems which

have enabled all libraries thus coordinated to extend greatly their educational service. They have demonstrated conclusively that small, poorly equipped, non-cooperating libraries, through carefully planned cooperation or inclusion in larger and more effective units, lose nothing inherently vital in individuality, but gain tremendously in educational efficiency and correspondingly increase the justification of their claim upon the taxpayer's dollar.

7. The seventh and final step which I propose is that of securing increased funds for library purposes. Alvin Johnson has said that the magic key to the pocketbook of America has long been the word education. He has expressed amazement that the library has made such slight use of this word. He insists that if the library will become a genuine educational institution money can be secured to support it. He insists that the librarian who serves a relatively few persons significantly, as the high school or college teacher who directs the studies of only forty or fifty individuals, is entitled to support similar to that received by the teacher in the school or college and that he can secure it. That, of course, remains to be demonstrated. But at all events the securing of such support should be one of the major objectives of librarians in their campaigns for state and federal aid. Through such aid the library should be able to staff and equip itself in such a way as to furnish adults all the resources essential to fruitful study and to provide all groups engaged in educational programs, leadership, materials, and physical quarters which would make the library an indispensable community educational center. This total program, if intelligently and persistently carried out, will tremendously increase the educational significance of the public library in thousands of American communities and fully justify its support as one of the principal promoters of the American democratic way of life.

For many reasons it is particularly fitting that this challenge to blue print and implement the course of adult education through the public library should be accepted by the librarians of the state of Michigan. Your state is the only state in the nation that, through its first constitution, made the support of public libraries mandatory. At the very outset, it recognized the importance of the library as an educational force in community life and assumed its support as a state responsibility. It was the first state to enact a comprehensive public library state aid measure with an appropriation large enough to effect substantial library development over a period of years. Its State Library Board is now giving thought to the reorganization of the machinery through which this support is to be administered and to methods of cooperation to increase the value of the service of every library, small or large, within the state. Through the public library of Detroit, it has furnished the libraries of the nation a notable example of effective reorganization and experimentation in the adult educational field. Through its district round tables, the Michigan Library Association has brought librarians and adult educational leaders in the state together to develop a more significant cooperative adult educational program, and it is now engaged in a study of personnel which is fundamental to high educational accomplishment. Finally, this conference has exhibited an expectancy and determination that would seem to insure that the steps which I have mentioned will be taken and that a program will be carried into effect which will tremendously increase the ability of the individual citizen of Michigan (1) to overcome limitations in his early training; (2) to maintain his vocational efficiency; (3) to deepen his understanding of the world around him; (4) to heighten his ability to adjust himself to the social and political order of which he is a part; (5) to quicken his understanding of himself; and (6) to increase greatly the permanent satisfaction of his inner life.

NOTES:

[1] Louis R. Wilson and Edward A. Wight, *County Library Service in the South* (Chicago: the University of Chicago Press, 1935) and William C. Haygood, *Who Uses the Public Library* (Chicago: the University of Chicago Press, 1938).

[2] Louis R. Wilson, *The Geography of Reading* (Chicago: American Library Association and the University of Chicago Press, 1938) and Robert B. Hudson, *Radburn, A Plan of Living: A Study Made for the American Association for Adult Education under the Supervision of John O. Walker* (New York City: American Association for Adult Education, 1934).

[3] *In The Role of the Library in Adult Education*, ed. L. R. Wilson (Chicago: The University of Chicago Press, 1937).

School Libraries

A Constructive Library Platform for Southern Schools

IN A GATHERING OF MEN AND WOMEN assembled to discuss matters pertaining to the advancement of general education, it may seem inappropriate to raise the question whether or not the modern library, whatever its form, is considered seriously as a helpful, constructive educative agent. Upon first thought, such a question seems wholly uncalled for. Its answer in the affirmative is so obvious that no good reason is apparent to justify its asking. This seemingly is especially true so far as the Southern Educational Association is concerned; for it has expressed itself unmistakably as to its conception of the importance of the library as an educational influence by providing in its constitution for a library department and by giving a place in its general program for the discussion of vital library topics. Furthermore, as members of this Association, we have written laws providing for the establishment of rural school libraries from Maryland to this great state, and all of us who, in our childhood years, hung upon our mother's lips as we heard of fairies and princes, or in our early teens followed the heroes of Cooper and Stevenson across the printed page, or in our maturer years have felt the ennobling, vitalizing influence of some great book, need no argument to win us to a belief in the library. We know it is an indispensable agent in any educational system, and absolutely so in one from which broad culture and enduring satisfactions are to be derived.

Such, seemingly, is true, and yet, with no spirit of faultfinding, but rather with rejoicing that every Southern state has made provision in its laws for school libraries, and with a desire that we may not fall into error by taking for granted what may not in the fullest sense be true, I ask the question in all seriousness, and I believe with

Reprinted from *Proceedings*, Southern Educational Association, Houston, Texas, December 2, 1911, pp. 272–284. The Association was discontinued and publication ceased in 1915. Also published in *Library Journal*, 37:179–185, April, 1912.

justifiable appropriateness, if an analysis of library conditions now prevailing in the South, and for which we are largely responsible, will show our works in full accord with the profession of our faith. Are we, as educators, convinced, and have we expressed our conviction in our works, that the library, as an educational instrument, is an absolute essential if the process of education begun in the child by means of the school is to be carried on and brought to full fruitage in the after-school life of the adult? I ask it seriously, are we? The question demands an answer, and I shall attempt to give it.

An analysis of library conditions now prevailing in the South will reveal the following facts upon which the answer may be properly based.

First, it will show that, beginning with the year 1900, or thereabouts, a definite forward movement was made by one or two of the Southern states to provide for state-supported systems of rural school libraries. An examination of the proceedings of this Association and of the Conference for Education in the South will show that from that date until the present, state after state has taken up the work, and from year to year has so added to the number of volumes in libraries already established, and has so increased the number of new libraries, that now scarcely a county in the whole South is without some sort of school library facilities. I refrain from figures with a long train of ciphers following in their wake, however imposing they may be, but the number of such collections runs high into the thousands, and the number of volumes is well beyond the two-million mark.

Second, it will show that fully fifty per cent of the graded school systems of our towns and cities have library facilities of varying kinds, and that in many instances the work done by the library is very vital.

It will show, in the third place, that through the personal efforts of schoolmen many well-equipped, serviceable public libraries have been established and library clubs and associations have been organized for the purpose of making the public libraries of the South more efficient servants in the field of general education.

These are facts of splendid achievement. If there were no others to be considered, I should withdraw the question. But a continuation of the analysis will show on the opposite side:

First, that with very few exceptions, no instruction in the administration of school libraries, in the use of books, and in the supervision of children's reading and literature has been given by the Southern states in their teacher's institutes, normal schools and state universities. Be it said to the very great credit of Winthrop College, of
South Carolina, whose very progressive head has led in many forward movements in Southern education, that for a number of years
it has given two courses of such instruction, with the view of equip-
ping its graduates with such a store of information concerning school
libraries as would enable them to administer them to the ultimate
good of their pupils. In my own state, with its state university and
four normal schools, providing instruction for 3000 pupils during
the year, and with its 2500 rural school libraries, not to mention
town and city school libraries, only fourteen students were given instruction in a regular course in school library methods last year. It
was our privilege to have this class at the state university, and to
give several talks before students on the subject of the library; but
this was the extent of normal training in this branch in North Carolina. From the reports I have had before me, I have been forced to
the conclusion that a similar proportion prevails throughout the
whole South between the number of school libraries and of teachers
prepared by the normal schools to administer them.

Second, it will show that of the Southern states holding teacher's
institutes, few, if any, offer in their courses of study any instruction
in the subject mentioned or prepare bulletins for the guidance of the
teachers in it.

It will show, in the third place, that although the movement for
state-supported high schools has been begun since the one for rural
libraries was inaugurated, adequate provision has not been made by
which the special and larger needs of the high school's library may
be met. The high school library has been placed on the same basis
as that of the rural school library, although it is clearly apparent
that a more comprehensive library is essential to the best work of
the high school, and a larger income for library purposes is absolutely necessary.

Fourth, it will show that, although with the establishment of high
schools, high school inspectors have been appointed and sent here
and there within the borders of the state to aid in the standardiza-

tion of courses and in the solution of local problems, no library inspectors have been appointed to do a similar work in the field for
the libraries, although, on account of the fact that no instruction
is given teachers in this all-important subject by the normal schools
and institutes, there is a correspondingly greater need for the services of such a field worker.

It will show, in the fifth place, that the State Teachers' Associations have yet to form library sections or to give place in their programs in a large way for the discussion of library problems. I note
with genuine pleasure a tendency last year and this on the part of
teachers' associations to give librarians an opportunity to present library topics. This year, at least in three states, the Teachers' Assem-
blies and Library Associations are meeting in conjunction and exchanging speakers; but this is as yet by no means the general practice.

Sixth, it will show that in securing legislation for the establishment of library commissions and for the operation of systems of
traveling libraries, or, to put it differently, in the endeavor to extend library privileges to the whole people, the betterment associations, the women's clubs, the literary and historical associations, and
the library associations have been the principal aggressors. They
have led the fight, and so far as victory has been won it has largely
been won by them.

Further analysis, however, is unnecessary. I think the point I am
trying to make is by this time clearly patent. There is, in all seriousness, a timeliness and appropriateness in my question; for if we but
admit the facts as they are, we are forced to acknowledge that in the
matter of providing such library training as will best bring out the
resources of our libraries we have been woefully negligent, and in
the work of general state-wide library extension we have been satisfied with too small a part. If we hark back to the ever-convincing
test that trees are judged by their fruits, we are driven to the admission that in this all-important matter our actions have belied any
professions we have made to the contrary. We have not thought
through the matter, and have not given it the large, careful consideration it demands and of which it is eminently worthy. We have
but made a beginning in the right direction.

A thorough analysis also reveals the causes producing this condi-

tion. In an attempt to formulate a plan by which the condition may
be remedied they must be taken into account. Briefly stated, they
are three:

First, we have been so obsessed with theories and methods of how
to teach that we have lost sight of the alarming fact that 80 per cent
of us are out of school by the time we are 12 or 14 years of age, and
that if we are not trained in that time as to the use of books and the
values of reading as a means of enriching our experience and quickening our inner life, the mere how of reading will avail us but little.
The object of our teaching has been too much to teach how to read
rather than the reading habit, and to cram our minds with unrelated
facts rather than to train us in the use of books from which in after
years we can find for ourselves the chart for our daily sailing.

Second, we have had, through keenest necessity, to provide the
schoolhouse, increase the length of term, and train the teacher in
what we have rightly or wrongly conceived to be the fundamentals.

Third, too many of us have not known how to use books ourselves,
and have experienced but little delight and inspiration in what we
have read. Today many of us stand helpless before an encyclopedia
which contains the information of which we are in need, and a card
catalog overwhelms us. We have not known how to help ourselves,
and failing in this we have not seen the necessity of training our
children to help themselves. Again, far too many of us have never
felt the fire of imagination kindled by nursery rhyme, fairy story,
and tale of heroic adventure. In my own experience I was twenty-five
before I became acquainted with "Alice in Wonderland" or read a
line of Aladdin and his wonderful lamp, and I expect to make my
first genuine acquaintances with Andersen and Grimm and their
troop of fairy folk during the next few years, while my two little
ones don their gowns in the evening twilight and climb and rest upon
my knee before they are off for dreamland. Through them I hope to
be led, even this late, if possible, into that wonderland which I failed
to discover in my childhood in which fairy and prince and little
dream-children of Eugene Field and the little boy and snowy-haired
Uncle Remus are forever at play. The very pathos of it, that so many
of us have grown to maturity without having experienced the subtler
influences of the book touching and moulding us in our tender
years! How can it be otherwise that we should be blind leaders of

the blind, having thus failed to see the light? Or how can we be other than strong, rugged men, if such we are, possessed of undisputed power, yet power not full and complete, because in our early years that which gave swiftness to fancy, alertness to thought, breadth to vision, depth to character, in so far as it is furnished through reading, was mostly lacking?

But to dwell too long upon the analysis of the conditions or the causes giving rise to them is beside the point. The real matter is yet before us, and I pass immediately to a very brief consideration of the subject of my paper, which, according to the official program, is a Constructive library platform for Southern schools, or a course of procedure by which the library conditions generally prevailing in the South may be improved by the efforts of the schools.

If it were my high privilege to assist in writing a platform for Southern schoolmen or in mapping out a plan by the operation of which the library would be made a more efficient agent in the work of public education, a privilege which I think it is the duty of the Southern Educational Association to avail itself, I should have it look to the accomplishment of the following ends:

Additional School Libraries

First, continuing the practice already so splendidly begun of placing libraries in the rural schools, every public school in the South should be equipped with the best school library possible. The few years constituting the school period are too brief in themselves, and the training too limited, to chart the pupil's whole course. He needs to learn how and where to find his bearings after the sheltering haven of the school has been left and he is driving before the winds on the high sea. In the case of the primary schools, a serious fault which injures the efficiency of the present system and which needs consideration is that of close supervision. Neither the state superintendent nor the county superintendent watches after the use of the library as carefully as could be desired. Of course, the difficulties involved are great and the failure is pardonable, but if it can be avoided it should be. To do this effectively it may be necessary to follow the plan recently adopted by California as a whole and by sections of other states—namely, of employing a county superintendent of school libraries. Another weakness of the system is that adequate provision is not made by which the individual collections can be freshened up from time to time. It is true that books are added occasionally, but some plan should be devised by which an exchange of collections could be made, if desirable, between neighboring schools. In this way each school would retain its reference books, but if its main collection was not a duplicate of that of the neighboring school, an exchange could be effected by means of which renewed interest could be created and each school would be benefited. Instruction in the use of books should be given, and such selections should be read and assigned for commitment to memory as would insure the formation of habits of reading and standards of taste.

In the high schools, a larger list of reference works should be provided, and the collection should be so amplified that in the special classrooms and the general library material could always be found at hand which would stimulate interest in the prescribed work, and would further develop the habit of reading and fix standards of taste. In other sections of the country, where the library has been used to great profit in the schools, the presence of from 25 to 50 volumes in each classroom, known as classroom libraries, insures, in connection with the general library of the school, the most effective method of providing library material for every pupil. In order that the range of choice might be larger than it is at present, the superintendents of public instruction, in connection with library commissions or individual library workers, should compile adequate lists from which every need of the high school library could be met. Among the many excellent lists of this kind which would be unusually suggestive and helpful, are to be mentioned the one prepared for the secondary school of Oregon, copies of which may be had from the Library Commission of that state, and the list prepared for the National Education Association and published at a cost of ten cents the copy, in its reports on the Relation of public libraries to public schools in 1899. These two lists, revised and adopted to meet the needs of special localities, are in every sense admirable, and I commend them most heartily to you.

Normal School Instruction in Library Methods

After the libraries have been secured and proper methods of administration of the system have been devised, provision should be made for the training of teachers in the use of books and children's literature. It is not sufficient to set the bookcase beside the teacher's desk or place it in a corner and let it stand there. It must be properly used. It is the clear duty of the departments of pedagogy of the various state universities, of the special normal schools, and of the conductors of summer schools and teachers' institutes to give this instruction. If we wish guidance in this matter, there are a dozen splendid manuals which can be had at a nominal price, and the extensive report of the National Education Association, submitted, adopted, and printed in 1906, are at hand.

School Library Inspectors

In continuation of this instruction, the state should provide a school library director or inspector, who should not merely have charge of the distribution of the state appropriations for school libraries, but should visit, as the high school inspectors do, the various school libraries in the state and give them the benefit of personal advice and suggestion in addition to that given from time to time by the central office through bulletins and special letters. This person should be a trained librarian as well as teacher, and his work should be the standardization of school library methods. The suggestion I am making is not an experiment. It has been carried out in practice in a number of large city school systems and in several states, and has yielded splendid results.

The recent experience of a congregation of which I know will possibly give point to what I have been urging. At considerable expense and very great sacrifice it purchased and installed a splendid pipe organ. The Sunday following the installation, the membership gathered full of pleasurable anticipation. The deep bass pipes, the tremulous flute notes, the subtle overtones and the splendid harmonies— the thought of all of these and the comfort and spiritual rapture they could impart possessed every mind. But when the moment came for the instrument to win joyous, reverent tribute from every heart, the minister arose and announced that as yet its stops were not fully understood by the organist. In the meanwhile, it would be necessary to use the old reed organ. And so the new instrument, capable of filling every heart with a glow of spiritual fervor, stood silent in its splendid beauty, while the congregation sat cramped in purse and starved in soul. In what whit is the case of the community different which has taxed itself to procure a school library without at the same time having secured a teacher so trained in the subtleties and power of books as will enable him to make its splendid resources touch the plastic boy and girl and enrich the fountains of his or her life with the perennial warmth of song and story?

Instruction of Pupils in the Use of Books

Instruction should not only be given teachers through normal instruction and library methods standardized through inspectors, but definite instruction should be given every pupil in the use of books. Special periods in the course of study should be devoted to this work. The pupil should be taught the purpose of the preface of a book, how to distinguish between the table of contents and the index, how to use the index, even if it is to a set containing two or more volumes; how to consult dictionaries, encyclopedias, atlases, maps, etc., and how to use a card catalog. If need be he should be taught to classify and catalog a small collection. In this day of modern business methods, when one cannot carry in his memory all the facts essential to the conduct of the business in which he is engaged, it is absolutely necessary that he employ scientific time and labor-saving devices. Among these, along with the adding machine and cash register, is the alphabetic card or printed index. The mastery of this index principle, whether the pupil is to be a librarian, a banker, a lawyer, a physician, a politician, a traveling salesman, a merchant, or what not, is one of the greatest assets he can acquire, because it enables him to aid himself. If he goes to college it opens the college library's resources to him. If he becomes a banker, he will find the principle employed in the handling of notes and loans. If he becomes a lawyer, he will use it in citing cases with which to support his brief. If he tends the man who is parching with fever, it will enable him to consult his medical library for the further study of the disease from which his patient is suffering. Even if we leave out of consideration the moral and cultural value of the reading which such training will lead to, the training in itself is invaluable, for through it the boy becomes a self-educated man and is capable of continuing his education in his after school career. In our manual training courses the boy is taught the use of tools; in our agricultural classes he is taught farm methods and the use of implements; in our business courses he is taught the administration of the store and the keeping of its accounts. It yet remains for us in our libraries to teach the use of books which will make of permanent value, through study after school, all that he has been taught in the other branches. In whatever work he engages, he will find this part of his training of service, and long after his geometry and Latin are forgotten he will find himself still in possession of a key which will unlock the store of information bearing upon the infinite problems of his daily life.

The Establishment of Library Commissions

Every schoolman should busy himself in securing legislation in his state providing for the establishment, equipment and adequate financial maintenance of a free library commission, which, composed of educators and librarians alike, should act independently of the superintendent of public instruction's office, but should maintain to all libraries in its state an advisory, helpful relation. It is the duty of the schools to aid in securing this legislation, although they are not the only ones who may be benefited by it. The experience of thirty or more states of the Union points unmistakably to the conclusion that library work for the whole people yields the largest returns when such a special board of library commissioners and library organizers maintain a public office and offer their services to any community, school or club for the improvement of its library facilities. These should be the active agencies for the formation of library sentiment, and by them every library problem should be considered and in so far as possible solved. They should maintain public offices at the state capitals, and be in readiness to serve anyone in the state at all times. In Maryland, North Carolina, Kentucky, Missouri and Georgia, such commissions exist as separate state departments, but only in Kentucky and Missouri is the appropriation made by the state in any sense adequate. In North Carolina, Missouri and Kentucky trained librarians have been employed as field secretaries and are rendering an enlarging, useful service. In Virgina, Tennessee, Alabama and Texas library extension is provided for by the state through the state library or the department of archives and history. This arrangement, however, even if appropriations are equal, is not as satisfactory as that in which the commissions are separate; for the work of library extension is apt to be subordinated to that of the department with which it is connected. It suffers, too, from the lack of standing out singly and distinctively as an office having special work to be performed and of an importance second to nothing.

Traveling Libraries

To do their work properly, it is a matter of wide experience that these commissions must not only publish bulletins for the dissemination of knowledge concerning library matters, send out library organizers, encourage communities to establish new libraries and to improve old ones, etc., but they must be enabled to aid schools, rural communities, villages and towns by sending out a well-organized collection of traveling libraries. Up to the present, Virginia, Missouri and Tennessee have been the only states in the South to operate an extensive system of this kind, but during the present year over six hundred cases of fifty volumes each are in circulation and are rendering a splendid service. By means of such a system, any rural primary school may have its library shelves replenished by a loan; the debating and reference sections of the high school library can be supplemented for a given period; a village community can be supplied with a collection of books on agriculture, public health, domestic science, etc., in addition to a representative list of fiction, travel, history, biography and other forms of literature; a town which has never had a public library can receive a case and make it the nucleus of a free public library. Books can be brought to all the people, and the library idea can be crystalized into a general forward library movement. Here, certainly, is a splendid field for co-operation on the part of the schoolmen with the librarians, and every effort possible should be made to bring about the proper establishment of these offices.

Enlargement of Service of State Libraries

The state library, whenever it is expedient, should be made to contribute to the library needs of the state. In the South state libraries have until recently been little other than documentary collections, and have served few others than the state officers and members of the legislatures. Under the newer order of things, when every genuinely progressive library is extending its usefulness in as many directions as possible, it should not be so restricted either in the character of its contents or in the extent of its services. In the South, especially, where large city public libraries are few and where distances to other large libraries of other sections are great, it becomes more and more imperative that the state library should build up a strong reference collection and extend its privileges to any individual or library in the state. Among the Southern states which have adopted this plan, Virginia has met with most signal success.

More Public Libraries

The services of the free public library must be secured for all of our towns and cities, and must be more systematically utilized by our pupils and teachers. Unfortunately for the South, development in this field has been slow. The library's place and usefulness must be more fully understood. Its work with children, its cooperation with the schools, its helpfulness to study clubs, its contributions of books and periodicals and sets of stereopticon views to surrounding rural comunities, its public lectures, its activities in a thousand helpful directions—all this is too far-reaching in its influence for good and in its educational import for the South to miss. It must be secured at whatever cost. If there are no constructive library laws upon our statute books which will stimulate the establishment of such libraries (and in several states there are not), they must be written and enacted. Public sentiment in favor of libraries must be cultivated. Vigorous local tax campaigns for the maintenance of libraries, as well as of schools, must be waged and won. The library must be directed intelligently and made to serve. This is our work as educators. If we perform our duties well our labor shall not be in vain, and our reward will be great.

The analysis of library conditions existing in the South today has been made, and a plan or platform, by the adoption of which it can be changed and changed for the better, is before you. I realize fully that it is one man's analysis and one man's plan, but until a more comprehensive and more thoroughly thought-out policy is laid before you, I present it to you, and in the name of the children of the

Southland, whose duty and high privilege it is ours to prepare for participation in a large, well-rounded life, I call upon you to adopt it and see to it that the good which it contemplates for your children and your children's children is happily realized.

Standards for High School Libraries

THE IMPORTANCE OF MAKING the high school library the heart of the work of the high school has within the past five years received two highly significant evidences of consideration. In the South generally, through the Southern Association of Colleges and Secondary Schools, the possession of specific library resources has been required of schools in order that they may enjoy the accredited relation. Throughout the North and West, in which a similar requirement had been made earlier, definite standards applicable to library organization and equipment for secondary schools have also been adopted.

In North Carolina, the State Department of Education has recently passed a regulation in accord with that of the Southern Association of Colleges and Secondary Schools, requiring minimum collections of 300 volumes for group B and 500 volumes for group A schools, and has printed a list of books from which it is suggested that the books be selected. The matter of high school library standards is now under consideration, and the following suggestions, based very largely on the Report of the Committee on Library Organization and Equipment of the National Education Association (American Library Association, 78 East Washington St., Chicago, 1920, 40c), are offered for the guidance of schools now attempting to build up efficient high school libraries.

Reprinted from *High School Journal*, University of North Carolina, 6:96–98, 110, April 23, 1923, by permission of the publisher. Also published in University of North Carolina *Extension Bulletin*, Vol. II, No. 14, June 1, 1923.

Requisites of a Standard Library Organization

According to the report mentioned above, the requisites of a standard library organization are: (I) appropriate housing and equipment of the high school library; (II) professionally trained librarians; (III) scientific selection and care of books and other material, and the proper classification and cataloging of this material; (IV) instruction in the use of books and libraries as a unit course in high school curricula; (V) adequate annual appropriations for salaries and for the maintenance of the library, for the purchase of books and other printed matter, for the rebinding of books, for supplies, and for general upkeep; (VI) a trained librarian as state supervisor to be appointed as a member of the state education department, as in Minnesota, or under the library commission in cooperation with the state education department, as in New Jersey.

I. Housing and Equipment

The library should be scientifically planned as an integral part of the high school building. The reading room (which should be used solely for library purposes) should be centrally located, preferably on the second floor and near the study hall, unless it is used by the community in the capacity of a public library. In that case it should be on the first floor near the entrance. In the small school it should have a minimum seating capacity of an average classroom. In larger schools provision should be made for from 6 to 10 per cent of the entire enrollment, an area of 25 square feet of floor space per reader being required for complete accommodations and service. It should have an exposure admitting plenty of light and sunshine, should be well ventilated, and should be equipped with electric ceiling fixtures of either the indirect or semi-indirect type. White ceiling, light buff walls, light colored woodwork and trim, and a sound-deadening floor covering of cork carpet or linoleum are highly desirable.

The shelving, set flat against the wall or built into it, should be open and adjustable at intervals of one inch. It should be 7 feet high, 8 inches deep, and divided into three foot sections. For very large books the bottom shelves of one or two sections should be made 10 or 12 inches in depth, and one section of 8-inch shelving should be set aside for magazines which can be laid flat on their sides. In estimating the book capacity of shelving, allow 8 books for each linear foot. Floor stacks will rarely be required, as the wall space is usually ample. Tables 3 by 5 feet and seating 6 pupils, a card catalogue case, a library changing desk, a dictionary and atlas stand, a periodical rack, a book truck, a vertical file case, pamphlet boxes, and chairs (tipped with rubber if the floor is not covered) complete a minimum equipment.

In schools that can afford it, the reading room should be connected with a librarian's work room and a library classroom. The work room should be at least 10 by 15 feet and equipped with a cataloging desk, a typewriter with card-cataloging attachment, a typewriter table, chairs, shelves, storage space for supplies, and running water. The classroom should be furnished with chairs with tablet arms, a small stage, lantern and moving picture outfits, reflectoscope, victrola, table, and bulletin board of corticine. Both rooms should be well lighted and ventilated. If the classroom is used by all departments, it should have other access than through the library.

II. *The Librarian*

Ideal qualifications for the librarian are a college education, one year's training in an approved library school and one or more year's experience in library work, an attractive personality, and a knowledge of how to make the resources of the library available to every teacher and pupil in the school. (1) Administrative duties of the librarian should include directing the policy of the library; preparing the annual library budget; supervising the work of student assistants; selecting and ordering books and periodicals; and assembling a working collection of pamphlets, clippings, and pictures to supplement the book and periodical resources of the library. (2) Technical duties include classifying, cataloging, indexing, and filing all the material of the library so that it is readily accessible; keeping a record of all material loaned; providing for the mending and binding of books and periodicals; and keeping correct records and statistics of the growth and use of the library. (3) Educational duties include assisting teachers and students in finding material on special topics; instructing students in the use of catalogs and reference works; and stimulating the interest of students in cultural and inspirational work and the forming of a taste for good reading.

In libraries of schools having 200 to 500 or more pupils, the librarian should have at least one year of special library training and should be given the same rank and salary as heads of departments. In smaller schools, if a teacher-librarian is employed, library training for six weeks at a summer school should be required. In this event the teacher's schedule should be divided between the library and the classwork. If student assistants are employed in addition to the librarian, in order that the library may be kept open throughout the school day, they should be trained and supervised by the librarian.

III. *Scientific Selection, Classifying, and Cataloging of Books and Other Material*

Books and other materials for the library should be selected by the librarian, with the approval of the principal, upon the recommendation of heads of departments and teachers, selection being made with reference to the educational aims of the school, the recreational and cultural needs of the students, and the particular interests of the local community. In making the selection the librarian should be guided by standard lists such as those issued by the United States Bureau of Education (Washington, D.C. *Bulletin* No. 41, 1917, 40c), by the various state departments of education, or in accord with suggestions offered in publications issued by the National Education Association, the American Library Association, and other publishers of handbooks on book selection and library management. The best reference books and periodicals should be supplied in abundance, while complete works of authors or books sold on subscription should largely be avoided. Books in great demand should be supplied in duplicate. All books should be marked with the school bookplate, accessioned, classified, cataloged, shelf listed, and made ready for circulation. The minimum requirements for North Carolina schools are 300 and 500 volumes. Standards recommended throughout the country are: for schools having an enrollment of 100 or less, 1000 volumes; 200 or more, 2000 volumes; between 200 and 500, 3,000 volumes; between 500 and 1000, 3000 to 8000 volumes.

Other material, such as clippings, post cards, pictures, lantern slides, moving picture films, maps, globes, etc., which are used on special occasions by different departments of the school, should be classified and kept by the library and loaned for use in the library classroom or other classrooms. The library should also administer the loans made to the school by other libraries, museums, and loaning agencies, but it should not have charge of text books, stationery, and other school supplies.

IV. *Instruction in the Use of Books*

The most important work of the library is that of training students in the use of books and libraries. (1) A minimum of 3 recitation periods per year should be given in each English course to graded instruction in these subjects; or, preferably, (2) a minimum of 12 lessons a year should be given, 3 in English, 3 in history, 1 in Latin, 1 in Spanish or French, and 4 in the sciences, manual training, and home economics. This instruction should be given by the librarian; it should be scheduled as a part of the curriculum, and credited as a separate subject.

The training in the use of the library should have three principal objectives: (1) Students should be taught the use of indexes and reference books as tools. Lessons based on the card catalog, indexes to books and magazines, dictionaries, encyclopedias, atlases, and other works of reference, should be carefully planned so that an exact knowledge of their use and contents can be acquired. (2) Education does not end with the high school. Consequently the training in the use of books should be related to the use of public, college, and reference libraries, and of material furnished by library commissions and university extension agencies, so that self-education may be continued throughout life. The connection between the school library and the public library should be particularly close and cordial. (3) Books also furnish recreation and amusement; they instruct and inspire. Students should be trained in discovering these values in the books they read.

V. *Annual Appropriation*

In North Carolina no special library fund has been provided for high schools. However, the salary of the librarian should be charged to instruction or administration, and books, magazines, and supplies to equipment. The library budget should be included annually in the total school budget and the school fund should meet the main cost of operation. The book fund should be carefully apportioned by the librarian according to the needs of each department, and it should be estimated on the basis of a minimum of 50 cents per student per year. For periodicals at least $40 per year should be estimated even for the smallest high school.

VI. *State Supervision of School Libraries*

Inasmuch as the building up of a successful high school library system involves a great deal of effort and the expenditure of a large amount of money, the whole work should be directed by a library expert. Through such an officer, connected with the state department of education or the state library commission, library standards should be established, proper lists of books and effective methods of procedure should be worked out, and the whole work of the high school library should be placed on a satisfactory basis. Where such an officer is not provided, the duties mentioned should be performed as far as possible by the state high school inspector.

Modifications

The standards set forth in the foregoing sections will, in many instances, necessarily have to be modified to meet special conditions. The small school that cannot provide a special library room should equip a regular classroom. Likewise, if it cannot afford a trained librarian, it should provide a teacher who has had a least a summer school course in library methods. If it cannot set aside every year 50 cents per pupil for books, it should spend what it can. However, in all circumstances it must be kept in mind that the library can be, and should be, made the real heart and center of the school, and inasmuch as the standards recommended contribute to that end, they should be applied at the earliest moment that conditions permit.

Increasing the Significance of the School Library

To THOSE WHO HAVE taken part in the development of the elementary and secondary schools of this country during the past three decades, it is a matter of common knowledge that no single thing has contributed more to the effectiveness of the school program than the change from the use of the single text-book-recitation procedure to the supervised study-use of many books and materials method of instruction. Likewise, it is a matter of common knowledge, or should be, that the school library has changed with the methods of instruction, and that it has been one of the principle means by which the change in the schools has been consciously effected.

The Twelfth Yearbook of the Department of Elementary School Principals of the National Education Association,[1] recently issued, is devoted to the organization and work of the elementary school library. My purpose in this paper is to indicate some of the ways in which the usefulness of the school library in both the elementary and secondary schools can be increased. This, in my opinion, can be accomplished in three ways. Teachers colleges and departments of education in universities can provide instruction which will give teachers, principals and superintendents a better understanding of the function of the school library; library schools can improve their instruction for school librarians; and teachers and librarians alike can subject the common problems arising in the school library field to systematic and extensive investigation.

Teacher training agencies can assist in achieving these desired objectives, in so far as they can be achieved through the teacher, as fol-

Reprinted from *School and Society*, 38:845–853, December 30, 1933, by permission of the publisher. An address delivered before the Phi Delta Kappa and the Pi Lambda Theta profession·l education fraternities for graduate men and women, respectively, University of Chicago, August 17, 1933.

[1]For notes, see page 110.

lows. First, the prospective teacher should be made familiar with literature which has been recognized by teachers and librarians as of particular significance to different groups of children and adolescents. She should have first-hand knowledge of this material. Responsibility for the direction of pupils in its use can not be shifted from the teacher to the librarian. She must not only know its content, but also the methods of employing it skilfully in carrying out the educational objectives of the school. A course of this nature seems to me to be fundamental.

Secondly, the teacher should be trained in the use of the special library materials relating to the teaching of her particular subject. Morrison,[2] in his "Practice Teaching in the Secondary School"; McGregor,[3] in "Supervised Study in English"; and Simpson,[4] in "Supervised Study in History," and many others, have illustrated the ways in which mastery of given subjects in the curriculum is secured through the extensive use of assimilative material drawn from the library. The teacher should be familiar with these and similar books and the methods which they present in so far as they involve the use of the library. She should know how to coordinate her work with that of the librarian, what opportunities the library provides for conferences with students, how free reading helps to promote permanent reading habits, and how proper attitudes of conduct are developed through study in a library room shared with other pupils. The courses in which this familiarity with literature, materials and points of view is acquired should be thought of as content courses and not as professional courses in school library administration.

The way in which departments of education of universities can assist in the improvement of the school library, especially in matters of administration through principals and superintendents, may be indicated as follows.

In the first place, the principal and superintendent should understand the exact function the library should perform in the school. Inasmuch as the library serves all departments and is used by all members of the school, the principal or superintendent should know the relation which it sustains to the total school organization.

In the second place, he should know what qualifications a librarian should possess and how to test the performance of the librarian in the school. Tests and devices for determining the effectiveness of the performance of teachers have been perfected and are regularly employed, but methods of appraising the work of the librarian have not been developed as fully,[5] although the librarian is charged with the responsibility of coordination and generalship in the field of supervised study in addition to the provision of materials appealing to different pupil groups for free reading.

In the third place, the principal and superintendent should be familiar with school library literature such as the works on administration by Fargo,[6] Logasa,[7] Wilson,[8] and Johnson[9] and the school library yearbooks,[10] and books dealing with the experience gained in the field by skilled school librarians. Acquaintance with these books is desirable because the library is the principal integrating agency of the entire school and, particularly, because the books with which the superintendent and principal are usually acquainted deal largely with general administrative problems and methods and only incidentally, if at all, with library administration. The recent yearbook of the Department of Principals of the National Education Association on Elementary School Libraries is a notable exception, but even this volume, in the three lists of books which it recommends for: (a) principals, (b) teachers, and (c) principals and teachers—one hundred and eighty-two titles in all—includes only one book dealing specifically with the library, namely, "The Elementary School Library," by W. E. King.[11]

Inasmuch as the support of schools and public libraries comes from the public treasury, it is important that the school administrator should know what school library service costs, and how such cities as Pittsburgh and Cleveland and such counties as Kern, in California, and Hamilton, in Tennessee, have provided it through city and county libraries. It is also extremely important for the school administrator to know that in rural areas where county library service has not been provided, cooperation between the school and library extension authorities may go far in bringing effective library service into existence not only for the school but for the county as a whole. The county library movement of California and the present effort on the part of librarians and the library committee of the Southern Association of Colleges and Secondary Schools to work out a cooperative plan for supplying school library facilities in Southern rural areas are cases in point which might be studied with profit.

In the fourth place, the school administrator should be familiar with the more important problems of school library administration with which he will be confronted in the general administration of his school. He should not only be familiar with them, but he should be equipped to participate in their solution, or assist his librarian and other members of his staff in their solution.

The part which the library school or teachers college may play in increasing the effectiveness of the school library may now be indicated. They should provide suitable training for the part-time teacher-librarian who, in addition to her teaching, administers the library in a school with small enrolment and few teachers, and for the full-time librarian in a large school who is responsible not only for the professional administration of the library but for the guidance of students in both academic and extra-curricular activities. Whether given by library schools or by library departments in teachers colleges, training for either type of position calls for the selection of only those candidates who possess ability and personal qualifications of a high order, who have an extensive general educational background such as is indicated by graduation from college or university, and whose knowledge of educational practice and psychology is sufficient to enable them to participate in the activities of the teaching staff and to adjust themselves intelligently to the school's program. Experience in teaching, interest in children and the ability to work with others will add to the prospective school librarian's effectiveness. It is taken for granted that the library school will see to it that she understands such technical processes as are essential to successful administration. In addition, it should see to it that she has an intimate knowledge of literature for children and adolescents, that she is skilled in evaluating and selecting new books that may be added to the collection, that she knows what the educational objectives of the schools are and the ways in which the library can be used in attaining these objectives, and that she understands the relationship of the library to teachers, administration and the school generally. Her training should also thoroughly familiarize her with the relation of the library to the public library and other library resources of the community or state, and with the implications of library service in the fields of continuation and adult education.

The value of the work of the school library might be further increased if the school librarian could occasionally alternate work in the library with the pursuit of graduate courses dealing with the recognition of problems arising in the use of the library and in the effective guidance of pupils. Advanced study and training in methods of investigation in this field would unquestionably yield many fruitful returns.

The third major effort to increase the significance of the library in the school should take the form of investigation. This effort should be participated in by librarians and graduate students and staff members of library schools, by graduate students and staff members of departments of education, by teachers and school administrators in service, and by psychologists and sociologists interested in the intellectual and social effects of reading. The problems peculiar to the school library which might profitably be investigated have as yet been only slightly considered. For the purposes of this paper, it will be sufficient to indicate what some of these problems are and the direction which this investigation might take.

1. *Problems concerning administration.* Problems in the field of school library administration are numerous. At the head of the list stands the question, How shall school library service be furnished? Shall the school board supply it, as in Detroit, the city library, as in Pittsburgh, or the school board and city library jointly, as in Cleveland? Although school administrators and librarians have worked together on this problem for many years and have answered the question in various ways, three of which have been extensively employed in different sections of the country, no adequate study has been made to determine the correct answer or the comparative effectiveness of the three methods generally followed.

Another aspect of this administrative problem is met in the case of rural schools in areas dependent upon county libraries or in areas without general library service. Obviously, in rural settings, where library materials are limited and where both students and communities require service, different procedures from those employed in the city must be discovered. However, in the event a program of county-wide library promotion is organized, it is apparent that such promotion can not hope to be successful unless there is complete cooperation between the schools and those working for county-wide library service. Accordingly, a modification of school library standards, in so far as they relate to the physical ownership of school library books and the provision of competent library personnel, may be highly desirable, as books read by pupils at home and during vacation have an important bearing upon the work of pupils in the school.

Still another sub-problem of this general problem relates to the school library budget. Literature on school libraries seems to contain but slight data concerning school library financing. Standardizing agencies have undertaken to indicate what school library service should cost. Their formulas, however, have usually been expressed in terms of expenditure per student for books and periodicals and have very inadequately covered expenditures for personnel, equipment, etc. In instances in which school library service is provided jointly by the school board and the city library, the difficulties of arriving at the proper budgets are correspondingly increased.

A study which would bring all these diverse elements under review, which would deal with the interrelationships between school library service on the one hand and city and county library service on the other, and which would indicate how such service could be put upon an approved and permanent financial basis, is greatly needed.

B. Lamar Johnson,[12] in his monograph entitled "The Secondary School Library," has pointed out other administrative problems. Among them may be mentioned the use of the study hall as library. Johnson reports that principals prefer the use of the study hall for library purposes, and that librarians are equally strong in their disapproval. The data secured by him indicate that greater use is made of library materials in schools in which the library and study hall are combined than where they are separate. He also records the existence of differences of opinion concerning the location of classroom collections in secondary schools outside the general library. Here the ancient controversy of centralized *versus* decentralized collections presents itself. In both instances the advantages and disadvantages have not been made the subject of careful objective study.

The status of the school librarian in the school organization is also a matter which should be carefully studied. New York, Wisconsin and California have defined this satisfactorily through certification, but in other states, rank, tenure of position and remuneration are frequently left in doubt. Indefiniteness concerning these matters inevitably reduces morale and makes effective administration more difficult.

2. *Problems concerning teaching the use of books in libraries.* Standardizing agencies have consistently emphasized the necessity of providing instruction in the use of books in school libraries. Librarians have developed outlines for instruction in the use of catalogs, indexes, dictionaries, atlases, works of reference, etc., and have urged that instruction of this nature be cared for in the curriculum. They have also formulated procedures for successful cooperation with teachers in carrying out programs of supervised study. Teachers, principals and superintendents, in turn, have given thought to the total organization of the schools, and have undertaken to adjust the library to the particular methods of instruction employed throughout the school generally. But they have also been confronted with the difficulty of introducing additional courses concerning the use of the library into the curriculum. The result frequently is that this course does not find the place in the curriculum which it deserves. While differences of methods in instruction adopted by a given school will always necessitate differences in methods to be employed within the library, studies dealing with the necessary adjustments in different systems would contribute greatly to the solution of this problem.

3. *Problems concerning standards.* Reference to standards for school library service has been made several times in this paper. The subject has frequently been considered by the National Education Association, the American Library Association, and by the various standardizing agencies during the past twenty years, and standards to meet the needs of different sections of the country have been adopted. They have embraced requirements concerning library rooms and equipment, number of books and periodicals, expenditures for general maintenance and personnel, training of the librarian, teaching the use of library materials, and technical processes dealing with the cataloguing, classification and circulation of materials. But in no instance that I know of have these requirements been arrived at on the basis of extensive objective data. Assumptions, opinions, and such experience as could be drawn upon without involving extensive investigation have been relied upon in the main. Now that twenty years have elapsed since experimentation with standards was begun and many individual school libraries have developed highly success-

ful plans of operation, the best practice should be brought under a painstaking, systematic review in an effort to formulate regulations which will insure the most effective use of materials.

4. *Problems concerning the distribution of library materials.* In 1921, at a meeting of the American Library Association at Swampscott, Massachusetts, a pamphlet containing data on the library resources of neighboring cities made vivid a fact that has frequently escaped notice, namely, that library facilities are very unevenly distributed in America. A comparison with the book resources of Salem, Massachusetts, and the State of North Carolina revealed the following facts: The public library of Salem (a city in 1921 of 43,000 inhabitants) contained as many volumes as the seven largest public libraries of North Carolina; the library of the Essex Institute of the city contained more bound volumes and pamphlets than any institution of higher learning in the state, and the law association library of the city contained more law books than the law libraries of the Supreme Court library of North Carolina and the three law school libraries of the state. In 1926, when the Library Extension Committee of the American Library Association made a nation-wide survey of library resources, it was found that 44 per cent of the population of the United States and Canada was without public library facilities.[13] When it is realized that less than 50 per cent of the high schools of the country have membership in the North Central, Southern, and other similar associations, which require member schools to provide specified library facilities, and that the elementary school library movement is much less advanced than that of the high schools, even in the larger cities, it becomes apparent that the book resources of many schools are at best extremely meager if they exist at all. The United States Office of Education compiles general data of this nature, but librarians and school administrators have thought too little about their educational implications. Studies of the library resources of the communities in which schools are located might go far in explaining the nature of the educational performance of the schools themselves, as well as of the contribution which the schools involved make to their communities.

5. *Problems concerning measurements.* No studies in the field of education seem to me to have yielded finer results than those dealing with the measurement of pupil attainment. Signal advance has fol-

lowed the investigations which have established the significance of eye movement and silent reading rate and increase in comprehension. But few objective data are available which throw light upon the differences of attainment of pupils in schools with and without adequate library facilities. I should be extremely interested to know why seniors in North Carolina high schools, when given the Thorndike vocabulary test in 1929 by M. R. Trabue,[14] failed to measure up satisfactorily with seniors in the high schools of the nation at large. As a matter of fact not only did they fail to reach the senior average, but only 48 per cent of them reached high school freshman average! I should also be extremely interested to know why one third of the pupils in the elementary schools of the state fail of promotion annually, or why there is such a high academic mortality of freshmen in the state's institutions for higher learning. I can imagine that shortness of school term, poor preparation of teachers, inadequate equipment, and many other causes have been operative. But I can not escape the conviction that the lack of adequate library facilities described above and the attendant lack of skill in silent reading rather than lack of natural ability are partly, if not largely, responsible for the situation.

Twenty studies summarized in the Twelfth Yearbook of the Department of Elementary School Principals deal with the interest of children in reading,[15] but few studies have been made dealing with the contribution which the school library makes directly to the pupil. Articles in the Yearbook hint at increased power of comprehension, but few objective studies of the effect of the library procedures upon the pupil have been carried out. Nevertheless a beginning in this field has been made which it is hoped will be increasingly followed. Eva Schars,[16] of the Detroit school library system, has undertaken to discover what effect school library procedure has in establishing appropriate attitudes of school citizenship on the part of the pupils. She finds that the school library is a highly successful integrating agency and that its procedures very definitely promote proper attitudes of conduct. Studies by Eurich,[17] the Presseys,[18] and Johnson[19] have undertaken to answer questions concerning the reading abilities of students at the college level, but no satisfactory answer has as yet been given to the question asked by Duffus,[20] Cheney,[21] and the American Library Association Committee on Readable Books,[22] why so many thousands of pupils who have read extensively in school are lost as readers when their school days end. And the question of the significance of reading in the school as a means to social adjustment is yet to be seriously considered. Miss Katherine Niles, a graduate student in the department of sociology of the University of Chicago, is now undertaking to find an answer to this question. She is attempting to find it through case study procedure of which the following is an example.

Miss X as a pupil in the grammar grades suffered from an inferiority complex due to the fact that she was the youngest member of her family, her family lived on the edge of the village and was without special status in church and community life. She, however, had learned to read without difficulty in the grammar grades and discovered that reading not only provided her with a means of escape, but gave her status at home, with neighbors and particularly in school. In the high school this sense of status was heightened by the fact that her reading was commended by the librarian and her teachers. This, in turn, led to her extensive reading of works selected and approved by the librarian and teachers, through which her standards of intellectual and artistic appreciation were definitely improved. The development of her power of appreciation and the extension of her intellectual and critical faculties gave her increased self-confidence and enabled her to make a satisfactory transition from early school life to a successful college and university career. At first, reading afforded release, later it gave status, and later still, it led to intellectual and appreciative mastery, which, in turn, led to effective social adjustment.

A second study recently undertaken deals with another aspect of after-school adjustment. This was made by Alice Horsfall, librarian of the Omaha Technical High School, Omaha, Nebraska, who attempted to discover what effect training in high schools with and without adequate library facilities had upon the reading of freshmen when they entered college. The first question she attempted to answer was whether or not training under these conditions materially affected freshman interest in reading. Her answer to this question is as follows:

> Subject interests of college freshmen are not noticeably affected by the presence or absence of an adequate library in the

secondary school. Doubtless the school curriculum, the newspaper, the radio and the general environment combine to render certain topics interesting to the group as a whole. The library provides reading material on the same topics, but does little to develop an original interest.

Other findings of her study are that students of low scholastic grades in schools with adequate library facilities upon reaching college do more free reading than do those of either medium or high grades and that students of low scholastic grades in schools with adequate library facilities read almost three times as much as similar students from secondary schools with limited library facilities. She also found that students who had become acquainted with good library procedure in secondary schools adjusted themselves very much more quickly to the library procedure of the higher institutions than the latter. In that respect they were able to make a quicker and, therefore, more effective beginning at the outset of their college careers.

Studies such as these may, or may not, be particularly significant in themselves. They are significant, however, in that they open up a new field of investigation—the field of the social significance of the after effects of reading in the school. Need for such studies concerning the development of reading interests, the fixing of permanent reading habits, and the establishment of standards of conduct and ideals through reading is tremendously important. Now that methods of supervised study have been elaborated, that library schools and teachers colleges have made an effective beginning in the training of school librarians, that teachers and librarians have developed library techniques through an extensive period of experimentation, the careful consideration of these more difficult measurements of the effectiveness of the school library should be begun.

In conclusion, I should like to ask these questions: What part is the school going to play in the field of adult education? What contribution will it make to the new social order in which leisure is to assume (has already assumed) a new importance? In asking these questions, I am still keeping in mind the improvement of the use of library materials in teaching. The formation of individual opinions by pupils, arrived at through independent study and the use of many materials in the school library, furnishes one part of the possible

answer. The development of proper social attitudes, through the socialized recitation and the self-imposed discipline of the school library, furnishes a second part. And the cultivation of taste and the
development of standards of appreciation through leisure reading in
the school library furnish a third. Whether the school is to be the
institution through which the community will undertake to answer
these questions concerning adult education and the use of leisure, or
whether it will undertake to answer them through the public library,
or through some other public institution not yet called into being, is
yet to be determined. The important immediate consideration for the
school is that through the training which it provides it shall make
possible for its pupils this kind of intellectual, social and cultural attainment. The school library, nicely adjusted to the entire program
of the school, may prove to be the school's best instrument to this
end. It goes without saying, then, that all who are interested in making it this sort of instrument, whether librarian or teacher, should
strive to bring it to the highest possible degree of effectiveness in
these or other ways that may be discovered.

NOTES:

[1] *Twelfth Yearbook of the Department of Elementary School Principals.* National Education Association, Vol. XII, No. 5, June, 1933.

[2] H. C. Morrison, *Practice Teaching in the Secondary School.* University of
Chicago Press, Chicago, 1927.

[3] Laura McGregor, *Supervised Study in English.* Macmillan, N.Y., 1919.

[4] Mabel Simpson, *Supervised Study in History.* Macmillan, N.Y., 1918.

[5] Martha Wilson, "School Library Score Card," *School Library Yearbook No.
II.* American Library Association, Chicago, 1928, pp. 59–74. *Twelfth Yearbook
of the Department of Elementary School Principals.* National Education Association, Vol. XII, No. 5, June, 1933, Chapter IX.

[6] Lucile F. Fargo, *The Library in the School.* American Library Association,
Chicago, 1933.

[7] Hannah Logasa, *The High School Library.* D. Appleton and Company, New
York, 1928.

[8] Martha Wilson, *School Library Management.* Minnesota Department of Education, Minneapolis, 1917.

[9] B. Lamar Johnson, "The Secondary School Library." United States Office of
Education *Bulletin*, No. 17, 1932.

[10] *School Library Yearbooks* Nos. I, II, III, IV, and V. American Library Association, Chicago, 1927, 1928, 1929, 1931 and 1932.

[11] W. E. King, *Elementary School Library.* Charles Scribner's Sons, 1929.

[12]B. Lamar Johnson, *Ibid.*

[13]Report of Library Extension Committee of the American Library Association on public library conditions and needs. American Library Association, Chicago, 1926.

[14]M. R. Trabue, See files of the Bureau of Research of the School of Education, University of North Carolina. Report of corresponding secretary of Committee on College Admissions of the North Carolina College Conference. Durham, North Carolina, November 23, 1926.

[15]*Twelfth Yearbook of the Department of Elementary School Principals.* National Education Association, Vol. XII, No. 5, June, 1933, pp. 486–507.

[16]Florence Eva Schars, "The Intermediate School Library and Character Education." Master's Thesis, College of the City of Detroit, 1932.

[17]Alvin C. Eurich, *The Reading Abilities of College Students.* University of Minnesota Press, Minneapolis, 1931. "Student Use of the Library," *Library Quarterly*, Vol. III, No. 1, pp. 87–94, 1933.

[18]Luella W. and Sidney L. Pressey, *Essential Preparation for College.* R. Long and R. R. Smith, New York, 1932.

[19]B. Lamar Johnson, "Stephens College Library Experiment," American Library Association *Bulletin*, Vol. 27, No. 5, pp. 205–211, 1933.

[20]R. L. Duffus, *Books, Their Place in a Democracy.* Houghton Mifflin Company, Cambridge, 1930.

[21]O. H. Cheney, *Economic Survey of the Book Industry.* National Association of Book Publishers, New York, 1931.

[22]Emma Felsenthal, *Readable Books in Many Subjects.* American Library Association, Chicago, 1929.

The Integration of Library Service with the School Curriculum

THE EXTENSIVE USE OF LIBRARY MATERIALS in the teaching process is one of the most significant aspects of supervised study in American elementary and secondary schools today.[1] It is my purpose in this article to consider ways in which this use of library materials, this integration of library service with the curriculum, may be success-

Reprinted from *School Review*, 42:657–666, November, 1934, by permission of the publisher.

[1]For notes, see page 121.

fully effected and the total work of the modern school correspondingly broadened and enriched. Specifically, I shall consider: (1) what effective integration of the library and the curriculum depends on, (2) by what methods it is effected, and (3) certain experiments that are being made through which, it is hoped, a higher degree of integration may be successfully achieved.

What Integration Depends On

In the first place, integration depends fundamentally on the organization and administration of the school. Buildings, equipment, curriculum, teaching staff—all are conceived in accord with a unifying aim, and each part of the entire school is so directed as to contribute to the achievement of that aim. The library, being a part of the school—primarily a central, integrating agency for the school—inevitably is dependent on the general plan for its particular performance.

Integration of the library and the curriculum depends, in the second place, on the understanding and the cooperation of the principal. Testimony from all sources points conclusively to the fact that it is extremely difficult for the school library to achieve its maximum service, however skilled the librarian and the teachers, unless the principal understands fully how the library is related to the school's program and the part which teacher and librarian, respectively, play in carrying out the program. The allotment of physical space; provision of books, periodicals, and other materials; the competency and the training of the librarian and his assistants; the scheduling of classes in separate study hall and library or in a combination study-hall library; the provision for leisure-time reading and individual study—all these rest ultimately in the hands of the principal. For these reasons, it is tremendously important for the principal to understand how great his responsibility in this respect is. His responsibility is far greater, I frequently fear, than the principal realizes or than he has the opportunity to realize. If he falls short of such realization, his failure is quite understandable and may usually be attributed to two causes: First, departments of education have failed to include in the courses on school administration adequate instruction concerning the importance of library materials and service in effecting the integrated program of the school. Teachers and librarians may be guided to a realization of the importance of the library, but this phase of administration has been, and continues to be, a more-or-less blind spot in the school administrator's course of study. The second cause is that, even in such books as Morrison's *The Practice of Teaching in the Secondary School*, every page of which contains library implications, specific reference to library organization and administration is largely lacking. Even though integration is logically and forcefully suggested and teaching procedures are indicated by which librarian and teacher may effect integration, the necessary administrative organization and machinery are not pointed out with equal clarity. I am making no plea for overemphasis on the library per se or for the trained librarian as such; I am urging an understanding by the principal of what library organization and training may have to offer in promoting the work of the school and an acquaintance on his part with the literature concerning the school library written from the librarian's point of view as well as from that of the school man. Each type of literature supplements the other, and both are necessary. Both should be as obviously and specifically labeled as possible.

In the third place, integration depends on the understanding and the cooperation of the teacher. It is largely through the teacher that materials made available by the library are integrated with the daily work of the school. Just which subjects taught in a school, a high school for example, involve an extensive use of library materials may be open to question. Some course with a large drill content or laboratory accompaniment may make slight demands on library materials. Mathematics, work in the shop, a part of the work in science possibly fall within this group. Even here, however, the single textbook does not completely suffice; wide reading for orientation and illustration are also required. The teacher who secures extensive participation by his students in the socialized recitation or a high degree of effectiveness in the completion of special units or projects in the study program, and genuinely interests them in their work, will see to it that they make extensive use of library materials and will base his teaching technique largely on the school library. He will do so, not because he has any predilection for the library per se, but because he knows that successful teaching is based on interest and that interest springs in many instances from the wide range of illustrative and assimilative materials which the library supplies. Needed materials will be at hand in the classroom, the laboratory, or the central library and will be employed as the occasion demands.

The fourth essential in securing integration is intelligent coordination supplied through the librarian. By "librarian" I mean a person, whether trained primarily as a teacher or as a librarian, who has a broadly based general education, who has been grounded in the essential principles of education, who understands the purposes of the curriculum, and who through knowledge of books and materials is able to supplement the work of the principal and the teacher with pupils, individually and collectively. The librarian should understand the total relationships of the various parts of the school, both those concerned with the curriculum and those having to do with the extra-curriculum, and be able to make the library the center of them all. Training in the theory and the practice of library organization and administration, which acquaints the librarian with principles and methods of procedure in effecting essential unity in the multiplicity of school relationships, as contrasted with experience gained on the job, proves invaluable at this point. It lifts the librarian out of the class of school administrators who have been styled "administrators of emergencies" and enables him, when confronted with problems of cooperation or integration, to formulate procedures for the solution of the problems which are dictated by correct principles of administration. The librarian's point of view, like that of the principal, should be school-wide, rather than departmental. If the librarian is to fill his position effectively, his training should be planned accordingly.

How Integration is Effected

The successful use of library materials in the program of studies may be effected in a variety of ways. Chief among these, as indicated by library standards, score cards, and various books and articles on the school library, is teaching the use of the library through a series of lessons running throughout the entire period of the school. Such instruction can be given effectively as a separate course by the school librarian, by the librarian of the public library, or by teachers of

English or the social sciences. Numerous books and manuals devoted to teaching the use of the library are available. The greatest obstacle, however, to the effective presentation of this unit, is lack of time in the school schedule. B. Lamar Johnson, in his study of secondary-school libraries, found that such instruction was not so generally practiced as recommended, and for the reason indicated.[2] Librarians and teachers who have had occasion to teach pupils how to use library materials know how indispensable this instruction is if all pupils in a school are to become familiar with a wide variety of reference books as sources of information for constant use.

Teaching the use of materials through cooperation with the teacher by means of assignments in specific subjects is a second highly successful means of effecting integration. This procedure involves the use of materials in individual courses and subjects and is elaborated in detail in many of the well-known books on various aspects of supervised study. One of the most interesting statements concerning this method is that of Alice R. Brooks, presented in *School Library Yearbook, Number Five*.[3] This article describes the results of an attempt to teach the use of the library through the daily assignments in the social studies. The results, in that they grew out of actual situations, were altogether satisfactory so far as they went, but they fell short of including the whole range of library tools and materials which were essential in other courses. Wherever this method of teaching is depended on, all courses must be taught in this way if pupils are to secure a knowledge of how all the library tools and materials are to be used, and even then some coordinating instruction given by the librarian is necessary if a high degree of unity in the course is to be secured.

A third and most important method of securing integration is that of providing an abundance of materials for free or leisure reading. Not only may reading rate and comprehension be increased in this way, but knowledge gained through the free reading of fiction, or stories of adventure, or books of travel, or biographies, or works of literature and science leads to a better understanding of materials useful in instruction and in many instances furnishes the interest and factual information essential to successful class work.

Integration may also be effected in many other ways. The librarian may assist individual pupils or groups of pupils in dealing with library problems. He may induce them to become members of book clubs or train them for positions in the library as pupil assistants. He may see that the library participates in assembly programs, dramatic performances, and extra-curriculum activities in general. The librarian's greatest contribution to the integrating process may result from his contacts with the principal and individual teachers and his participation in the staff meetings of the school. The list of effective methods of integration might easily be extended, since countless librarians and teachers employ these and other means daily. It is sufficient merely to mention these few and to pass on to a consideration of some of the experiments which are being carried out today, not only at the various school levels, but at the junior-college, college, university, and adult-education levels, to discover effective measures of enriching the modern educational program through the use of the library.

Experiments in Integration

The report by Miss Brooks already referred to is based on an experiment worthy of special notice because the study of the social sciences is receiving unusual consideration today and means of enriching the subject through the library are correspondingly important. The reason given for making the experiment is stated by Miss Brooks as follows:

> Library instruction is given at present in the majority of cases as a separate series of lessons or as lessons correlated with certain subjects of the curriculum. But to teach the use of the library as a separate course or through correlation, having library instruction as an end in itself, is to attempt to teach by means of artificially created situations. The pupils fail to absorb the practical value of material learned in this manner and miss the opportunities of applying it to the work of their other courses. Since the trend of present-day education is to "learn by doing" in answer to "a felt need," this study suggests the possibility of a close integration of library instruction with the various courses, to be given whenever and wherever the problems or activities of a course require it.[4]

At Cleveland in February, 1934, at a meeting of high-school inspectors and principals held in connection with the meeting of the Department of Superintendence, G. H. Reavis, of the Ohio State Department of Education, gave informally a graphic description of the way in which he determines the effectiveness of the performance of a high school. Naturally, he discusses the organization of the school with the principal. He looks over the plant and goes through the usual routine procedures. He makes it a point to see all the teachers who have recently been added to the staff, those who normally are not far from retirement, and those concerning whom he has any occasion to make special inquiry. In order to ascertain the real effectiveness of the school, he uses the library as a barometer. He discovers through the pupils and the librarian which teachers base their work most effectively on the library. He finds this test one of the most satisfactory he can apply in getting at a real understanding of the character of the work of the school.

At Stephens College, Columbia, Missouri, a junior college, President Wood is frankly attempting to determine whether complete integration of library materials and instruction can be achieved through the reorganization of the program of studies. B. Lamar Johnson fills the double position of librarian and dean of instruction. As dean, he is concerned with the formulation of the curriculum and the techniques followed in instruction. He maintains contacts with faculty members, discusses books with them, sees that new books are available for their use, and supports such plans as they may develop which involve the use of books in teaching. As librarian, he is concerned with the instruction of the students in the use of the library and particularly with the stimulation of reading. Classroom libraries, current magazines in dormitory parlors, and dormitory libraries are so distributed over the campus that they can be reached easily. Teachers take classes to the library for instruction in the use of materials, the librarian gives courses in library orientation, students are urged to suggest new books for purchase, and every incentive is made to encourage reading. Students whose rate of reading is slow are organized in silent-reading groups, and an attempt is made to improve their power of comprehension as well. This experiment is now two years old, and the results are being watched with keen interest by college teachers and students of reading at advanced levels.

The New Plan for Freshmen and Sophomores, adopted in 1930 at the University of Chicago, rests squarely on the idea that individual reading, with appropriate guidance through lectures, syllabi, and skilled advisers, provides the surest basis for genuine education. In the autumn of 1933 the idea was extended down into the last two years of the University High School, and with the beginning of the autumn quarter, 1934, it is proposed to reduce the period of formal class instruction in many of the upper classes—composed of Juniors and Seniors in the Divisions and the professional schools—from eleven or twelve weeks to eight weeks, the last three or four weeks of each quarter being left largely free for reading, for consultation with instructors, and for the preparation of reports. Examinations may or may not be given within the last week of the period, depending on the decision of the instructor. For Freshmen and Sophomores enrolled in what are known as the four general courses in the Humanities, the Social Sciences, the Biological Sciences, and the Physical Sciences, and for many other courses pursued during the first two years, extensive syllabi with required and optional readings are provided. For the general courses a special library has been developed with offices for professors (advisers) surrounding the reading rooms. A library containing many of the same books, particularly the optional works suggested, is provided in one of the large dormitories for men. In the first calendar year in which examinations were offered in the courses (June, 1932, to June, 1933, inclusive) 131 students took examinations after having attended corresponding courses only two of the three quarters, 62 after attending only one quarter, and 78 without attending at all. When numerical values were assigned to the marks made by these students (A = 4, B = 3, C = 2, D = 1, and F = 0, with D or 1 representing a passing mark), the average of these 271 students was found to be 2.31, while the average of all students taking the examinations was 1.90. The percentage distribution, according to their marks, of the 271 students who took examinations before completing the customary three quarters of the course was: A, 14 per cent; B, 30 per cent; C, 36 per cent; D, 12 per cent; and F, 8 per cent. The distribution of the entire group taking the examinations was: A, 9 per cent; B, 18 per cent; C, 41 per cent; D, 18 per cent; and F, 14 per cent.[5]

Integration in the colleges of the North Central Association of

Colleges and Secondary Schools is being sought through new stand-ards for college libraries. These standards have been in the process of revision for three years and have been worked out on a qualitative rather than a quantitative basis. They attempt to disclose the effec-tiveness of the work of the colleges instead of indicating the amounts of their endowments and other data of that kind. The results of their first application, so far as the effectiveness of library service is con-cerned, are being studied by Professor Douglas Waples and some of the students of the Graduate Library School of the University of Chicago. A number of colleges which have filled out returns have been asked: (1) to describe the method used in allocating book funds to the various departments; (2) to list methods used to in-crease student use of the library; (3) to list loans to members of the faculty, indicating particularly titles which are professional and either related to the respective fields of the individual instructors or to the problems of college teaching; (4) to give the total number of titles purchased and the expenditure for books in each of the past five years; (5) to list any library problems being studied by the li-brary staff or other student-reading problems being studied by others by means of library data; and (6) to furnish data indicating use made of the library during the year, including gross circulation of reserves and other books and studies of student use based on individ-ual reader records. From the answers to these questions the review-ing body can see what use is made of the library by each member of the faculty and can review the total reading record of each student by author, title, and classification. When such data on student use are accompanied by college-aptitude scores and the marks of stu-dents, a definite picture of integration can be secured, and the part which the library plays in the college can be indicated.

Questions concerning the school library are being raised on every hand. They relate not only to integration but to many other matters. Librarians and school men are familiar with them. If these questions are to be answered properly, teachers and librarians alike will have to answer them as other questions relating to elementary and sec-ondary education have been answered in America during the past thirty years—by careful, detailed scientific study. School librarians and principals may well consider what their part in such study will be. They may well ponder the suggestions made by Professor Charles

H. Judd in an article on "New Standards for Secondary Schools."
In this article he suggests a method of determining whether a school
is really alive to the requirements made of it by society. He proposes
three standards by which to determine the school's alertness:

> (1) From the principal of each secondary school applying for
> approval [shall be] required a report indicating some particular
> in which experimental modification has been undertaken during
> the past year in the curriculum, class organization, methods of
> dealing with the public or pupils, or in some other phase of
> school work. . . . (2) [The principal must] report six cases in
> which pupils showing signs of maladjustment in their courses
> or in their general social relations were fully readjusted through
> special attention given them by the school staff. Describe the
> way in which these cases were discovered, the way in which
> they were treated, and present the evidence that the treatment
> was successful. . . . (3) The principal of the school shall cause
> to be transmitted to the inspector one or more statements from
> committees of the faculty with regard to plans which they have
> matured during the year for the cultivation in the pupils of the
> school habits of reading or independent effort wholly outside
> the assignments of any course. Lists of books read or of con-
> structive activities undertaken or of excursions organized and
> carried to successful completion should be submitted as a part
> of each statement.[6]

In so far as successful integration of the library with the curriculum depends on teachers and librarians, this statement of standards
is a challenge which may well receive thoughtful consideration.
Today it is almost certain that not less than 60 per cent of the population of high-school age is enrolled in American high schools. The
American population is becoming more and more an adult population. Leisure is here, and there will be still more leisure. The function of the library, in school and out, is to assist these Americans of
tomorrow to a greater knowledge of the world about them, to a hap-
pier participation in the work in which they will be engaged, and to
a more creative use of the leisure which will be theirs. If I am not
mistaken, the library cannot perform this function properly unless
it receives more adequate support, unless its importance is better

understood by the school and the public, and unless all phases of its activities are subjected to sustained experimentation and investigation.

NOTES:

[1]a) Henry C. Morrison, *The Practice of Teaching in the Secondary School.* Chicago: University of Chicago Press, 1926.

b) A. Laura McGregor, *Supervised Study in English for Junior High School Grades.* New York: Macmillan Co., 1921.

c) Lucille F. Fargo, *The Library in the School.* Chicago: American Library Association, 1933 (revised).

[2]B. Lamar Johnson, "The Secondary-School Library," p. 43. National Survey of Secondary Education Monograph No. 17. United States Office of Education *Bulletin* No. 17, 1932.

[3]Alice R. Brooks, "The Integration of Library Instruction with the High-School Social Studies," *School Library Yearbook, Number Five,* pp. 121–144. Chicago: American Library Association, 1932.

[4]Alice R. Brooks, *op. cit.,* p. 122.

[5]C. S. Boucher, "Phi Beta Kappa Prospects at Chicago under the New Plan," *University of Chicago Magazine,* XXVI (June, 1934), 275–278.

[6]Charles H. Judd, "New Standards for Secondary Schools," *Proceedings of the Eighteenth Annual Meeting of the Department of Secondary-School Principals,* pp. 9–11. Bulletin of the Department of Secondary-School Principals, No. 50. Berwyn, Illinois: Department of Secondary-School Principals of the National Education Association (H. V. Church, Executive Secretary), 1934.

College and University Libraries

The Place of the Library in College Life

WHAT IS THE PLACE OF THE LIBRARY in an American college? This is the question I shall attempt to answer in this address. What I shall say grows out of my experience as a student assistant in an excellent Pennsylvania College for three years and my service as librarian of the University of North Carolina since 1901.

I shall answer it positively and in direct contradiction to an idea expressed a few years ago by a Sophomore to a Freshman as they concluded an inspection of the University Campus at the beginning of an academic year. They had visited the gymnasium, the swimming pool, the athletic field, the Book Exchange in the YMCA building, Memorial Hall, and the "Davie Poplar," and were on their way down town to the soda fountain and Post Office. Their way led past my office. The Sophomore had evidently been serving as a guide to his less sophisticated companion and was enjoying to the full the feeling of superiority in which he was indulging himself. As they passed my window, the Freshman paused and asked, "And what building is that?" "Oh, that," replied the Sophomore, "that's the library. But it's a side issue."

The first thing I wish to say and to say most emphatically, is that the library is not a side issue. On the contrary, it is the pulsing heart which is to quicken every activity which goes on upon the campus; it is the easily accessible mentor to which every alumnus, after his days of privilege within college walls have ended, should look for guidance; and it is a beacon light whose rays should illumine more and more the path of those leaders of men who are entrusted with the conservation of equality of opportunity and the solution of the problems of civilization that daily assumes a greater and ever increasing degree of complexity.

Reprinted from *Bulletin*, Elon College, 20: 12–18, November, 1924, by permission of the publisher. An address delivered at the Dedication of the Carlton Library Building, Elon College, September 27, 1924.

I. *Service to the College Community*

The function of the college library, therefore, is threefold. It has a service which it must render first of all to the college community. It must follow with gracious assistance the men and women who have passed out from the college walls into the active work of the world. And it must become a positive influence in the state and nation for the increasing of knowledge and the quickening of the sons of men in their quest after truth.

Taking up these services in their order, the duty of the college library to the college community is six-fold.

Its first duty to the campus I conceive to be that of furnishing background for the work carried on in the classroom, in the laboratory, and in the society hall. Few courses of instruction are given today without reference to the literature on the particular subject; and no instructor should consider this task fully performed who has not generously supplemented it with references which carry his pupils to the library for investigation of what others have thought and written. This duty is so obvious and is so universally recognized from the grammar grades up through the graduate school, that it requires no elaboration here.

The second duty of the library is that of imparting to the student the ability of using books and indexes as tools. The day has passed when men carry in their memories all of the facts essential to the performance of their varied duties. But the public in North Carolina is just beginning to realize that the most important training which a pupil in the common school or the student in college can receive is that of the precise use of books. Too frequently books have been conceived of by us as of value to the lawyer or doctor or minister or teacher, but not to the banker or farmer or man of affairs. They have not been thought of as tools; and the student, while he has been taught to use the axe, or the saw, or the plane around the house or in the manual training class, has not been taught the special uses of yearbooks and dictionaries and encyclopedias and the handbooks on business administration and banking and textile manufacturing, and the thousand and one pursuits in which we engage for our livelihood. The use of the principle of the card catalogue, the method of consulting indexes, of filing clippings and pictures and letters and material of all sorts on any particular subject, is invaluable, and the library that fails to impart this information both through the provision of experimental material and special instruction by the library staff, is failing at the point where it can be of greatest assistance and where, in the past, I am convinced it has most signally failed here in the South.

A few days ago I ran across a verse on a bookplate which quaintly illustrates the point which I have just made as well as the third service which the library should render. If you will listen rather closely I believe you will be able to catch it. It is taken from the bookplate of an engineer and evidently it expresses the two chief services which he expects of his books:

> Ye Engineer his booke profound,
> Him helpeth make ye wheels go 'round:
> Also ye bookes in lighter vein;
> They Soothe ye Engineer—his brain.

Sometimes I find myself wondering whether, with the multiplicity of holidays with which our college year is honeycombed, and with the minimum of study evidenced by some of our students, it is essential for the library to furnish the students "Ye books to soothe his over-fatigued brain." But when I think of those students who do burn the midnight oil, or of those others who, like Englishmen of the James Bryce or Arthur Balfour type, devote their leisure periods to recreational reading and study, I am convinced that one of the fundamental functions of the library is to provide recreation. One of the great defects of our college life today is not that we do not take time off, but that we have not fully learned to use our leisure profitably. And I can conceive of no finer way, in this day of the phonograph and the movie and the automobile and the radio, of a student's filling his leisure hours than that of allowing the great thoughts of those who have written of life in its universal terms to sink into his plastic, growing mind.

A quotation from Thomas Carlyle aptly suggests a fourth service —that of broadening the outlook on life of the student. "In books," says Carlyle, "lies the soul of the whole Past Time: the articulate audible voice of the Past, when the body and material substance of it has altogether vanished like a dream. . . . All that mankind has done, thought, gained, or been; it is lying as in magic preservation in the pages of Books." Like the recently discovered, though centuries-old, tomb of Tut-ankh-Amen, they bring back, as if it were but yesterday, the past, while the telegraph and the newspaper and the magazine make vivid the present and the probable future. To me there has always been something challenging in the vow taken by the Athenian youth to pass on to the generation following him a civilization "not only not less, but greater and better" than that he received from his fathers. Certainly this should be the high endeavor of this student body, and it is the sacred mission of this library which you are today setting apart to enable these young men and young women to visualize clearly both the past and the wonderful present in order that they may achieve a more glorious future.

There are two stories, the truthfulness of which I cannot vouch for, which illustrate the fifth duty your library owes to your community. The first is of the poet Whittier when a boy in his father's cottage. One night a traveler drew up his horse in front of the Whittier home and asked for lodging for the night. After supper, while the traveler and host were talking, young Whittier noticed lying on the traveler's saddle-bags a book. He picked it up, lost himself in it, and did not lay it down until his father summoned him to bed. It was a volume of poems by Robert Burns; and in those moments while Whittier read, there flashed the spark of poetic genius which set his poetic soul aflame.

The second is of Abraham Lincoln while a clerk in a crossroads store in Illinois. One day while the wagon trains of immigrants from New England to the middle west were rolling by, one of the wagons, to lighten its load, threw out a barrel of trash, which, among other things, contained a volume of Blackstone's *Commentaries on the English Law*. The book came into the hands of Lincoln, and from that hour he marked the beginning of that wonderful legal and forensic career that led him to a place among America's supremely great. From the hills of New England and the plains of Illinois to the back side of the desert where Moses caught the vision of his life's work in the glory of the burning bush, may be a far call; but yet, in different ways, men throughout the ages have come to know the tasks to which it was meant they were to put their hands. And so it should be still. Here while young men and women are laying the foundations for their careers, it is not too much to hope that some of them, many of them upon laying down some great book, may see no longer as through a glass darkly, but face to face, the heavenly vision and go forth obedient to it.

I conceive it the duty of the library not only thus to inspire the youth who pass this way, but to quicken their appreciation of the beautiful and to kindle within them a passion for truth. President Chase, of the University, in an address to the student body on the 19th, declared it to be the duty of every college to instill in its student body a proper conception of intellectual freedom. No theory of education which denied the necessity of weighing evidence and arriving at truth was, he declared, worthy of acceptance, and progress conditioned on anything other than knowledge and understanding was futile. I have the feeling that, owing to the far too limited funds which have been available for the support of our libraries, many of our colleges have not been able through a wealth of material, a variety of manuscript, and picture, and rare book, and beautiful binding, and special edition, and map, and stereotype, and musical score to develop within their student bodies this sensitiveness to beauty and the appreciation of truth they should. But whether they have or not, here where a magnificent organ has recently been installed, and where today the doors of your splendid library are being thrown open, in study, in class-room, in laboratory, in society hall, in fact everywhere upon this campus, under the influence of these stimuli there should be continued and intensified the immemorial search for beauty and truth which make men free. For, in the language of the seer:

"If thou criest after knowledge, and liftest up thy voice for understanding; if thou seekest her as silver and searchest for her as for hid treasure—

"Then shalt thou understand the fear of the Lord, and find the knowledge of God."

II. *Service to the Alumni*

Mr. President, these are in brief some of the services which the library should render to your immediate college community. I am happy to believe, however, that it has a wider field of service, which includes your alumni and the denomination which you represent as well. The time, I believe, has forever passed when an institution's duty to its student ends with the termination of their college careers. Accordingly, your alumni and those whom this institution is particularly set apart to serve, are your special concern and can be ministered to through your library. If I may, I shall indicate what I mean by reference to a movement set on foot twelve years ago which today has grown to large proportions and which, I believe, is productive of far-reaching good. I refer to the Extension Movement of the University which, in large measure, had its beginning in the University library and grew out of the recognition by the library that its service to students should not end upon the receipt of their diplomas. The first bulletin in the long series of helpful publications sent out by the Extension Division was a handbook on a debate query to be used by University and other college men who were teaching and who were particularly charged with the direction of high school literary societies. The second was a list of one hundred books of special use for the professional training of teachers, the books being loaned upon request. Today the list of publications, many of them based on the resources of the library, runs into the hundreds, and the boys and girls and men and women of this state who profit from some form of Extension activity run well up into the thousands. I do not know what special requirements your graduates make of you for continued assistance, but I am convinced that through your library you can, as many other institutions do, serve them with books from your shelves which will keep them growing intellectually; and that in promoting the effectiveness of the leaders of your denomination, through special institutes and reading courses, your library can play no inconsiderable part. It, more than any other part of your college, can be and should be the daily means of strengthening the bond between you and the constituency which you serve.

III. *Service to the Nation*

Furthermore, the library, in common with the college as a whole, has a general duty which it shares with all other colleges and universities—the duty of training more adequately the leaders of a state and section who will both know and find joy in service to a civilization whose complexity daily becomes more manifold. Men and women who are thoroughly informed, who know the use of books as tools, who have learned to seek after wisdom, and have found joy and inspiration in the doing of their tasks, are demanded of every college worthy of the name; and this institution, true to its traditions and the ideals which it maintains, will send them forth in ever increasing numbers.

And when I point this out, I have in mind a situation in North Carolina and the South with which the dedication of this library may be particularly concerned. I refer to the fact, for it is an indisputable fact, that ours is a section which today is not making the use of books and magazines and bookstores and publishing houses that it should make and must make if we are to work out a balanced, finely conceived order which will not only minister to our material and physical needs, but will abundantly satisfy your intellectual and artistic aspirations as well.

Sometimes I think probably I have over-emphasized the limitations of the South in these respects. But the exercises of today bring them back with renewed vividness to my mind. They remind me that in the number of books which North Carolina has in her public libraries per one thousand inhabitants, she ranks forty-seventh in the sisterhood of states; that in the number of the popular magazines and daily newspapers read by her citizens, she ranks approximately forty-fifth; that, to build up a collection of books within her borders numbering more than 100,000 volumes, it has taken her 128 years in three centuries, while far larger collections have been assembled in other states in a much briefer period; that to the support of her public libraries her average annual expenditure per inhabitant has been from twenty to thirty cents instead of the one dollar set up as a standard by the American Library Association for the country at large; that throughout her length and breadth there are to be found only a third or a fourth of the number of book stores to which, by averages for the country at large, she is entitled; and that, with other Southern states, she has yet to build up even in her colleges and state offices, journals and publishing businesses intended to stimulate her intellectual growth commensurate with her development in the fields of agriculture and engineering and industrial activity.

When I contrast this situation, this lack of these essentials which are so fundamental to the development of a civilization of learning and culture and spiritual enrichment, I say when I contrast this condition with the splendid provision which has been so wisely made here and the forces which have been released thereby, not only for the cultural and spiritual growth of those who are privileged to be students here, but for the intellectual and artistic stimulation of the State and South as well, my mind harks back to the dramatic situation which confronted the Jews in the days of King Ahasuerus, and to the message sent by Mordecai to Queen Esther, "Who knoweth whether thou art come to the Kingdom for such a time as this?"

To have placed here at the heart of this college this beautiful library, to have adequately and generously equipped it, to possess it and to use it for these high ends, is to conceive and to execute in a way that today and through the years will bring to all those who pass this way a greater power of intelligent, helpful service, and a finer comprehension of the fuller, deeper issues of life. To support it bountifully, to develop its resources of book and journal and picture and rare edition, to make it a place in which youth find beauty and truth and a great mission in life, to make it the mentor to which alumni and public turn for guidance, to multiply and enrich its contribution to the intellectual and spiritual growth of the state and nation—these are some of the coveted privileges, Mr. President, which you and your honored donors, your librarian and institution possess. Again, I congratulate you, one and all, and bid you God-speed in the complete realization of the splendid opportunities which are yours.

Library in Modern Education

TWO·FACTORS HAVE ELEVATED THE LIBRARY to a position of great importance in the modern university. The first is a rapid increase in the production of books; the second, a new conception of educational methods within the last quarter-century.

Books and the Faculty

There was a time when professors made extensive collections of books important to their subjects. This day of the large private library is passing. Fewer and fewer men are able to purchase the swiftly growing number of publications in their fields. Nowadays universities gather for common use by their faculties all important books of the past and present which lie within the scope of their study and investigation.

What books does the professor need when he undertakes research? He needs all the new books bearing on his problem and all the old books. To discover what these books are he must have indexes and bibliographies. And if he cannot have all these books at hand, then he needs aids to finding them, such as catalogs of other libraries. Few researchers can provide themselves with even a tithe of this required material. It is the university which must do the providing, and the library is the university's agent in the provision.

No item of the university's educational activity is carried on without reference to the library. Even the work of a scientific laboratory —in a hasty view, the most characteristic element of a university— would be greatly hampered without access to published investigations made all over the world. It is the library which collects and makes available these publications.

Twenty-five years ago a knowledge of his subject, a set of lecture

Reprinted from *The University Library*, p. 5ff., University of North Carolina Library, 1929, by permission of the publisher.

notes, and a single textbook constituted the average instructor's stock in trade. Now the picture is different. The instructor keeps abreast of learning, revising his lectures as new discoveries are made, by reference to the latest books—supplied by the library. His students are sent to the library to examine the same material, from which they are expected to form their own judgments.

Books and the Student

Not only does the university library serve the teacher, the researcher, the laboratory investigator with old and new books, card catalogs, indexes, etc. It also serves the student who has come to college to discover the wisdom accumulated by diverse and clearer minds, to secure a richer background of fact and knowledge, to be spurred toward right values and creative accomplishment in his own life.

Some of that wisdom is in the books which his instructors have carefully selected to emphasize and expand classroom lectures. Some of it is in the books he will choose for his own reading. These books are an important concern of the library, for what the student learns from recreational reading is often fully as important and valuable as what he learns from his teachers. It is the university's and the library's business to see that he is lured into the realm of books and taught how they can be a source of endless delight.

What a Library Is

Is a library only a collection of books? Is it books-in-a-building? Both of these are popular conceptions of a library, but if the first is true is not the junkman's yard with its fine assortment of old books and magazines a library? And if the second is true, must we not call the publisher's warehouse a library?

A library is much more than this. It is a collection of books brought together to serve a particular purpose. In the case of a university, this purpose is education and research. To serve this end the collection must be constantly growing. The books must be arranged and indexed so that all material on any subject, whether books or parts of books, is readily available. The collection must be housed adequately in a building so equipped that the books may be used with a maximum of ease. Finally, it should be administered by a staff of trained specialists.

It is in this last feature—the staff—that the library is distinguished from the mere aggregation of books. With increasing publication the problem of keeping up with learning becomes each year more difficult, and the demands made upon the personnel of the library by its clientele require more and more competence on the part of the librarians.

The University of North Carolina And Its Library

How is the University of North Carolina Library meeting the varied and complicated demands made on it by faculty and students? To what degree is it fulfilling its obligations to them in the matters of building up its collection, of making this collection available, and of properly housing the books?

The New Building

It is to meet this latter obligation that a great new library building is now rising on the campus at Chapel Hill. It is a magnificent structure costing $625,000, but so confident are its creators of the future of the University and of the importance of a library in that future, that the new building is but one unit of the great library to come. Closing the quadrangle, the sides of which are South Building, Venable Hall, and the group of buildings which includes Steele Dormitory and Murphy Hall, it extends over a front of 210 feet and to a depth in the center of 140 feet, and rises to the height of four stories, including basement. Yet some day it will be necessary to build wings on either side to a depth of 150 or 200 feet, and, later still, to close these wings at the rear with a section as large as the front of the present building. The stacks now being erected for books are nine stories high and will shelve approximately 400,000 volumes. Later extensions can be provided at the rear to a depth of 150 feet and a height of from nine to sixteen stories, with a capacity of more than a million volumes, when the future demands it.

Planning A Library Building

This age has learned the value of specialization. The manufacturer does not look upon just any factory as suitable for his business.

Nowadays he studies the problems peculiar to his work and plans accordingly. So it is with a library building.

The modern library structure is not merely an edifice architecturally acceptable in proportion and decoration. The building's plan and equipment are a concrete expression of the organization of the library within. Ideally speaking, the new library building at Chapel Hill is the expression of the dignity of learning; practically, it is planned with cold and remorseless efficiency. Every inch of space in it has been utilized for one purpose: to house books and to make these books available to persons who want to use them.

Those changing conditions which, within the last quarter-century, have marked out new acres for the library in the field of education have left their impress on the design of library buildings. Twenty-five years ago the average student used eleven books in his senior year; the senior of 1928 borrowed sixty.

Even this astonishing increase does not take into account the new usefulness of the library, for the modern senior uses library materials within the library to a greater degree than did his predecessor. Study halls must be furnished to make easily available to undergraduates the collateral reading so important in the university course of study. Whereas it used to be thought sufficient to provide seats for ten or fifteen per cent of the student body, new libraries at Dartmouth and Yale are planned to provide seats for fifty per cent of the students, and the University of Iowa library provides a seat for every freshman. The new library unit at Chapel Hill, planned in accordance with modern ideas, provides seats for thirty-three and a third per cent of the student body.

With the increase of faculty and advanced graduate research provision must be made for study in proximity to the books which will be used by the investigator. To this end each floor of the bookstack has been edged with alcoves, each with a window, table, chair, a shelf for books, and a light. For graduate classes and discussion the third floor has been divided into special seminar rooms where advanced classes will meet.

The growing number of books published every year together with a genuine need for more books for study has brought inevitably a larger staff for the competent administration of such a collection. For this staff small but, for the present, adequate quarters have been provided. It should be noted that, if the collection is to expand as it should to keep pace with knowledge, the staff must grow. Further room for this increased staff must be provided in the not too far distant future in the wings indicated on the plans in these pages.

In these various ways has the University of North Carolina sought to meet the problems of housing a modern university library so that the collection may be used to the best advantage.

How Many Books?

Any attempt to determine how large a university library should be is like trying to answer that celebrated witticism of two decades ago: "How far is up?"

Discrepancies between examples are wide. Harvard University places 2,600,000 volumes at the service of its students and faculties. The University of Michigan Library increases each year by 30,000 to 50,000 volumes. The new University of Illinois library is planned with stacks twelve stories high, and Yale with a veritable book tower capable of shelving four million books.

Those competent to judge hold that work of university caliber cannot be offered in an institution with less than 400,000 volumes. The Library of the University of North Carolina houses something over 200,000 books and receives annually 2,500 periodicals.

A university library must keep pace with knowledge. It must be a source of supply for a dozen major schools. The plain truth is that the state of North Carolina, like the South in general, is only on the eve of the development of its library resources. The University is looking forward to the future. The past, however worthy, the present, however commendable, are of less interest than what is to come. The University has high hopes that its Library may become *a great national library in the South*. To this end a definite program of expansion has been developed. The new library building represents one side of this expansion. Other needs are presented here.

Bibliographical Tools

One of the jobs the special investigator most frequently faces is the necessity to find out all that has been written on a particular subject. Once he would have had to discover all the books himself. Now others have done it for him.

What he needs in beginning an investigation is organized catalogs of books to tell him what to read; finding-lists—catalogs of great libraries—to tell him where these books may be seen. He wants indexes to periodical literature and to transactions of learned and scientific societies to unlock the vast stores of thought in these publications. These are bibliographical tools—as necessary to the student as hammers and saws to the carpenter. The scholar needs not only books, but books about books, and without them he is helpless, so complex has modern knowledge become.

In collecting such apparatus the Library of the University of North Carolina has made a notable beginning. The Library of Congress, one of the three or four great libraries of the world, issues to a few selected institutions complete duplicate sets of its catalog cards —cards listing millions of titles housed at Washington including thousands of books rarely found outside the Library of Congress. There are only two such duplicate sets in university libraries in the Southeast, and one of them is at Chapel Hill—an immense aid to the seeker for some special book who can learn in five minutes whether it is at Washington, and who can, in most cases, borrow it through the inter-library loan system.

But there are other great libraries in the United States—Harvard, Chicago, Michigan, Illinois, California, each rich in its peculiar treasures, which have published cards for those rare portions of their collections not to be found in the Library of Congress. It would be equally a saving of time and energy if duplicate sets of these special cards were also at hand, as they are in many large university libraries elsewhere. Yet there is no library east of the Mississippi and south of a line running from Washington to St. Louis where a union catalog of these cards can be consulted. In other words, investigators in the South begin their work under a handicap not felt by their rivals in the North and West. Until the Library of the University of North Carolina obtains such files of cards, its graduate work and the investigations of its professors must suffer in comparison with similar activities of universities in other sections.

Fundamental Reference Materials

Scientists and scholars not happy enough to be born in the United States or the British Dominions have an unfortunate faculty of not writing in English. Nor do foreign countries go out of their way to publish works of reference in a tongue not their own. But knowledge is international. The physicist must know what goes on in laboratories in Cracow, Berlin, Tokyo, and Petrograd. The authority on world trade has to find out the possibility of navigating the Ob river and what the country is like around Tomsk. The psychologist may need a list of psychological laboratories in Vienna, and the professor of art will be unhappy until he finds out whether an obscure Italian gallery houses a particular painting.

At present the reference collection in the University Library might seem to the uninitiated quite ample. Here are encyclopedias, dictionaries, handbooks, yearbooks, almanacs, biographical collections, government documents, gazetteers, atlases, maps, statistical abstracts, and collections of clippings. But if he is a special student, he will not be so complacent, for, when he looks deeper, he will discover that the majority of them are English or American publications; or (to put it another way) that the Library is not sufficiently well equipped in foreign reference material. What it needs is similar collections of reference works for the foreign nations of the world; and, in addition, files of their journals and learned publications to a degree that the librarians do not like to talk about.

Distinctive Exhibit Materials

Mr. Henry Ford is reported to have said that his interest in engineering really began when he was placed in charge of the engine room of an industrial plant. Handling machinery suggested new types of machines. Mr. Ford is doubtless a genius, but his experience is a common one. We learn by handling things. A fragment of Babylonian tablet makes a whole civilization flash into being. A page from an ancient manuscript, and the ancient Greeks suddenly become real. A good replica of a great masterpiece is worth a chapter of talk, and an early edition of Shakespeare or Milton makes us feel a little less pleased with a modern novel, and a little more pleased with the legibility and cheapness of a contemporary book. If the experience of such institutions as the New York Public Library means anything, it means that the exhibit of such collections by a library awakens interest and fires imagination—is, in fact, an educational achievement of the first order. Lacking such exhibits and the means to make them public, the University Library lacks the power to make scholarship vivid. The institution at Chapel Hill has some collections of this sort, but it needs a great many more.

Specialized Collections

In the public mind it would sometimes seem that universities are rated by their football teams, but to the scholar they are often rated by their special collections of books and their zeal in adding to them. For example, the richest amount of material on Dante is found in the Willard Fiske Collection at Cornell. The Goethe Collection at Yale draws investigators from the whole country. The Browning specialist wants to know what there is in the library of Baylor University before he looks elsewhere, and so on.

Such collections usually begin as some specialist in a given field (whether it be botany or chemistry, history or literature) purchases books for his own use. His collection grows. At his death it comes as a gift to a particular library, or it is thrown into the market and is often bought up as a whole by some institution. The institution then adds to the collection from time to time, and so its peculiar richness and its reputation grow. The North Carolina Collection of 40,000 titles at Chapel Hill has been developed during twenty-five years in this fashion. When such opportunities offer, they must be seized at once, and they can be seized only by instantly supplementing the normal book fund of a university library by special gifts—a practice that is increasingly common among the friends of Eastern and Middle Western libraries, but which is, alas! all too rare in the South although the requisite sums are often not large, and the South is becoming increasingly prosperous.

A National Southern Collection

The story of the South's part in the building of the nation, as compared with that of New England or the West, has never been adequately told. And yet the South has lived a life—social, economic, industrial, political—as distinctive as that of any other section. It has played a part in national history second to none of the others. Its contribution of leaders, particularly in the realm of politics, has been striking.

What, then, is the reason? The answer cannot be given in a single paragraph. There have been many causes. But the one fundamental cause has been that no individual or institution in the South has ever brought together in one great collection the materials—the books, pamphlets, newspapers, letters, diaries, and other human documents —on which to base the story. Nowhere in the South is there anything comparable to such great collections of Americana as the John Carter Brown Library at Brown University and the Clements Library at the University of Michigan, the collections of Middle Western materials of the Burton Library of Detroit and the Wisconsin Historical Society at Madison, the Bancroft Collection in California of Spanish and Pacific materials, and the University of Texas collection of materials dealing with the Southwest and Mexico. Their resources have been available to writers and scholars.

The University, with its collection of more than 40,000 titles dealing directly with North Carolina (and incidentally with Virginia, South Carolina, and Tennessee) has indicated what can and should be done by way of forming such a collection, and eagerly awaits the opportunity to undertake this task.

A Library School

If the need of a library school at the University has not been more keenly felt, it is because the South has lacked modern library facilities. Long ago crotchety Thomas Carlyle said in his decisive way that the public library was the people's university. The South must have more such "people's universities." Whereas the average per capita circulation of public library books in the United States is 3.20, in the South it is only .465. In the New England states only 2-3/5 per cent of the inhabitants are without public library facilities; in the South 71 per cent of the people lack them. As the University of North Carolina through its graduate school is training experts for the state and for the South; as, through its Institute for Research in Social Science, it is studying the special problems of Southern life; as, in its University Press it is endeavoring to encourage the publication and reading of books by Southerners, so it is the hope of the Library at Chapel Hill that there shall soon be established a library school for the training of librarians and teachers in these Southern states.

Public libraries are on the increase. Public schools and high schools are putting in library books. Yet, south of the Mason and

Dixon line, there is at present only one institution available to train librarians among the white people. So far the University has been able to provide merely casual instruction in library work—classes in the summer school, and random courses in the regular session. As a part of the program of social welfare now being worked out at Chapel Hill, a library school is needed, where librarians, like lawyers and doctors and teachers, may secure expert professional training. With its magnificent new building as a laboratory for the school, such an institution would not only be in harmony with the program on which the University has embarked, it would offer opportunity through the sending out of trained librarians for the South to tap the vast reservoirs of human knowledge.

If the Library is to add to the distinction which it has achieved and is to serve the University to the fullest extent it is capable of, it is important that, when the building is dedicated on University Day, 1929, the University be able to announce additional endowment sufficient to provide both for the general upbuilding of a number of sections of the Library and to make possible a high degree of specialization in certain fields. For the former, the book fund of approximately $40,000 for the past two years should be greatly increased, and for the latter, such amounts should be made available as specialization in particular fields may seem to warrant.

In the foregoing pages, fundamental reference material, bibliographical tools, a great Southern collection, and a library school have been singled out, not only on account of their special importance, but also by way of illustration. History or philosophy or literature or the fine arts or science or the social sciences or the professions could be selected as well, and University Day, 1929, is set apart as the day for the perfection of plans for their permanent enrichment and support.

The Emergence of the College Library

THE PURPOSE OF THIS PAPER is threefold: (1) To comment briefly on the efforts made by American schools and colleges to redefine their educational objectives and procedures; (2) to review the studies which have been made of the status and functions of the college library and (3) to suggest ways and means by which the college library may be more effectively utilized in achieving the educational objectives of the modern American college.

I

For the past twenty-five years the American school and college (particularly the college) have undergone a continuous bombardment of criticism. From press and platform, classroom and office, both have been taken sharply to task for their seeming lack of purpose and effectiveness. They have been urged to reexamine their functions, to redefine their objectives and to perfect their procedures so as to guarantee a quality of training that will maintain an intelligent and vital democracy.

Fortunately for the school, it has been able and willing to submit its case to the experts in the major university schools of education and research foundations for diagnosis and prescription. Its entire procedure from the first grade to graduation from high school has been investigated in the most minute detail. Its functions and objectives have been restudied and redefined, its curricula reorganized, its methods of instruction revised, its technique and measurements refined. School boards and administrators, state and national education associations, state departments of education, university schools of education, teachers colleges, summer schools, journals and graduate dissertations have allowed no aspect of its procedure to escape

Reprinted from A. L. A. *Bulletin,* 25:434–446, September, 1931, by permission of the publisher. Also published by *School and Society,* 34:483–492, October 10, 1931, and by the Carnegie Corporation of New York, November, 1931.

investigation and publication. The result is that the seven cardinal principles of education for the lower schools are as well defined and as generally known by the present generation as were the seven deadly sins in the Middle Ages. Not only are they known, but the school is consciously attempting to carry them into effect.

In consequence of this exact definition and statement of objectives, the place of the library in the school and the part it is expected to play are likewise clear. Courses on the purposes of the curriculum and the functions of the library for teachers and library workers, instruction in the use of materials for pupils, socialized recitations, individual assignments, project and problem procedures, the "Dalton Plan" and the "contract" technique place the library at the very center of the school and make of it the principal synthesizing instrument in the modern school educational process.

In the case of the college, self-examination has not been nearly so extensive. The college and the university, while quick to investigate the practices of the lower schools, have not shown an equal ambition to investigate themselves or to have their procedures investigated. Respect for tradition, and an insistence upon knowledge of subject and ability in research as the principal essentials to effective college performance have frequently stood as barriers against the search for knowledge of method and clarity of objectives. Only a few of the major universities have engaged in extensive experimentation or carried on systematic investigations of college and university methods of instruction, or have provided courses for training in methods of teaching at the college level. The University of Minnesota is one of the most notable examples. The difficulties in the situation have been further accentuated by the unprecedented increase in college enrolment during the past decade, the great expense involved in handling different groups within an institution in different ways, the absorption of the interest and time of deans in routine duties rather than the improvement of scholarship, and the lack of mutual understanding and cooperation on the part of colleges of liberal arts and schools of education in the solution of their common educational problems. On account of these conditions it naturally follows that the educational aims of the college and the part which the library should play in achieving them are less clear than they should be.

Nevertheless, significant studies have been made by the more com-

petently staffed and adequately financed colleges and changes have
been made with great benefit to the student bodies concerned. Books
like President Wilkins' "The Changing College,"[1] Dean Hawkes'
"College—What's the Use?"[2] Dean Kelly's "The American Arts
College,"[3] Dean Johnston's "The Liberal College in Changing Society,"[4] Dr. Robert Kelly's "The Effective College";[5] honors courses
such as those at Harvard and Swarthmore; courses in reflective
thinking at Columbia and Chicago; the Wisconsin experimental college; deans of men and student advisers; freshman week and orientation courses everywhere; intelligence tests and college aptitude ratings
for admission; and the sudden development of the junior college
movement—all these represent aspects of this attempt at redefinition,
and all have resulted in extensive modification and clarification of
college objectives and procedures.

II

While the college library has received but slight consideration in
these studies, it has received extensive and notable consideration by
librarians and members of library school faculties in an effort to integrate it more effectively with the college program. "College and
University Library Problems," by Works;[6] "Library Facilities of
Teacher-Training Institutions," by Rosenlof;[7] "The Library in Land-
Grant Colleges and Universities," by Brown;[8] "Budgets, Classification
and Compensation Plans for University and College Libraries," by
the American Library Association;[9] the Hilton[10] and Hester[11] book
lists for the junior college and the Shaw[12] list for the senior college
libraries; the study of reading interests, by Waples and Tyler;[13] the
studies concerning standards in progress by the North Central[14] and
Southern[15] Associations of Colleges and Secondary Schools; the
statement by Reeves and Russell[16] of the new duties imposed upon
the library by the new teaching procedures in the social sciences and
the projected book by Randall[17] growing out of the work of the Advisory Group on College Libraries of the Carnegie Corporation under the chairmanship of Dr. Bishop, all deal with the status of the
library in the college of to-day. They pick up the work where it was
left by the American Library Association Survey[18] and their value is
apparent in the following particulars:

[1] For notes, see page 155.

(1) In the first place, they have made available a general body of new, significant data. The Works[19] study treats of the financial support, resources for research, departmental collections, status of staff and other incidental matters of the libraries of eighteen major universities and colleges. The Rosenlof[20] investigation presents extensive data concerning books and periodicals, the training school library, the library staff and budget from libraries of 69 four-year teachers' colleges and 46 normal schools. The Brown[21] survey brings together data from 51 land-grant colleges and universities, covering functions of the library, requirements for good library services and methods for facilitating use, book collections, financial support and budgets. The Hilton[22] book list recommends 2,388 titles for 32 basic junior college courses, the titles checked by 928 junior college instructors and 265 instructors connected with institutions of university grade. The Hester[23] list comprises 3,500 titles grouped according to academic courses most commonly offered. The Shaw[24] list contains 14,190 titles distributed over 24 major subjects, with books to support every subject presented in the arts college curricula. Its preparation involved the services of many of the most gifted instructors in American universities and colleges, and it has been checked by the libraries of more than 250 institutions. The Carnegie Corporation Advisory Group on College Libraries has assembled returns, supplemented in many instances by data acquired through visits, from 200 institutions. The active participation of presidents, instructors and librarians has been secured in the answering of the questionnaire,[25] and has resulted in an emphasis on the importance of the library as a teaching instrument. Supplemented as the data in all these studies are by the bibliographies in the three numbers of the "College and Reference Library Yearbook,"[26] the problem of discovering the practice and procedure of the college library has been made far more simple than ever before.

(2) In the second place, these investigations have resulted in a restatement and clarification of the functions of the college library. There is fairly common agreement that its functions are as follows: (a) To furnish material for instruction to students in appropriate environment and through a personnel competent to serve as efficient liaison officers to connect instructor and student with library resources; (b) to develop general reading interests through open

shelves, browsing rooms, attractive bookstores, book lists and a stimulating readers advisers' service; (c) to furnish new technical books and periodicals which enable the members of the faculty and library staff to keep abreast of their subjects; (d) to meet the needs of such members of the faculty as are engaged in productive investigation; (e) to continue book service to students after graduation; and (f) to make materials available to students involved in correspondence courses and extension classes.

(3) A third result of these investigations is that greater exactness and objectivity have been given to standards and procedures essential to the performance of these functions.

(a) Dr. Randall,[27] in his visits to many of the 200-odd colleges applying for grants-in-aid from the Carnegie Corporation for their book collections, found that the college library is housed either very well or very badly—in the majority of cases, badly. Non-fireproof buildings have been erected as late as 1929. Of the stacks of 96 college libraries, 60 are crowded beyond their working capacities, or will be in ten years. One hundred and eighteen of 201 buildings have one seat for each 4.4 students. Space for administration and cataloguing has been so grossly neglected and so carelessly overlooked that proper performance of these duties is rendered extremely difficult. The data assembled in the chapter entitled, "Suggestions for Minimum College Library Standards," in the second "College and Reference Library Yearbook,"[28] plans of the more notable recent buildings contained in both the first and second Yearbooks,[29] and the eleven requirements recommended in Chapter V of the Brown[30] study set forth the requirements as to building, seating capacity, reading rooms for special groups, cubicles, etc., essential to the appropriate housing of the college book collection. Klauder and Wise contribute additional data in their volume on college architecture.[31] Drs. Randall and Gerould will add still further to the picture in the volumes which they now have in preparation on the college library and college library buildings.

(b) These studies reveal the fact that college executives frequently know less about the duties of a librarian and the services he should render than of any other officer or teacher on the college staff. This is evidenced in a number of ways. The process through which the college goes in the selection of the librarian will serve well as an example. The selection of the head of an English department is a procedure with which the average college president is entirely familiar. Members of the department concerned and presidents, deans and acquaintances in other faculties are asked for recommendations. A thorough sifting goes on until a person is chosen whose scholarship, teaching ability, interest in investigation and general personal effectiveness are such as to make him suitable to the institution's needs. But not so in the case of the selection of the librarian. The probabilities are that the president and dean have had but slight acquaintance with librarians. Their contacts with the library staff, library schools and library extension agencies are limited. Their understanding of the functions which the library should perform and the way it should perform them is so hazy that a selection based upon knowledge of qualities desired in the appointee is exceedingly difficult. Frequently a librarian is secured fresh from library school and without experience in or special gift for integrating the library in the instructional program of the college. The salary paid is low, and the librarian, if called elsewhere at a larger salary, is replaced by a new recruit. Neither the importance of the selection nor the desirability of the retention of a thoroughly qualified librarian is sufficiently understood by the administration to result in an appointment which will insure the proper development of the library as an integral, vital part of the institution, or maintain its policies consistently over an extended period.

(c) Similarly, institutional policies concerning the libarian's rank, pay and vacation, his control of book collections and library personnel, and his participation in the selection of books and coordination of the objectives of the library with those of the instructional staff have hitherto lacked clarity and have often been left to casual decision. The professional qualifications of the library staff and its number in relation to enrolment and teaching staff have also lacked definition. Information concerning these matters is furnished in the aforementioned studies in sufficient detail to insure more intelligent procedure.

(d) Standards regarding adequate book and periodical collections have also received additional clarification. The Hilton[32] and Hester[33] lists for the junior college effectively ban the book shower as an appropriate means of meeting the requirement as to number of volumes owned by the library. Instead they emphasize the desirability of the careful selection of books for appropriate courses rather than large collections which bear no special relation to the curricula. Their use by the librarian and the teaching staff of the junior college will secure a higher degree of effectiveness in the selection of parallel readings for basic courses. The Shaw[34] list, developed along more extensive lines, performs an equally admirable service for the four-year college. The mere checking of these lists by instructors and members of the library staffs has resulted in a fine educational service to both groups. It has revealed the inadequacy of the collection of books and periodicals, and has indicated an orderly method of enriching the library's total resources and insuring proper library support of each instructor's work.

(e) In like fashion, study by presidents and deans of the application blank for grants-in-aid from the Carnegie Corporation, with its queries concerning hours of service, special service to students and faculty, circulation within and without the library, honors courses, professional fitness of staff, has been a very illuminating exercise. It has left no doubt of the desirability of close integration between library and instructional staffs in creating a genuine library-mindedness on the part of the personnel of the arts college. Like the ancient Mosaic law, which the author of the book of Hebrews said had served as a teacher to the Israelites, the questionnaire has been a schoolmaster to the schoolmasters. It has given some college executives their first thoughtful lesson on the importance of the library in the college.

(f) The formulae for measuring the adequacy of financial support have also been more exactly stated. College executives have been given new yardsticks by which to determine this. The library should be thought of as a department, or rather as the equivalent of two departments, so far as support is concerned. It is urged that salary levels for the library staff, including the librarian, heads of departments and other members, should be equal to those for deans or heads of departments and the instructional staff. It has been convincingly shown that less than 7 per cent of the total educational budget, or $20 per student, will not provide effective library service. Ten per cent and $30 to $40 per student will be far better. Nor should the total library budget, providing adequately for personnel, maintenance and book and periodical collections, be thought of as something apart from the administrative, instructional and maintenance budget of the college, but as an integral part of the whole.

(4) The study by Waples and Tyler[35] on reading interests of adults breaks new ground for the publisher, bookseller and librarian, on the one hand, and the sociologist and psychologist, on the other. It presents the results of an extensive scientific investigation of the subjects which interest the minds of mature groups. Heretofore the college library collection has been built upon the basis of the knowledge of the librarians and the instructor of the subject-matter of books. In the future the librarian and the instructor will be able to add to this knowledge the further knowledge of whether the books will appeal to the interest of the student or alumnus. In this highly important respect, the study contributes new criteria for the selection of the book collection and emphasizes the value of the library as a teaching instrument.

III

Valuable as these studies are on account of the data assembled and the specific recommendations made, they are additionally valuable for certain suggestions they offer and ideas they evoke. If, however, the college library is to make its full contribution to the college of tomorrow, it is essential that the suggestions and ideas called forth be acted upon by the following groups and in the following manner:

(1) The colleges must bring themselves to a further serious consideration of their objectives. They must submit themselves to the same sort of scientific investigation which they have insisted on applying, and with profit, to the lower schools. They will have to arrive at conclusions concerning educational issues by means of extensive experimentation and scientific evidence, instead of by decrees from the president or dean or the easy-going methods of faculty majority vote and committee compromise. This does not mean that every state university will have to set up a "college within a college" as the Experimental College (now passing) at Wisconsin, nor that every institution will undertake honors courses, comprehensive examinations or other devices now being extensively employed to secure greater unity in educational purpose or closer application of

students to the performance of intellectual tasks. But it does mean that administrative officers and faculty must recognize the necessity of knowing and being interested in students as well as in subject-matter and research. It means that they must discover the best methods of teaching the preparational, cultural and professional courses embraced within their curricula so that the objectives of the college may be most completely achieved. And certainly it means that they must understand and consciously determine the part which the library as an educational instrument is qualified to play in realizing college objectives. The relation of the library to the methods of instruction through lecture, laboratory, assigned readings, individual study, as they are employed singly or collectively, and the library's function in making these methods richly fruitful in the intellectual development of the student, must be discovered and understood by every teacher. These matters are far too important to be left, as they too generally have been, to hazy thinking or to chance.

The idea must also be given up that the library is an adjunct, something added (like a department of home economics or journalism); that it is something, to quote Dr. Randall's[36] experience in talking with a number of presidents, which the college "was just going to do something about." It is not an adjunct. It is an integral element about which the whole college, if alive and alert, should be doing and is doing something today. It is, like the instructional staff, a teaching agency; and teaching in the best sense, as many secondary schools and library-minded colleges have discovered to their very great advantage, can not go on apart from it.

(2) The college administration must make adequate budgetary provision for such a teaching instrument. The idea of library support by means of fees is utterly untenable. A laboratory fee of $5 may take care of the expense of materials used in a given course in chemistry, but it will not pay the salaries of the departmental staff nor provide for effective departmental maintenance. Effective library service must be thought of in terms of administrative and instructional expense, and must be based, as are all essential divisions of the college, upon appropriations, income from endowments, tuition, fees and gifts, all combined. And it must not be the first of this fundamental educational trinity—administration, instructional staff, library—to feel a reduction in revenue when times are out of joint, as

now, but it must be given its proportionate, well-considered share, as a matter of major importance.

(3) The library staff also has a part to play in the perfection of the college library. At present it is probably purchasing and organizing materials as effectively as it can under existing conditions. The Waples study should provide it with new and valuable criteria for the selection of books. But with more adequate support it must better understand the objectives of the college and function more effectively as a liaison agent between student and book collection in attaining them. As compared with the librarian, it is possible that the college registrar fills entirely too important a place in the mind of the student today. The registrar is too often the only college officer who knows all the students by name and in turn is known by them. The unit of the college over which he presides is no side issue in their thought. The registrar is the official keeper of their credits—their educational attainment, their educational salvation! It is the librarian's privilege, however, and it might well be his ambition and that of his staff, to know the mind of the student and to help him enrich it. But he can do this only by contact and suggestion through an organization that not only selects and organizes books for use, but presents them to the student in an environment and in a manner that will contribute to the development of his personality and character, and lead him to intellectual mastery. Today the library's task does not end with the collecting and preserving of books; it should go on to instruct the students in the best use of them. It must know how to use its materials as a teaching instrument. It must assume a positive teaching function. Instruction in the use of the library during freshman week, friendliness and helpfulness at the circulation desk, open shelves, browsing rooms, exhibits, all have their place in this scheme of things. But there must be something more. Student assistanceships in the library, courses about books by members of the staff, conferences with students by members of the staff qualified to advise on books of the day or books essential in optional attendance procedure, work for honors or comprehensive examinations, attractive bookshops within the library which stimulate book ownership should be added and other means steadily sought to increase the library's teaching effectiveness. Such an understanding of its functions and such an employment of its resources by the library staff will go far

in laying the foundation in college of a kind of education which now only a few students take with them into life.

(4) The library school likewise has a duty to perform in relation to the teaching function of the library. Mr. Brown[37] has pointed it out in the case of the librarians of the land-grant colleges. He finds them lacking in knowledge of science. Dr. Works[38] discovered it in other institutions. He found that many instructors complained that librarians were lacking in knowledge of other subjects. It is apparent to any investigator that the college librarian frequently knows less than he should of the major subjects of the college curricula as well as of the purposes of the curricula and the best methods of coordinating the teaching objectives of the library with those of the instructional staff. Probably not much more can be accomplished within the one-year library training course than is now being done by way of providing instruction which will enable the librarian to integrate the library with other departments within the college. But a knowledge of the point of view of the scientific departments, an insight into the methods of investigation, a conception of the functions of the college which are to be performed through the combined effort of the library, the faculty and the administration, a knowledge of the student himself and the way in which books stimulate his mind and lead to the foundation of sound moral and social judgments are matters of fundamental importance to the librarian if he is to make the library the fine instrument it should be. These matters, as well as book selection and cataloguing, reference work and administration, should be emphasized somewhere in the librarian's training if he is to coordinate the fine educational influences of the library with the dynamic educational forces of the college teacher.

(5) A fifth and final obligation is one which rests especially upon the members of the College and Reference Section of the American Library Association. It is that of continuing and extending the sort of investigation begun by the American Library Survey, Works, Waples, Tyler, Randall, Rosenlof, Hilton, Brown, Shaw, Hester, the Advisory Group on College Libraries and others.[39] This obligation also rests upon the national associations and foundations devoted to the promotion of education. The advance attained in the school and the college has been attained in large measure by profound study of the underlying theories and principles of education, by extensive ex-

perimentation, and by careful analysis of educational technique and procedures. The synthesis of the school curricula was not achieved solely by the teacher in the classroom, harassed as she is by the details of the day. The research student and the investigator had to be called in before the seven cardinal principles of education could be nailed to the doorposts of the school and more skilfully devised techniques could be perfected for making them operative. The health and lifespan of each of us here is preserved and increased, not so much by the medical practitioner, skilful and patient though he may be, but by the investigator toiling in his laboratory far removed from us in space and time, to whom the family doctor looks for new principles and new methods of protecting and prolonging life. Today the body of data applicable to the college library, valuable as it is, is far too short of what it must be if college administrators, faculty and library staffs are to increase the power of the library as a revealing, synthesizing force upon the modern American college campus.

In the library of the American college of today, much is found that is disquieting. There are thoughtful observers who consider it the weakest link in the college chain. There are libraries that are housed in basements or in wooden huts of the wartime Y.M.C.A. type. Their equipment is meager and their atmosphere forbidding. Some of them are open for not more than thirty or forty hours a week, are insufficiently staffed, and are under the direction of librarians who have not been selected on the basis of general and professional training and special fitness for the positions they occupy. Some receive only 2 or 3 per cent of the college's total educational budget. In others the collection of books and periodicals has been brought together with slight relation to the courses which they are supposed to support. Their variety and timeliness are not such as to broaden the vision or kindle the imagination of the students who, were they otherwise, might be stimulated by them. I know of one college in which honors courses were offered when it was spending only 2 per cent of its total educational budget, or less than $8 per student, for library service. Its dean had worked out an elaborate paper set up for study in major fields, but he had not taken stock of his librarian and library resources to see that they properly reenforced and extended the work outlined. In this respect his planning might be compared to that of a quarterback who plans a brilliant end run without coordinating and utilizing his backfield in running interference and carrying the ball.

But, happily, this is only one side of the picture. There are other colleges that clearly reveal the emergence of the library as a well-coordinated, effectively employed teaching instrument. The building is planned with emphasis upon these features which are conducive to study—reading rooms conveniently located, offices for consultation with faculty advisers, open shelves, browsing rooms, cubicles in the stack. Hours of service are adequate. Books and periodicals are available in sufficient variety and number. The staff understands the objectives of the college and coordinates its effort with that of the instructors, and the administration provides a budget commensurate with the services to be rendered. Librarians here and there, the Carnegie Corporation Advisory Group on College Libraries, members of library school staffs and of the College and Reference Section of the American Library Association, are increasingly subjecting the library to intensive study. In these and other ways the college library is steadily emerging as a major force in American education. It is evident that if the course now being pursued is pursued steadfastly, the influence which the college library can be made to exert in preparing students for effective participation in the affairs of life will be significantly multiplied.

NOTES:

[1]Ernest H. Wilkins, *The Changing College*, Chicago, 1927.

[2]Herbert E. Hawkes, *College—What's the Use?* New York, 1927.

[3]Frederick J. Kelly, *The American Arts College*, New York, 1925.

[4]John B. Johnston, *The Liberal College in Changing Society*, New York, 1930.

[5]Robert L. Kelly, Ed., *The Effective College*, New York, 1928.

[6]George A. Works, *College and University Library Problems*, Chicago, 1927.

[7]G. W. Rosenlof, *Library Facilities of Teacher-Training Institutions*, New York, 1929.

[8]Charles H. Brown, "The Library in Land-Grant Colleges," *Office of Education Bulletin* (1930), No. 9, Vol. 1, pp. 609–713.

[9]American Library Association, *Budgets, Classification and Compensation Plans for University and College Libraries*, Chicago, 1929.

[10]Eugene Hilton, "Junior College Booklist," *University of California Publications in Education*, Vol. 6, No. 1, pp. 1–84, Berkeley, 1930.

[11] Edna A. Hester, *A Junior College Book List*, Chicago, 1931.

[12] Charles B. Shaw, *A List of Books for College Libraries*, New York, 1930.

[13] Douglas Waples and Ralph W. Tyler, *What People Want to Read About*, Chicago, 1931.

[14] Douglas Waples, "The North Central Association's Study of College Libraries," *College and Reference Library Yearbook*, No. 2, pp. 85–89, Chicago, 1930.

[15] Association of Colleges and Secondary Schools of the Southern States, *Proceedings*, 1930, pp. 280–281.

[16] Floyd W. Reeves and John Dale Russell, "The Relation of the College Library to Recent Movements in Higher Education," *Library Quarterly*, Vol. 1, No. 1, 1931, pp. 57–66.

[17] Chapters in manuscript from a book in preparation by William M. Randall.

[18] American Library Association, *A Survey of Libraries in the United States*, 4 vols., Chicago, 1926–27.

[19] Works, *Op. cit.*

[20] Rosenlof, *Op. cit.*

[21] Brown, *Op. cit.*

[22] Hilton, *Op. cit.*

[23] Hester, *Op. cit.*

[24] Shaw, *Op. cit.*

[25] Questionnaire prepared by the Advisory Group on College Libraries for the Carnegie Corporation of New York City.

[26] American Library Association, *College and Reference Library Yearbook*, Nos. 1, 2, 3, Chicago, 1929–31.

[27] Letter from William M. Randall, April 17, 1931.

[28] American Library Association, Nos. 1 and 2.

[29] *Ibid.*

[30] Brown, *Op. cit.*

[31] Charles Z. Klauder and Herbert C. Wise, *College Architecture in America*, New York, 1929.

[32] Hilton, *Op. cit.*

[33] Hester, *Op. cit.*

[34] Shaw, *Op. cit.*

[35] Waples and Tyler, *Op. cit.*

[36] Letter from William M. Randall, April 17, 1931.

[37] Brown, *Op. cit.*

[38] Works, *Op. cit.*

[39] See earlier citations.

The Service of Libraries in Promoting Scholarship and Research

ON APRIL 23, 1932, two new libraries, devoted exclusively to the purposes of scholarship and research, were dedicated in America. I refer to the Horace Howard Furness Memorial Library of Shakespeareana of the University of Pennsylvania[1] and the Henry Clay Folger Library of Shakespeareana[2] located on Capitol Hill in Washington, D.C., across the way from the Library of Congress. The former contains 12,000 volumes of priceless Shakespearean and Elizabethan dramatic literature assembled by Dr. Furness and his father during their distinguished careers as Shakespearean scholars. The Folger Library contains 75,000 volumes. Among these are a remarkable sequence of early folios, quartos, first editions, and 1,400 copies of collected works. Copies of the single plays of *Hamlet* and *Macbeth* number 800 and 500, respectively. Paintings, etchings, prints, musical scores, and phonographic records having to do with the dramatist's works or the parts which persons associated with the presentation of Shakespearean plays have taken are also included. Not only is there in the Folger Library a concentration of material concerning Shakespeare equaled nowhere else in the world, but it has been accompanied by a $10,000,000 endowment for future growth, provision for a librarian, a director of research, special studies for visiting scholars, and a theater designed in the Elizabethan style for the presentation of Shakespearean plays.

Reprinted from *Library Quarterly*, 3:127–145, April, 1933, by permission of the publisher. An address delivered at the dedication of the Mary Reed Library, University of Denver, October 28, 1932. Also published in *The Contribution of the University Library to Civilization*, A Series of Symposia at the Dedication of the Mary Reed Library, October 26, 27, 28, 1932, pp. 125–138, University of Denver, Denver, Colorado.

[1] For notes, see page 173.

Thus, on one day, in two cities on the Atlantic seaboard only 135 miles apart, library resources were opened to American scholars which will profoundly influence Shakespearean study for the future and add to the significant foundation which American libraries have been laying in the past for the advancement of scholarship and investigation in many fields of learning.

Let us consider briefly, and largely by means of illustration, five types of service which American libraries are effectively rendering the scholar today. They are: (1) the accumulation of materials; (2) making materials available; (3) personal assistance to scholars; (4) directing research and publication; and (5) aiding scholarship through international cooperation.

I. *The Accumulation of Materials*

One of the most notable features of reports of American university presidents and of proceedings of associations of university professors and learned societies from 1910 to 1930 was the frequency of references to the necessity of placing research on a more adequate basis and of organizing research councils in various national scholarly bodies.[3] The Association of American Universities, the American Association of University Professors, the American Historical Association, and other like bodies dwelt constantly on this theme until 1919, when the movement toward organization and cooperation resulted in the foundation of the American Council of Learned Societies embracing fifteen societies. At the same time, concerted action was urged to enlist support for the research programs of the cooperating associations.

While evidences of actual organization and cooperation on the part of American libraries to provide essential source materials for the scholarly undertakings of these organizations do not appear as frequently in the proceedings of library associations as in the proceedings of the associations mentioned, American libraries have constantly been aware that their first duty to the scholar, wherever located in the 3,000,000 square miles of territory comprising the United States, was to secure these essential materials for him. This has been particularly true of the Library of Congress, the libraries of the great metropolitan areas, the universities, and special libraries dealing with subjects of peculiar interest to scholars, and has shown itself in carefully considered plans of acquisition.

Two American librarians who have extensive knowledge of European library resources have expressed the opinion that no American library can probably meet the total requirements of the investigator with the same degree of satisfaction as the British Museum or the Bibliothèque Nationale.[4] But both of these librarians have recognized the fact that this disparity of resources is being equalized in the favor of the American scholar who wishes to carry on his work on this side of the Atlantic. This change has been effected through the enormous increase in American library holdings since 1900. At that date the Library of Congress contained slightly less than 1,000,000 volumes. Since then, the number has grown to 4,300,000.[5] Its holdings are also supplemented in Washington by the very extensive collections in the libraries of the Surgeon General's Office, the Federal Office of Education, the Department of Agriculture, the Smithsonian Institution, and other departments. To these resources it is constantly adding highly specialized materials such as the following. In 1931 it purchased 3,017 incunabula in the Vollbehr Collection. It added 5,246 volumes to its Chinese Collection, which now contains 142,018 volumes. It acquired 27,589 maps, which raised the total number in the map division to 1,219,682; and from 1927 to 1931 it secured 500,000 sheets of photostatic reproductions of materials in foreign archives dealing with American history.

The first duty of the great metropolitan libraries may easily be thought of as general service to their constituencies. But in this field also the obligation to provide highly specialized materials for the individual scholar is clearly recognized. The Lennox-Astor-Tilden foundations of the New York Public Library are devoted exclusively to reference uses. More than 2,000,000 of its 3,250,000 volumes have been acquired primarily for scholars. In the central building, where these materials are housed, they have been organized in specialized departments in which manuscripts, prints, documents, newspapers, and scientific and economic publications are drawn together from every possible source. The scholarly materials in the Ticknor Collection on Spanish literature and history in Boston, on folk lore in the White Collection in Cleveland, on local history and genealogy in the Burton Collection in Detroit—to mention only three of a long list of special collections to be found in public libraries—have been built up to provide the scholar with resources that are indispensable in carrying on investigations in these fields.

Important, however, as these accumulations of materials are, the responsibility for the training of scholars and the maintenance of sustained scholarly work is recognized as one of the two major functions of American universities. This is true even though teaching, in many instances, seems to consume the greater part of the money and time of universities and their staffs. Even though special institutes and foundations are engaged exclusively in research, the universities "are the principal springs and reservoirs of pure learning."[6] Their libraries recognize this responsibility and are meeting it in a constructive way. The record of their acquisitions demonstrates this conclusively, as the following examples will show. The Widener Library at Harvard added 193,800 volumes to its collection in a single year, 1930–31. This unprecedented total brought its complete holdings to 3,165,400 volumes[7] and entitled it to rank seventh among the world's greatest libraries. The scholarly character of these additions for the year was illustrated by the Nelson H. Gay Collection of Italian history of over 42,000 volumes and pamphlets bought *en bloc*.

The record of other university libraries for the thirty years from 1901 to 1931 is similar to Harvard's. The chief difference is in the number of volumes acquired. In 1901 the Harvard Library contained 576,900 volumes.[8] Its growth for thirty years was 2,588,500 volumes. At the University of North Carolina, in the southeast, the number of volumes grew in the same period from 33,000 to 230,512; at Texas, in the southwest, from 35,000 to 459,873; at California, from 90,000 to 773,354; at Illinois, from 53,792 to 887,884; at Chicago, from 300,000 to 966,195. During the past ten years thirty-two of the larger college and university libraries spent $18,446,397 for 6,803,138 volumes, and in 1931 possessed a total of 19,245,719 volumes. Inasmuch as the average number of volumes in 202 American college libraries was 35,000[9] in 1931, it is evident that even in universities where the undergraduate enrolment is large and where the work of the junior and senior classes is not closely integrated with the preliminary work in graduate fields, a high percentage of the total expenditure is for materials at the graduate level. Several librarians[10] of universities of this character have estimated that 50 to

75 per cent of the book fund was used for strictly graduate purposes; and at Johns Hopkins University, where undergraduate work has been held at a minimum, the whole organization of the library has been planned largely for graduate use. One of the great satisfactions of the university librarian is that he usually has special funds at his disposal which he can spend in cooperation with scholars in furthering their special investigations, and that over a long period of years he can develop a consistent plan of important acquisition.

University libraries have frequently advocated the increase of the total amount of unduplicated materials for scholarly use by limitation of fields and cooperative buying. The desirability of these procedures has generally been recognized; but in practice it is difficult to employ them because university administrations, faculties, and supporters, rather than librarians, largely determine what fields of learning are to be comprised within universities and what objects shall receive special support. Nevertheless, cooperation in limited ways is being achieved. The Library of Congress, in cooperation with several university libraries, has carefully considered important lacunae in their holdings as well as its own, and, through its foreign representatives, attempts to fill them. In New York, the Library of Columbia University and the New York Public Library have a working agreement with respect to newspapers. The Public Library subscribes for and preserves files of 135 domestic and foreign papers, while Columbia limits itself to 9.[11] In Chicago, the Newberry and the John Crerar libraries specialize in separate fields. The Newberry concerns itself with the humanities; the John Crerar, with technology and science. The Chicago Public Library attempts to serve the general needs of the city. The University of Chicago Library recognizes these specializations on the part of its sister-institutions as far as it can; but, as has been indicated above, finds it necessary to support the work of the schools and departments on the campus by means of its holdings.

Cooperation of another sort in the accumulation of materials is now being developed between the Committee on Public Administration of the Social Science Research Council and American libraries with respect to the collecting of federal, state, county, and municipal documents.[12] One library has been designated as a document center in each state; and the cooperating libraries are assisting each other in securing, through exchange, documents that otherwise would be acquired with difficulty. Scholarly work in the social sciences should profit tremendously as a result. Investigation in the field of modern languages has been assisted in a similar way. By means of a plan in which the Modern Language Association of America and university libraries participate, the Library of Congress has been enabled to secure photostatic reproduction of 182 manuscripts[13] of significance to scholars in the field, and it loans them to scholars through the participating libraries. Two other proposals, now being studied by the newly formed Association of Research Librarians, the American Library Association, and the Joint Committee on Materials for Research of the American Council of Learned Societies, relate to the publication of scholarly manuscripts, which commercial publishers cannot publish with profit, and to the reproduction of rare books and manuscripts by means of films and inexpensive reprints. The object of the study is to devise means by which these materials hitherto unavailable may be made accessible to students and libraries.

Another unorganized, but nonetheless significant, movement on the part of university libraries to aid scholarship through accumulation of resources is seen in the plan for the building-up of manuscript and original source materials in sections in which such collections have heretofore not been carefully developed. This is true particularly of the South, in which extensive foundations of newspapers, letters, diaries, plantation records, pamphlets, documents, and books locally printed have recently been begun at Duke University and the Universities of Virginia, North Carolina, Louisiana, and Texas. The development of extensive collections of negro history and literature in the South has been stimulated by the completion of adequate library buildings at Atlanta and Fisk universities and an important addition to the Library of Hampton Institute.

Surveys to which American universities have been subjecting themselves in recent years have also had an important bearing on the library needs of the scholar. The general survey of the University of Chicago now in progress furnishes an excellent example. The Director of the University Libraries has sought the cooperation of scholars in all of the schools and departments of the University in determining the nature and extent of acquisitions required to put their work on an appropriate basis. Bibliographies and holdings in all fields covered by the University have been systematically studied and checked, and a definite working program for the future is in the making. Such self-appraisals of university libraries lead to the formulation of policies of great importance to scholarship.

The rise of the special library concerned primarily with business and industry has been one of the notable library developments in America since 1900. In that year the number of such libraries probably did not exceed 50. It now exceeds 1,000. Many of them are members of the Special Libraries Association formed in 1909, and meet annually to consider measures for promoting their efficiency. Although they are not generally regarded as of interest to investigators outside the special field with which they are concerned, they have accumulated extensive resources which are frequently of importance to scholars and furnish data that cannot be secured elsewhere.

The role which historical society libraries have played in accumulating and preserving materials has long been recognized. Without the resources of such societies as those of Massachusetts, Wisconsin, and Virginia, the history of certain periods could not be written. Similarly, libraries of museums, municipal and legislative reference bureaus, state libraries, and other special libraries of learned societies and like organizations have also built up collections which are admirably suited to the needs of scholars.

The emergence of the private library built up by an individual collector, and later set apart for public use, however, is a fairly recent phenomenon of the greatest importance to the student. The Clements, Huntington, and Folger libraries fall within this classification and may serve as excellent examples of this very important type of library. In a very real sense they can be thought of as foundations for the study of the humanities; and the accumulation of their materials has been regarded with the greatest interest on the part of librarians, collectors, and scholars in all parts of the world.

The Huntington Library, for example, is essentially a "library of libraries or a collection of collections." Mr. Huntington transferred his technique as a business man to his book-collecting; and from 1904, when he began collecting, until his death in 1927, he was the most spectacular buyer of collections *en bloc* that America has

known. Confining his interests primarily to the history and literature of America and England, with occasional purchases of incunabula and Spanish-American documents, he bought collection after
collection with seeming abandon, but always with a view to securing
items of unusual rarity and value. In the twenty odd years of his collecting he assembled more than 175,000 volumes in the fields mentioned, 800,000 pieces of manuscripts, and many paintings and other
works of art. Concerned solely with the acquisition of rare items, he
disposed of duplicates which did not add to the value of the library
and left it to the trustees of the foundation which he established to
see to it that the essential catalogues and critical apparatus should
be provided later for its use.

II. *Making Materials Available*

The second service which American libraries render the scholar is
that of making their resources available. This is done in several
ways. The first of these is through the organization of space in the
main library building and departmental libraries. Plans of the larger
university libraries erected within recent years show this clearly.
Undergraduate reading-rooms either are provided on the first floor
of the main building or are found in classrooms or other buildings
designed for that purpose. The major portion of the central building
not devoted to administrative and technical purposes is devoted to
the general reference room, graduate reading-rooms, seminars, studies for professors or specialists, and, within the stack itself, numerous cubicles or tables where the materials most needed for investigation are near at hand. This organization of space is not accidental
but is planned with the sole object of making scholarly work possible under the most advantageous conditions. At Johns Hopkins University, the principle has been carried out in a particularly organized
tri-partite scheme. Tables for graduate students in English, for example, are provided in the section of the stacks where English materials
are located. The English seminar is in close proximity, and the studies
of the professors of English are immediately adjacent. At the University of Minnesota, while graduate reading-rooms have not been
provided as such, 39 seminars, discussion rooms, survey-rooms, 8
studies, and 143 cubicles in the stack are available for graduate stu-

dents and members of the faculty. At Yale the whole central tower, or book stack, is organized in such fashion as to bring the holdings of a given discipline upon a given floor, with cubicles in the stack, and studies and seminars at the corners. Space in the Huntington, Folger, and other special libraries is organized almost exclusively for scholarly purposes, and the studies at the Widener Library and the Library of Congress have always been eagerly sought by scholars. South Hall, the new library building of Columbia University, the cornerstone of which was laid on October 3, is planned primarily for graduate work. It will contain general reading-rooms, reserve reading-rooms, and seminars solely for graduate use. Approximately 1,000 desks will be installed in the artificially lighted, air-conditioned stack for graduate students; and desks in special rooms and 200 small private, practically sound-proof studies will be provided for the use of students engaged in writing theses and for members of the graduate faculties.[14]

The second means which a library has of making materials available is that of the development of a complete dictionary catalogue of its holdings, with duplicate catalogues for departmental libraries, indexes of periodicals and proceedings of learned societies, printed catalogues of other notable libraries, and bibliographical and critical apparatus concerning all the subjects contained in the holdings of the library. The part which the libraries themselves play in this way in behalf of scholarship may be easily overlooked but its significance to the advancement of learning is very considerable. In addition to these aids, fifty-one municipal, university, and other libraries in the United States possess depository catalogues containing the main printed cards for all the books owned by the Library of Congress and catalogued by it. Forty-three other libraries, mostly libraries of departments of the federal government, are depositories for partial sets. In many of the full depository catalogues this basic collection of approximately 1,250,000 Library of Congress cards is supplemented by cards for books in other libraries, but not in the Library of Congress. Harvard, Chicago, Michigan, Illinois, California, and other American and foreign libraries—fifteen or twenty in all—issue such cards which, if added to the Library of Congress set, constitute an indispensable finding-list for scholars. The fact that these depository sets are widely distributed increases the significance of this scholarly aid, as no scholar is apt to be too far removed from one of the centers to make consultation impossible.

The Library of Congress has developed this service to an even higher degree. It not only has combined its own cards and those issued by the other libraries referred to into one great union catalogue or list, but it has added to them cards received from 500[15] special collections throughout the country and cards for titles taken from 118[15] of the largest printed catalogues of libraries. All of these are merged into one great union catalogue which, with its auxiliary aids, contains more than 11,000,000 cards.[16] Here, then, is a cooperative service, sponsored by libraries and one of the educational foundations, which is fundamental to effective scholarly work. The effectiveness of this great finding-list is even more apparent when it is thought of in connection with other major cooperative bibliographical enterprises carried on by the Library of Congress, such as the *Union list of serials in the libraries of the United States and Canada*, the *List of serial publications of foreign governments, 1815–1931*, and the *Union List of European Manuscripts in American Libraries*, and the printed catalogues of the British Museum, the Bibliothèque Nationale, and the German libraries in the publication of which American libraries have been greatly interested.

Catalogues and finding-lists however, do not meet all the requirements of the scholar. These are not fully met until he has the materials in hand. Libraries have largely achieved this by the perfection of systems of interlibrary loans and photostatic reproduction service which have brought the resources of many of the greatest libraries to the scholar however far he is removed from extensive library holdings. The various lists and union catalogues referred to above constitute his first source of information as to where the desired volume or manuscript can be found. Failing these, the Library of Congress, through its Union Catalogue and various special lists, can be called upon either for information where the volume or manuscript can be secured or for the material itself, as its regulations governing interlibrary loans are very liberal. Although the libraries of the various cities, states, and universities are not under a single control as are the libraries of many of the European countries, and although the materials in some of them can be used only on the local premises, the scholar can at least know where a given volume or manuscript is, where it can be consulted, from what library it may be borrowed, or where a photostatic reproduction of it can be secured. When it is realized that all of these cooperative developments have been undertaken since 1900, and that such major undertakings as the *Union list of serials* and the Union Catalogue have been carried out within the last ten years, the importance of the service of libraries to scholars in this particular is instantly apparent. What it may become in the immediate future, by means of air transportation of materials, reproduction by films, and the possible reproduction by television or other devices now being considered, is even more fascinating to contemplate.

III. *Personal Assistance to Scholars*

Dr. Herbert Putnam, librarian of Congress, in concluding a paper on "The Relation of libraries to scholarship and research" before the World Conference of Librarians and Bibliographers in Rome in 1929, pointed out the service which the Library of Congress was rendering scholars through what he termed "its human resources." He did not have in mind the experts in the order, catalogue, and circulation departments—essential as they are even when not called upon for expert assistance—engaged in accumulating and systematizing materials and handing them over the delivery desk to borrowers. He had in mind, rather, the bibliographers, the chief reference librarians, the experts in various fields in charge of special divisions, and, more particularly, the specialists who, in recent years, have been added to the Library of Congress as expert consultants and who serve as personal advisers to the administration concerning the development of collections and interpreters to scholars of the collection and the apparatus for their use. In most libraries emphasis has very naturally been placed on the acquisition of materials and their preparation for use. Too seldom has it been placed on assistance in use. But this is changing. In one southern university the success of a special institute for research in social science was greatly promoted by the skill of a reference librarian in acquainting his colleagues, through abstracts of articles and bibliographical aids, with literature pertinent to the field. No detective story is more exciting than the recital by the chief reference librarian of Columbia University of the clues she followed in locating for a professor the letters hitherto not

collected of Ralph Waldo Emerson. Obscure obituary notices in
European papers yielded leads which probably would never have
been discovered otherwise and about which biographical dictionaries had nothing whatever to say. Some worker in the Huntington
Library discovered a sketch of the original building of the College
of William and Mary, which has been utilized by Mr. John D. Rockefeller, Jr., in the restoration of the city of Williamsburg. A recent
investigation by a noted scientist has convinced him that the investigator in the field of the humanities has not had nearly so much
assistance of this sort provided him as has his colleague in the sciences through skilled laboratory assistants. This year, as a result of
this investigation, expert reference librarians are being provided in
three American universities to assist scholars in their investigations
in the humanities and the social sciences. The addition of specialists
such as these to library staffs, and the visiting scholars and consultants at the Huntington Library and the Library of Congress indicate that scholarly libraries are seriously asking themselves the
question whether they might not serve scholarship more adequately
by adding experts to their interpreting staffs than by unlimited acquisition of materials. Stricter limitation of fields with greater provision of expert service might easily result in a more fruitful procedure than that now usually followed.

The part which the private library is playing in making materials
available, both through technical and personal service, is splendidly
illustrated by the Huntington Library. Founded by Mr. Huntington
in 1919, this library was expressly devoted to the "advancement of
learning, the arts and sciences, and to promote the public welfare."

These purposes are carried out by a staff consisting of a director
of research, a librarian, a curator of rare books, a curator of manuscripts, three bibliographers, a chief binder, a curator of art materials, and two staff members in charge of photographic reproductions
and public exhibitions, respectively, together with library and other
essential personnel. A group of distinguished visiting scholars,
which has grown since the publication of the first annual report in
1928 to 10 in 1931, has been associated with the staff. In connection
with the Harvard University Press, three series of publications have
been begun, entitled "Huntington Library publications," *Huntington
Library Bulletin*, and *Annual reports*. All of these convey information

to scholars about the nature of the materials of the library and the conditions under which they may be used. At first a collection of 175,000 books and 800,000 manuscripts, relating especially to English and American literature and history and characterized by the high percentage of unique or excessively rare items in the fields covered, its book resources have recently been systematically catalogued, and an extensive scholarly apparatus for its use and interpretation has been acquired. More than 800 of the rarest manuscripts and books and hundreds of less extensive materials have been photostated, either for use in the Library or for the use of scholars elsewhere the world over. Scientific methods of restoring wax seals, of protecting manuscripts and books from deterioration through exposure to moisture, light, and insects, and for reproducing portions of badly faded manuscripts by specially devised photostatic procedures have been effected which will have wide application in libraries wherever similar materials are stored. The life-span of priceless materials for research has thus been extended through the application of scientific principles; and the debt of the scholar to the librarian as accumulator, preserver, and interpreter of the materials of research has been further increased.

IV. *Directing Research and Publication*

The director of the large American library is usually so pressed with the details of administration that he does not become a productive scholar in the sense that directors of many European libraries do. Nevertheless, names of librarians like those of Winsor and Gilman (who was librarian of the Sheffield Scientific School at Yale before he became the first president of Johns Hopkins) find their place in the list of American scholars; and American librarians have had, and are having, a direct and important part in the promotion of scholarship. This is shown in at least four ways. In the major universities the librarian is more and more being added to the directing boards of special research institutes or of faculties of graduate schools in order that the purposes of these organizations and of the library may be closely coordinated. On account of his institutional, rather than departmental, point of view and of his knowledge of the resources of all departments, he is in position to suggest the joint use of materials or special lines of cooperation that cut across departmental boundaries and make an effective attack upon given problems possible.

In many institutions, the librarian also exerts the influence of the library through contacts with graduate clubs and through instruction offered in the subjects of bibliography. The chief librarian of Yale holds the title of professor of bibliography. At Princeton a member of the library staff gives a course in bibliography which has been departmentalized for the benefit of students in the classics, modern languages, English, art and archaeology, history, politics, and science. The offering by librarians of lectures or courses for the purpose of orienting graduate students in the literature of various fields of learning is becoming more frequent.

The librarian has also become, in connection with graduate library schools, not only a teacher of bibliography in the general sense, but the director of special investigations in librarianship and related fields. In this respect he has become a director of study and investigation in his own right. The doctoral dissertation on library subjects is in the way of becoming a less novel and infrequent phenomenon; and students in library schools, librarians, and members of library school staffs are carrying on investigations which promise fundamental significance.

The role of the librarian as compiler, editor, and publisher is also one of importance. His service to bibliography, the starting-point and foundation of all sound investigation, has been of inestimable value as he has given it precision and form. His participation in the preparation of notable catalogues of the past and of recent publications such as the *Check-list of newspapers* issued by the Duke University Library, the *Catalog* of the John Carter Brown Library, the *History* of the New York Public Library, and the *Union list of serials* affords illustrations of valuable scholarly work for which librarians are largely responsible. The part which librarians have taken in the organization and direction of university publications and presses at McGill University, the University of Toronto, and the University of North Carolina—to mention but three institutions—is also illustrative of the importance which librarians attach to scholarly undertakings and of the many-sided service rendered in promoting them.

V. *Aiding Scholarship Through International Cooperation*

Scholarship knows no national boundaries. Inasmuch as its quest is truth, it seeks it wherever it may. Consequently, a unity of purpose binds libraries together wherever they may be located. American libraries have been quick to recognize this and have taken an active part in establishing relationships with librarians of other countries for the benefit of scholarship throughout the world. Through its Committee on International Relations, the American Library Association, at its Fiftieth Anniversary Meeting at Atlantic City in 1926, began a movement which has resulted in the formation of an International Federation of Library Associations which meets quadrennially and in the intervals between meetings carries on its work through a committee composed of distinguished librarians representing a score or more of countries. The objective of this Federation is the establishment of relations among the libraries of the world by means of which their resources may be pooled in behalf of the scholar wherever located. Cooperative enterprises such as the publication of the British Museum *General Catalogue of printed books* and the speeding-up of the publication of the *Catalogue général* of the Bibliothèque Nationale furnish examples of this interest. The cooperation of American libraries with the authorities of the Vatican Library in organizing its materials in accord with modern procedures is another. The assistance of American librarians to the visiting commissions from the libraries of Oxford and Cambridge universities in working out plans for new buildings for those seats of learning is still another. All of these demonstrate the way in which the American library of today is attempting to make itself indispensable in all fields where scholarship is involved. To the librarian also, more than to any other, has fallen the task of perfecting the machinery by which exchange of materials between libraries in different countries is made available. Thousands of copies of theses and proceedings of learned societies thus exchanged, cross the high seas annually, for which the Smithsonian Institution provides free transportation; and library committees study the simplification of postal and custom regulations in order that obstacles to the flow of materials for the scholar from one country to another may be reduced to the minimum.

The emphasis in this paper thus far has been placed upon the services of libraries of scholars and to scholarship. Seemingly, the importance of libraries as the source of ideas and ideals and as the stimulator of scholarly interests and attitudes has been overlooked. What have libraries done, and what are they doing to kindle the enthusiasms of youth and to make men scholars?

Some time ago I received a letter from a former student and instructor at the University of North Carolina, now a research student at the British Museum, which may be considered in the nature of an answer to this question. I scarcely knew the student when he was at North Carolina, but he sat down in London and wrote a long letter to the library in gratefulness to it for something which it had contributed to him which moved him profoundly and started him on the way of the scholar. He spoke of the classic dignity of the façade of the library building at Chapel Hill; of the aesthetic spaciousness and lightness of the reference room; of the adequacy of the data on the cards in the catalogue; of the quickness of the service at the loan desk; of the skill of the reference librarian in aiding graduate students in the use of indexes and reference tools; of the convenience of the cubicles in the stack and the close intimacy of the books; of the attractiveness of the exhibits of special materials; and particularly of the freedom of access to the rare books and manuscripts.

His letter stopped here, but I can imagine something further. One day, while at work with rare books or early manuscripts, or in conference with his instructor in the library, a new spirit stirred within him. The passing of graduate courses, as such, ceased to be a goal. Knowledge of the civilization of which the books or manuscripts were evidences became a passion, a passion which since has kept him in the great libraries of Europe.

Just how libraries produce such changes of point of view I cannot say; but without the library, without its resources and services, without the contacts with librarian, teacher, and fellow-student in a place where books and materials find a congenial home, this change in attitude could not have been effected. They served as the flux of the village blacksmith shop which causes two pieces of white-hot iron to unite under the hammer. Until it is applied, no amount of hammering will firmly unite them; but once applied, they instantly lose themselves in a single, perfectly welded union.

Such is the work of the scholarly American library. These are some of the ways in which it serves and stimulates scholarship and research. It was this that President Butler of Columbia University had in mind on October 3 when he guided the cornerstone of South Hall into position and said it was the purpose of the university to make that building its chief instrument of productive scholarship and public service.

NOTES:

[1]*School and Society*, XXXV (1932), 558.

[2]George Wicher, "The Folger Shakespeare Library," *Theatre Arts Monthly*, XVI (1932), 108.

[3]F. A. Ogg, *Research in the Humanistic and Social Sciences* (New York, 1928).

[4]W. W. Bishop, *The Backs of Books* (Baltimore, 1922), p. 277, and Herbert Putnam, "American Libraries in relation to study and Research," *Library Journal*, LIV (1929), 694.

[5]U. S. Library of Congress, *Report of the Librarian of Congress*, 1930/31.

[6]Ogg, *op. cit.*, p. 20.

[7]Statistics of university libraries, 1930–31.

[8]*The World Almanac and Encyclopedia*, 1902.

[9]W. M. Randall, *The College Library* (Chicago, 1932), p. 67.

[10]Letters from university librarians.

[11]University of Chicago Libraries. Current newspaper program of thirteen American libraries outside of Chicago and of six libraries in metropolitan Chicago (unpublished).

[12]*Bulletin of the American Library Association*, XXXVI (1932), 533.

[13]Library of Congress, *op. cit.*, p. 72.

[14]Letter from Dr. C. C. Williamson, director of libraries.

[15]Letter from Mr. Ernest Kletsch, curator, Union Catalogue, Library of Congress.

[16]Library of Congress, *op. cit.*, p. 106.

The Use of the Library in Instruction

In this paper I shall undertake to answer two questions. (1) What forces or influences within and without the modern American college have increased the use of the library in college instruction? (2) How may library use and instruction be more effectively integrated in achieving the educational goals of the college in the future?

Library use in collegiate instruction made a distinctive advance in the past decade. The forces or changes which effected this improvement fall into three categories: (1) forces outside the college; (2) changes within the college; and (3) changes within the library.

I shall consider first the forces outside the college which have significantly affected library use. Four of these are worthy of special note. The action of the Carnegie Corporation of New York stands at the head of the list. This foundation, through its various college library advisory committees and library examiners, studied the libraries of approximately 750 liberal arts, junior, teachers, and Negro colleges from 1929 to 1941, and granted a total of $1,-609,000.00 to 235 institutions[1] to support the instruction offered by them. While these grants were under consideration college presidents, deans, faculties, and library staffs spent a great amount of time discussing library problems with library examiners, studying library budgets, filling out questionnaires concerning the qualifications of personnel, and checking book lists[2] dealing with the use of the library in instruction. This detailed, illuminating study and the addresses and articles by the chairman and members of the advisory committees revealed the actual status of the college library as a teaching instrument in a light in which it had never been seen be-

Reprinted from *Proceedings*, Institute for Administrative Officers of Higher Institutions, 1941, pp. 116–127, University of Chicago Press, by permission of the publisher.

[1]For notes, see page 184.

fore. And, more important still, it revealed it to the college president, who, in the final analysis, is the person most responsible in any college community for the adequacy or inadequacy of the college library as an instrument of instruction.

The second influence outside the college which affected the library favorably during the decade was exerted by the various accrediting associations of colleges and secondary schools. The influence exerted by the North Central Association was particularly notable. This organization set up qualitative measures for the evaluation of the part the library plays in the achievement of the college's educational objectives, and published a volume entitled *The Library*[3] to guide colleges in the improvement of library service. It discarded purely quantitative measurements, and undertook to determine the effectiveness of the library in attaining definitely conceived educational aims by means of qualified staff, interested faculty, and the use of books, periodicals, pamphlets, pictures, maps, films, musical recordings, and other materials.

Research and publication in the college library field constituted the third means by which library use was promoted during the decade. The examination for the Carnegie Corporation by Randall of the libraries of 200 liberal arts colleges when they were being considered for grants-in-aid resulted in 1932 in the publication of *The College Library*.[4] It presented a realistic and unflattering picture of college library development. It was soon followed by Gerould's *The College Library Building*,[5] which dealt with the housing of library facilities. Five years later it was followed by Randall and Goodrich's *Principles of College Library Administration*[6] which not only dealt with problems of college library administration, but set forth a philosophy of college library development which is now widely accepted by college administrators, faculty members, and college librarians. The decade brought forth a number of Master's and Doctor's theses and other studies which dealt with the reading of college students and the selection of books and periodicals for college libraries. As the decade closed, *Vitalizing a College Library*, by B. Lamar Johnson,[7] of Stephens College and *Teaching with Books*, by Harvie Branscomb,[8] of Duke University appeared. The former described the results of a carefully planned experiment in integrating instruction and the use of library materials in a junior college. *Teaching with Books* set forth the results of a nation-wide study of various means employed by American colleges in using library facilities effectively in instruction. The study was undertaken under the auspices of the Association of American Colleges. Consequently, it became a marked item in the reading of college presidents, deans, librarians, and those members of college faculties who were most alert to means of improving the quality of their teaching.

The fourth influence which has tended to increase the effectiveness of the college library was exerted by library schools. Prior to 1926 no American library school was concerned primarily with advanced instruction and research in librarianship. Since then five library schools connected with major universities have developed carefully organized graduate programs, one of which is devoted solely to graduate work and research. In varying degrees these schools have insisted that the college librarian must not only have a mastery of the fields of bibliography and librarianship, but must be broadly educated and be well equipped in some subject field as well. They have also insisted that he must be thoroughly acquainted with the educational goals of the college and must know how to work in close cooperation with the teaching staff and students in attaining them. Consequently, library school students have been required to attend courses offered by other university departments in order to insure their familiarity with the administrative and educational policies of higher institutions and to acquaint them with the subject matter of special subject fields. Prior to 1925, two-year courses in librarianship based upon the completion of a four-year college course were offered at two library schools,[9] but the programs of study were not organized under graduate schools and were not integrated extensively with other university departments. From 1927 to 1939, 570 Master's degrees and 25 Doctor's degrees were awarded to library school students by graduate schools upon the conclusion of from 6 to 8 years of university study and the completion of extensive Master's reports or theses and Doctor's dissertations. The percentage of students entering library schools with higher degrees in subject fields likewise increased from 6 to 10 per cent from 1928–29 to 1937–38, the total for the period being 700. Since the summer of 1936 the Graduate Library School of the University of Chicago has annually held a seminar which in reality has been a workshop on the college library, and in two of its institutes dealing with trends in librarianship and book selection, it has emphasized the modern concepts of the college library through papers by Presidents Wriston and Davidson and other speakers. During the present summer its activities will be coordinated with those of other workshops in the University in an effort to effect greater integration in library use and instruction.

The forces which I have described above originated outside the college. I shall next consider changes which have developed within the college. These have been principally curricular. The adoption of a new type of curriculum inevitably produces a corresponding change in the character of library use. Three such changes which have markedly affected library use will suffice as illustrations.

The first is the curriculum of the junior college which grows out of the interests and needs of the individual student and is implemented largely by individual guidance and counseling. In such situations the library becomes one of the principal means for the integration of instruction. H. M. Adams, in *The Junior College Library Program*,[10] states the aims of the library in such situations and illustrates how such a program may be carried out by referring to that of Menlo Junior School and College, developed in 1936 after a self survey of its library service.

In carrying out this program, a reading council was appointed; space in the library for chairs, tables, open shelves, and facilities for displaying library materials was more than trebled; instruction in improving silent reading was instituted; students were encouraged to keep daily reading records; and reading records and the results of reading tests were made available to faculty counselors. The book collections were approximately doubled in four years; a divisional collection for the social sciences and classroom and dormitory libraries were set up; musical recordings and reproductions of pictures were provided; and a college-wide stimulation of desirable reading was inaugurated. Through a reading council the combined library instructional efforts of the institution were coordinated, and an evaluation of the program in terms of the attainment of objectives was undertaken.

The second curricular change that has greatly increased library use has grown out of the interest of colleges in general education.

This interest has manifested itself through the survey or orientation course in junior colleges and the lower divisions of four-year colleges. While survey courses date well back of the 1930's, their most notable development has occurred within the past decade. Their nature requires little comment. Their library implications, however, call for consideration. Here at the University of Chicago their library implications were fully considered before they were put into effect. A special library was provided to house the materials selected to support them. An extensive syllabus including required and optional readings was developed for each of them. Reading materials were selected to cover all the objectives of the courses. Recency of publication was strongly emphasized. Duplication of titles was stressed, and, although the total number of individual required and optional titles for the courses was only about 2,000, approximately 12,000 copies were secured at a cost of about $25,000 and annual additions have been made in support of the program.[11] An extensive rental library service was also provided to supplement this service.

This has been only one part of the program. Constant revision of the syllabi and consequent revision of the list of titles have been regular routine. Faculty counselors have offices in the library quarters and are available for consultation about any phase of the individual student's work, including his use of library materials. Discussion groups meet regularly under discussion leaders in addition to the general class meetings, and assistance is given concerning methods of study and library use when these are desired. The use of the card catalog, of encyclopedias, of periodical indexes, and of the principal reference materials of the main library is taught as an integral part of an English course required of all freshmen, and, in the event students seem unable to keep up with their reading assignments, they are sent to the reading clinic of the University Laboratory Schools for testing and training in speed of reading and reading comprehension. Specially prepared motion pictures are also provided to supplement lectures, reading, and discussion.

At other institutions the details vary, but library councils, faculty counselors, discussion leaders, library coordinators and advisers have been provided, library regulations have been liberalized, student difficulty in carrying out reading assignments has been discussed by student, instructor, and librarian, and close integration of instruction and library use has been effected.

Junior colleges and the lower division of four-year colleges in many parts of the country have been able to carry out such programs because of their freedom to break with tradition and of their willingness to apply the results of experimentation and research to college teaching. Upper divisions of a number of colleges and universities have likewise increased library use during the decade, but they have been less aggressive in experimentation than the lower divisions. Where such increased use has occurred it has expressed itself through honors courses, tutorial or preceptorial programs, house plans, and other means.

E. B. Stanford, a student in the Graduate Library School of the University of Chicago, has recently completed a study to determine the extent of the involvement of the library in 130 colleges which have been reported to offer some form of instruction through honors courses or other independent study programs. In these courses the candidate (usually a senior or a junior of demonstrated superior ability) is assigned to a particular member of the faculty, who is thereafter known as his adviser, preceptor, or tutor. Working under the direct supervision of this faculty member, the student undertakes a program of independent reading and study based on a long-range goal of achievement. Stanford's findings are disappointing, not because they fail to discover the use to which the library is put in such courses, but because they show so few students enrolled in them. Of the 130,052 students enrolled in 86 colleges reporting, only 5,046 or 3.87 per cent were honors students. The library extended special privileges to such students in 82 of the colleges; it called new materials to their attention in 57; librarians discussed the bibliographical needs of honors students with their faculty counselors in 55 colleges; in 42 faculty advisers held conferences in the library with such students; and in 25 the library maintained a list of individual honors projects. Other special services furnished honors students by the library included inter-library loans, extended loan periods, purchases of special materials and microfilm, loans for vacation and off-campus use, stack privileges, and the use of bound periodicals and rare materials outside the library. At Williams College certain members of the Reference Department have been informally designated Library Consultants, and at Wellesley the Librarian, the Head of the Reader's Division, and the Assistant in Charge of Public Documents, give specific attention to the needs of honors students. In a number of institutions the effect of the reading program of the honors students was said to be reflected throughout the entire student body, but methods by which the effect could be appropriately measured have not as yet been devised.

In the case of tutorial and preceptorial programs, the student is usually expected to consult with his adviser not only concerning his academic problems but concerning his personal problems as well. The tutor is supposedly interested in the student's emotional and social growth as well as in his intellectual development. The impact of this type of program upon the library has been carefully recorded at Southwestern College, at Memphis, Tennessee, where the total number of book withdrawals (overnight reserves and home circulation) increased in a six-year period from 46.02 books per student to 78.86 per year, the size of the student body (500) remaining fairly constant.[12]

Other modifications of the curriculum have effected corresponding modifications in the use of library materials in instruction. Through house plans, Harvard has placed libraries of from 5,000 to 12,000 volumes in each of seven residence halls to support supervised study under tutors as well as to provide recreational reading. Through reading periods, during which classes are suspended, the University of Chicago has provided an opportunity for extensive reading, writing, and consultation with instructors. Through "great books" courses, St. Johns has centered attention largely upon a hundred or more of the classics. All of these devices involve the library in varying degrees and have as their object the development of the student in directing his own study and thinking.

Changes within the library which have promoted its use may now be mentioned. I regard three of these as particularly significant. Of first importance is the attempt members of many library staffs have made to understand the educational program of the college as it relates to the library and to participate intelligently in carrying it into effect. As indicated above, 1200 or more librarians have taken advanced degrees either in subject fields or library science during the

past decade. Sixty-five per cent of all the students enrolled in advanced courses in library schools during the summers of 1935–37
were members of college and university library staffs. Many of them
were taking courses dealing with the objectives of the college curriculum, the administration of higher institutions, methods of educational counseling, and subject fields which would increase their pro-
ficiency as student consultants and advisers. They have also carefully
studied the new types of curriculums and have undertaken to discover how each involves library use. This effort has been made in
many instances by college librarians in spite of limited vacations, in-
definite academic status, lack of recognition within the college that
the library staff may perform an important role in instruction, and
low salaries which are generally characteristic of college libraries.

The second change which librarians have helped to effect has involved the physical reorganization of library materials for specific
uses and the modification of library buildings or the arrangement of
new buildings to secure conditions which are conducive to effective
study. The library at Haverford has recently added a new wing by
means of which it has greatly extended its open shelves for books
and periodicals. The library at Wellesley has provided a new series
of alcoves in its main reading room to give greater quiet and intimacy of contact with books. Brown University has reorganized its
library along divisional lines and has greatly increased the student
use of books, and the new library building at the University of Colorado has been built on a divisional basis, the effect of which upon instruction has been reported to be very pronounced. Proposed plans
for a new library at Stephens College call for a building which will
house under one roof the general library, divisional and classroom
libraries, classrooms, conference rooms, and faculty studies.

Librarians have, in the third instance, taken the leading part in the
study of college-student reading. They have long been aware that
student failure in college work has often been due to the student's
inability to read sufficiently rapidly to keep up with class assignments or his inability to comprehend what was assigned to be read.
They have taken part in the diagnosis of reading ability and have
attempted to relate reading records to academic records in order to
assist the college in raising its total educational efficiency. Theses
and articles written by college librarians have constituted the princi-

pal source of information available concerning various aspects of college-student reading. The findings of these studies would make valuable reading for college executives and deans of instruction, but unfortunately they do not often find their way into such hands.

So far, I have considered three types of forces or changes which have increased the use of the library in collegiate instruction in the past decade. In conclusion I wish to offer certain proposals for further increasing such use. In doing this I have in mind the fact that the efficiency of the modern Diesel railway engine in converting fuel energy into hauling power has been tremendously increased over that of the early steam locomotive. From decade to decade the efficiency of the railway engine has been steadily pushed up by the constant study and experimentation of the physicist and the engineer. I believe the efficiency of the library as an educational instrument can likewise be further increased, provided the problem is steadily and intelligently attacked by college administrators, faculties, librarians, and research students.

Any statement of proposals for accomplishing this should include:

1. Provision, by the college administrator, of a library budget sufficient to insure the steady support of the instructional program with library materials and to secure a library instructional staff competent to administer the library at a teaching, rather than at a stripped-down administrative, library housekeeping level.

2. The placing, by the administration, of the librarian in such administrative and educational relationships as will enable the library to participate in the formulation and execution of administrative and educational policies in which the library may be involved to the profit of educational goals. Service on the curriculum committee, the library committee or reading council, the writing-speech-reading laboratory committee, the educational counseling and guidance committee, and the college self-survey committee should be automatic.

3. Provision, by the administration, of opportunity for the librarian and members of the library staff who serve students and faculty in a consultative or advisory capacity to continue to prepare themselves for such duties through study in professional, bibliographical, and subject fields. Opportunities should be made available to members of the library staff to acquire competence of this character just

as they are to other members of the instructional staff to pursue advanced study.

4. Formulation, by the librarian and faculty, of a program of systematic book selection which will bring under constant review the adequacy of materials available for the support of all parts of the curriculum. Recent studies have shown conclusively that many libraries do not have such a program, and that the procedures for selecting books are decidedly ineffective.

5. The establishment, by librarians and members of the instructional staffs, of a journal or section of an already existing journal devoted to reviewing and evaluating books and other materials intended for use in college teaching. A recent analysis of titles included in syllabi of survey courses shows such a lack of agreement concerning essential materials as to lead to the conclusion that present reviewing media do not provide information that facilitates effective selection or that, if they do provide such information, they are not sufficiently available to college librarians and instructors.

6. Stimulation, by the faculty, of student use of library materials through lectures, conferences, and suggestions growing out of an intimate understanding of the different kinds of material available, their suitability for the purposes of instruction and the difficulties which students encounter in carrying out reading assignments.

7. Provision, by the college, of a course or units of courses in subject fields, on the use of library materials for freshmen. Even though training in the use of the secondary school library may have been provided (in many instances it has not), such training is inadequate to insure the understanding of the greater complexities of college library use. Where reading, writing, and speech laboratories are provided by colleges, tests to determine student ability in the use of the library can be easily administered.

8. Provision, by university graduate schools and libraries, of courses or other means which will familiarize prospective college teachers with materials used by undergraduates in survey courses, honors programs, and other forms of instruction which involve extensive use of the library. Materials used in graduate study are very different from those used in college instruction at the freshman and sophomore levels. It cannot safely be taken for granted that a new college instructor will be familiar with the materials which will be

available to undergraduates or that he will understand automatically what are the most effective means of stimulating book use or of building up book collections.

In a study which I am now making 89 of 126 instructors and librarians expressed the opinion that college instructors needed formal instruction which would give prospective teachers information of this character. Others agreed that instructors should possess such information but thought it should be secured informally. Eells and Branscomb, who have recently made extensive studies of junior and liberal arts college libraries, estimated that 95 per cent of college instructors would profit by such information.[13]

9. A self appraisal, by the college, of the library's effectiveness in the attainment of the college's major goals. Such appraisal participated in by faculty members, library staff, and students may be very revealing and may add greatly to the college's understanding of the strengths and weaknesses of its library program.

These examples of what has been accomplished in the past decade and proposals for the decade ahead by no means exhaust the possibilities of increasing the efficiency of the library in collegiate instruction. They provide a pattern, however, which, if followed, should enrich and make more meaningful the educational program of the American college.

NOTES:

[1]William Warner Bishop. *Carnegie Corporation and College Libraries*, 1929–1938, Pp. 53,58. New York: Carnegie Corporation of New York, 1938.

Carnegie Corporation of New York. *Report of the President and of the Treasurer for the Year Ended September 30, 1939*, Pp. 54–55. New York: Carnegie Corporation of New York, 1939.

Carnegie Grants for Books. *Library Journal*, LXV (Dec. 15, 1940), 1086.

[2]Carnegie Corporation of New York, Advisory Group on College Libraries. *A List of Books for College Libraries*, Charles B. Shaw, Compiler. Chicago: American Library Association, 1931, Pp. xii, 810.

Carnegie Corporation of New York, Advisory Group on Junior College Libraries. *A List of Books for Junior College Libraries*, Foster E. Mohrhardt, Compiler. Chicago: American Library Association, 1936, Pp. xiv, 300.

[3]Douglas Waples. *The Library*. The Evaluation of Higher Institutions, Monograph IV. Chicago: University of Chicago Press, 1936. Pp. xviii, 86.

[4]William M. Randall. *The College Library*. Chicago: American Library Association and the University of Chicago Press, 1932. Pp. xii, 166.

[5]James Thayer Gerould. *The College Library Building, Its Planning and Equipment.* New York: Charles Scribner's Sons, 1932. Pp. x, 116.

[6]William M. Randall and Francis L. O. Goodrich. *Principles of College Library Administration.* Chicago: American Library Association and the University of Chicago Press, 1936. Pp. xii, 246.

[7]B. Lamar Johnson. *Vitalizing a College Library.* Chicago: American Library Association, 1939. Pp. xviii, 122.

[8]Harvie Branscomb. *Teaching with Books; A Study of College Libraries.* Chicago: Association of American Colleges and American Library Association, 1940. Pp. xviii, 240. Reprinted 1964 by The Shoe String Press, Inc., Hamden, Conn.

[9]The New York State Library School, from 1902, and the Library School of the University of Illinois, from 1912, offered a two-year curriculum, following a subject bachelor's degree, leading to the degree of B. L. S. Under this program, the New York State Library School awarded 344 B.L.S. degrees. Emphasis in these curriculums was placed somewhat more extensively upon technical and bibliographical aspects of librarianship, and less upon related subject fields than is the case in the curriculums of today.

[10]Harlen Martin Adams. *The Junior College Library Program.* Chicago: American Library Association; and Stanford University, California: Stanford University Press, 1940. Pp. xii, 92.

[11]Chauncey Samuel Boucher and A. J. Brumbaugh. *The Chicago College Plan,* p. 198. Chicago: University of Chicago Press, 1940.

[12]Branscomb. *Op. cit.,* p. 66.

[13]Private correspondence.

The Significance of the Joint University Libraries

THE DEDICATION OF A NEW LIBRARY BUILDING to serve the students and scholars of a great modern university is always an occasion for special ceremonial. And well it should be. It marks the addition to the varied resources of the university of a new, carefully planned building set apart to aid the university in achieving the ends for which the university has been established and maintained by society. It tremendously reinforces the university's efforts to conserve and revitalize knowledge and ideas from the past, to discover new knowledge and develop new ideas, and to pass this cumulated heritage on to succeeding generations through instruction, publication, and public service. It signalizes the supplementation of old forces and the release of new forces within society which inevitably contribute to its increasing understanding and cultural enrichment.

The dedication of the Joint Library of Vanderbilt University, George Peabody College for Teachers, and Scarritt College for Christian Workers shares this general significance with the dedication of all university libraries. But it does not stop there. It does something more. It has a significance peculiar to itself which derives from other causes than those just mentioned. This significance is at once so great and so unusual that we may do well to take time to analyze it in order that we may better understand just what it is.

First of all, the dedication of this building marks the culmination of a full decade of institutional planning by educational foundations, higher institutions of education, and libraries which has resulted in a clearly defined, purposeful program of educational cooperation. It

Reprinted from *College and Research Libraries*, 3:102–108, March, 1942, by permission of the publisher. Also published in *The Development of University Centers in the South*, edited by A. F. Kuhlman, Pp. 82–92. Nashville, Tennessee: Peabody Press and the Vanderbilt University Press, For the Joint University Libraries, 1942. A paper read at the dedication of the Joint University Library, Nashville, Tennessee, December 6, 1941.

makes concrete in brick and stone a type of planning of which there have been all too few examples in the past and of which it may be hoped there will be an increasing number in the future. Here the normal loyalties and rivalries of three institutions which usually tend to keep institutions apart have given place to the united consideration of means for enriching teaching and research insofar as this can be accomplished by the elimination of duplication in teaching at the undergraduate level, by the concentration of facilities and resources in the fields of graduate and professional study, and by the provision and support of a great joint library. Here is an enterprise involving three student bodies, three faculties, three libraries, and two educational foundations, which brings them all together in a unified program of education, of which this splendid new library building is the visible symbol. In these respects, the dedication of this building, to the usefulness and beauty of which librarians, builder, and architect have contributed, stands out as an instance of a new and significant type of educational statesmanship.

This dedication is significant for a second reason. It marks the emergence of a new type of educational administrative device. Prior to the 1930's, the attitudes of American institutions of higher education were characterized by rugged individualism. Funds for higher education were relatively abundant in the 1920's, and every university and college looked to the day when it would be bigger and richer and capable of outdistancing all its competitors. University libraries shared this spirit and attempted to make themselves self-sufficient. In the two decades of the 1920's and 1930's, while they more than doubled their holdings, they constantly bid against one another for rare materials and thereby increased the cost to themselves and to other libraries alike. They, and the boards of control of the institutions of which they were parts, did not set their legal staffs to work to devise means by which they would cooperate. The legal instrument, however, by means of which this joint library has been brought into being, is a newly conceived type of educational document. Although cooperative agreements among educational institutions and libraries have existed heretofore, the educational authorities and legal staffs who drafted this instrument did not find an educational model ready at hand. It is a document that renounces competition among institutions and libraries as a way of life and sets up in its stead a plan of cooperation for common benefits. It calls into being what, for lack of a better term, may be called an educational holding company organized not for financial profit but for the continuous cultivation of men's minds. It has already been widely studied. Principles very similar to those which it embraces have been applied by the libraries of Harvard University and other New England institutions in providing a common storage library for little-used books. It will continue to be studied by other colleges and universities which seriously seek to maintain and improve library facilities for instruction and research under the steadily increasing financial difficulties of the time.

Program of Curriculum Revision

The arrangement by which the joint library was brought into being is significant for another reason. It was worked out as a part of a program of curriculum revision in which not only the curriculums of all three institutions were considered together but the demands which the curriculums made upon the libraries of all three institutions were also considered. This again is an instance of an educational procedure which has likewise been all too infrequently employed by institutions when they have been involved in curriculum revision. Many institutions develop new plans for improving instruction or for carrying on investigation in new fields without including their libraries in the planning, and then are surprised when the effectiveness of the program is not so great as they had thought it should be, because proper library provision had not been made in the planning. It is only recently that a certain college president was heard to remark with evident, but ill-founded pride, that he had just finished putting through an extensive curriculum revision in his institution, that next year he was going to concentrate his attention on the development of facilities for the study of art, and that after he had completed these programs he was going to do something about the library! It did not seem to occur to him that unless these undertakings were properly supported with library resources and integrated with intelligent library use, the results he expected from them could not be achieved. The success of the survey courses at the University of Chicago and of the house plan and tutorial instruction at Harvard is attributable in part to the fact that both institutions devoted as much consideration to the selection and provision of the library materials which were to support the programs as they devoted to their organization and general content.

Staffs United

Here on these campuses a significant procedure was followed. The instructional and research staffs united to consider the elimination of competition and duplication of effort at the undergraduate level in order that work at the graduate and professional levels might be increased. They were conscious of the fact that no effective program of collaboration in these fields could be worked out which failed to include within it a plan of library development as well. Consequently, plans for providing library resources to support specialization and research in desired fields were made an integral part of the whole program. All of the planning went forward together, and the provision for this new building, for securing additional endowment for library purposes, and for increased library operating funds was, in fact, precedent to other developments which may now be expected to follow.

This is the kind of curriculum planning involving the careful integration of curriculum and library use, which, if followed from the elementary school, through high school, college, and university, will tremendously increase the effectiveness of American teaching and research.

Role of Library in Higher Education

On a number of occasions I have spoken of the role of the library in higher education and especially in higher education in the South where library resources have not been nearly so abundant as they have been in other parts of the nation. This audience knows the nature of the limitations which result from this lack and their effect upon productive scholarship. It knows that most Southern universities have been unable to undertake graduate work in many departments leading to the doctorate because essential library resources are lacking. It knows that thousands of graduate students have been lost to the schools and colleges and the business and professional life of the South because they went elsewhere for graduate training, and, after completing it, did not return to the South. It knows that the training of thousands of other students who were unable to use such materials in Southern universities has been less effective than it should be because of this lack. The dedication of this new library is of the greatest significance to higher education in this region because it marks the firm establishment of a new concentration of library resources upon which distinctive graduate work can be confidently based. With this concentration of four hundred thousand volumes, supplemented by the services of union catalogs and microphotography laboratories, which bring the total library resources of the city to more than eight hundred thousand volumes, students and scholars in Nashville can go about their daily work with new confidence. Nashville in a truer sense than ever before becomes a university center which not only can support the work of scholars here, but can make more fruitful the work of scholars on all the university campuses of the South. This installation of new resources not only reinforces work here but adds to the combined resources of all the centers of learning stretching from the nation's capital to the Mexican border.

Contribution to Resources for Research

A further significance of the dedication is to be seen in the contribution which the joint library makes to the total resources for research of the nation. In the official year 1935–36 of the American Library Association the status of the Committee on Resources of American Libraries was changed from that of a committee to that of a board, with enlarged powers, and a committee on microphotography was established. Since that date a conscious, well-conceived library program has been developed which has had two major objectives. The first has been the location and description of library materials essential to research. The second has been the increased provision of bibliographical apparatus and films for the use of scholars. Librarians and scholars in all parts of the nation have participated in this undertaking and have had the satisfaction of witnessing its successful development. Union catalogs and bibliographical apparatus have been provided in a number of the major libraries in various regions of the country for the location of research materials.

The resources of the Union Catalog of the Library of Congress have been greatly extended by the inclusion of cards from hundreds of libraries and regional union catalogs. It has, as a result, become the ultimate source to which the scholar, wherever located, may confidently look for bibliographical assistance. A number of notable microphotography laboratories have been established in university and research libraries for the reproduction of rare yet indispensable materials. Machines for the satisfactory reading of films have been developed and are to be found in reference rooms and special collections on campuses everywhere. The resources of a number of major research libraries have been systematically described by subject fields and significant titles through library surveys and other publications. A conference of national scope and attended by librarians, officers of universities, and members of learned societies has been held, which dealt with many phases of library cooperation and specialization. The Library of Congress, through the aid of an educational foundation, has set up a temporary Division of Library Cooperation, by means of which further aid to libraries and scholars is anticipated. A report growing out of a nationwide study of union catalogs and describing the nature of their services is now in press, and two editions of a publication describing the resources of libraries and special collections useful in national defense have recently been made available to the public. Altogether, this program is one of the most notable undertakings in America for the advancement of scholarship and it is one in which the librarians of Southern universities have played a leading role. In this movement the joint library, through its librarian and the librarians of Nashville, has taken a conspicuous part. Through their planning with the instructional and research staffs here, and their cooperation with librarians throughout the country, they have aided these three institutions to make a splendid contribution to the human and cultural resources of the nation.

Will Attract Other Gifts

A sixth significance of this dedication is to be found in the fact, for it is a well-proven fact, that this concentration of library buildings, resources, and staffs will attract other collections and gifts devoted to library service. Great libraries attract great gifts. Individual friends of the library, organized friends of the library, alumni, and nonalumni, will inevitably be impressed with the concentration and multiplication of resources represented here, and when seeking ways through which to contribute to educational effectiveness will find in this library the means which will aid them to this end. Splendid evidence of this fact is already here. I have spoken of the educational foundations, of the three institutions, and of the three libraries which have participated in bringing this new resource of learning and investigation into being. But I am not unmindful of the fact that supplementing their effort has been the significant support of students and members of these faculties and of men and women of this city, of this state, and of the nation, who, through their interest and gifts have made this library their very own. Without their aid, this building would not have been possible. They will be succeeded tomorrow, and in the lengthening future, by others who will add to what they have so generously helped to begin.

The final significance which may be associated with this dedication is the part which this new library should play in preparing teachers and librarians for more effective teaching and research. In 1931 in a paper which I read before the American Library Association at Yale entitled "The Emergence of the College Library," I presented evidence which seemed to me conclusive that the college library was then moving forward into new areas of usefulness in the field of higher education. The evidence seemed to be of many kinds. New curriculums were being established here and there which called for greater use of library service. Libraries were expanding their book collections and adding to their staffs personnel imbued with new educational ideals. Books and articles by college librarians, college presidents, and officers of educational foundations dealt with the larger role which the college library should play in the educational process. The college library in reality could be said to be entering upon a new period of usefulness in which teaching with books was becoming an important method of teaching.

Similar Movement in Other Libraries

Today it seems to me that a similar movement can be detected in other types of libraries. From the elementary school through the junior college, similar stirrings are to be noted. Better library quarters have been provided; more books have been purchased; more periodicals have been placed on the shelves; more radios, records, slides, and films have been secured; more librarians have been put into service; more superintendents, principals, and teachers have gained some understanding of the role of the library in teaching; and more school boards and state legislatures have provided increased funds for library purposes in many types of libraries. This situation presents one of the greatest challenges to the institutions located on these campuses. These institutions, including as they do a university, a teachers college, a school for the training of librarians, a practice school library for elementary and secondary schools, and a library embodying all the best features of modern library service, have the opportunity of training prospective teachers and librarians at all levels of education in such a way as to enable them better to integrate library use and teaching than teachers and librarians have been able to in the past, and thereby tremendously increase their educational efficiency. If I am not greatly mistaken, it is just at this point where library use and teaching unite that American education will make its greatest advance in the next decade. Here in the libraries and classrooms of these adjoining campuses, the foundation has been laid for uniting teachers and librarians in a program of training which should make certain that all prospective teachers and educational administrators will understand how to utilize library materials in effective teaching. Unfortunately, many teachers do not know how to do this today. Furthermore, graduate study is generally so preoccupied with specialization and the use of highly specialized source materials that the prospective teacher has little opportunity while working for advanced degrees to become familiar with materials which can be used effectively in teaching at other levels. The foundation has likewise been laid here that should make certain that prospective librarians at all educational levels will understand the educational aims of the institutions which they serve and the best methods by which library materials may be used in their attainment. Fortunately for the improvement of teaching, the institutions which share in the use of the library resources of these campuses likewise share the philosophies of education and librarianship which insist upon the combination of these important understandings without which teaching cannot achieve its greatest effect. If those who teach and those who administer libraries here imbue prospective teachers and librarians with these philosophies and send them thus equipped into the schools and colleges of the nation, education will take on a new and fuller meaning.

Forty Years' Development

Forty years ago this December I wrote my first report as librarian of a neighboring Southern university. In the four decades that have intervened I have constantly studied the growth of libraries in higher institutions of education in this region. I have witnessed the movement for greater library resources, for more ample library support, for more adequate library buildings, go forward. I have seen the book collections reach the first one hundred thousand mark, then the quarter and half million marks. Now two are on the climb to the million mark. I have watched budgets grow to $10,000 annually, to $50,000, to $100,000, and more. I have seen special collections of a few hundred or a few thousand titles become so extensive as to give distinction to any institution which might possess them. I have witnessed from Virginia to Texas the erection of university library buildings that in their organization and size reflect the expanding conception of the importance of library resources and service in higher education. At times this movement has been slow. But at all times it has been forward.

Today as I consider this new achievement, I congratulate you, individually and collectively, who have made this building possible. Through the plans which you have perfected and through the building which you have added to the enduring resources of these three institutions, you have made a contribution to the extension and enrichment of education, the full significance of which cannot now be foreseen.

You have placed here at the center of these campuses a library building functionally designed to serve the varied interests of a distinguished community of students and scholars. Rooms for leisure and required reading and for the consultation of periodicals and reference works are available to the undergraduate; carrels in the stacks and special reading rooms are at the disposal of the graduate student; seminars and studies are set apart for the faculty member;

space for bibliographical apparatus, for microphotography, for the exhibition and use of special collections, and for the administration of the library as a whole, rounds out the full complement of the requirements of a modern university library. And all of these essentials have been skilfully organized in a building which in beauty of line and impressiveness of form stands as a symbol of the dignity and worth of learning. These are the obvious results of your conscious collaboration. But what you have so splendidly begun will, I am confident, demonstrate what has so frequently been demonstrated of the work of planners and builders heretofore. It will demonstrate that, splendid as have been your vision and accomplishment, you have actually planned and built better than you knew.

The Library in the Graduate Program of Institutions of Higher Education in the Southeast

WHAT IS THE PLACE OF THE LIBRARY in the advancing graduate program of the institutions of higher education in the Southeast? In this paper it is my intention to sketch, in rather broad outline, the answer to this question. I have in mind particularly the libraries of the teachers and land-grant colleges and the universities and professional schools in the region that are concerned with the training of the teachers and scholars in school and academic subjects and the experts in the professions and the fields of agriculture, engineering, and the various industries.

The answer to this question is important today and for a number of reasons.

1. The whole field of graduate instruction in the South has been subjected to increasing study during the past 25 years, and particularly within the decade of the 1940's. One of the most notable evi-

Reprinted from *University of Tennessee Library Lectures*, 1952, pp. 17–31, by permission of the publisher. This was the second lecture of the series and was delivered at Knoxville, Tennessee, April 21, 1950.

dences has been the establishment of the Conference of Deans of
Southern Graduate Schools in 1927, and its setting up of standards
for the master's and doctor's degrees in 1935 and 1947 respectively.
The publication of *The Development of Library Resources and Graduate Work in the Cooperative University Centers of the South*, by
Davidson and Kuhlman in 1944; of *Higher Education in the South*,
by the Committee on Work Conferences on Higher Education of the
Southern Association of Colleges and Secondary Schools; and of
Graduate Work in the South, by Mary Bynum Pierson, in 1947,
further emphasized the importance of graduate training, showed the
region's lack of graduate personnel and facilities, and set up objectives for higher attainment in the future.

Three other major developments in graduate and professional
study have taken place which mark significant advances in the field.
They are the development of university centers, described in a book
under that title published following the dedication of the Joint University Libraries in 1941, the special consideration given the subject
of graduate and professional education for Negroes since the decision of the Gaines Case by the U. S. Supreme Court in 1938, and the
organization of the Board of Control for Regional Education in the
South in 1949. During the Quarter century 1925–50 cooperative arrangements among the universities and colleges of Chapel Hill–Durham, Athens–Atlanta, Nashville, and New Orleans were perfected
which made possible graduate work more soundly based than previously especially through the cooperative provision of library resources, union catalogs, and other library facilities and apparatus.
The Board of Control for Regional Education in the South is coming to grips realistically with the problem of providing graduate and
professional training for both whites and Negroes through regional
support which cannot be provided through the individual effort of
institutions. And since the decision of the Gaines case requiring
states to provide equal facilities for whites and Negroes, Southern
legislatures, educational foundations, the Conference of Deans of
Southern Graduate Schools, and Negro educators have cooperated
in projecting graduate programs for Negro students.

The most compelling influence, however, has been the growth in
number of students seeking graduate and professional training of a
high order. In 1936 the enrollment of graduate students stood at

5,521 in the institutions covered by the Conference of Deans of Southern Graduate Schools. In 1944, when enrollment reached its lowest point in the war, it dropped to 2,121. But in 1949 it had climbed to 22,090 including Negro institutions, with the enrollment in summer sessions in 1949 for both races reaching a total of 31,451.

Research Organizations Have Emphasized Need

Demand for increased graduate and professional training at higher levels has come from another quarter. Today the idea of research is more firmly established in the region than formerly and institutions are being urged to increase their personnel and facilities in order that they may supply an adequate number of research workers to man the institutions, laboratories, and industries of the region.

Within the institutions themselves a number of research institutes have been established with fine records of achievement behind them. In the social sciences the Institute for Research in Social Science at the University of North Carolina and the Southern Regional Training Program in Public Administration at the University of Alabama, with which the Universities of Kentucky, Georgia, and Tennessee are associated, are cases in point. In 1948 the Southern Association of Science and Industry, established in the early 1940's, listed in its monograph, *Research in Southern Regional Development*, the following separate research agencies in Southern colleges and universities: 13 in agriculture, 15 in engineering, 25 in natural science and medicine, 8 in social science, 11 in government and public administration, 12 in education, and 14 in other unclassified fields. And in the humanities the Carnegie Foundation for the Advancement of Teaching and several of the national associations have stimulated research through grants-in-aid and through the establishment of regional divisions of their organizations. The Carnegie Foundation grant was made to four university centers for a five-year period. Each center associated with itself four colleges, the funds from the Foundation and institutions totaling $180,000 annually. The American Council of Learned Societies has assisted the Southern Humanities Conference organized in 1947 in the promotion of research in the humanistic fields.

Research in industry has also been greatly extended. The organization of the Southern Association of Science and Industry marked the conscious development of this movement, and the publication by the Association of monographs on research, forestry, industry, and other subjects has made clear the impressive role research is to play in the region. The Association has also furnished a medium or sounding board for the promotion of research throughout the region. In 1945 the University of North Carolina held a three-day symposium on various aspects of research, the papers presented before which were published in *Research and Regional Welfare*. The Southeastern Research Institute began the publication of its *Journal* in 1949, and industrialists generally have associated themselves directly or through a veritable rash of newly established foundations with the land-grant colleges and universities in providing funds for research professorships, research assistantships, and fellowships and scholarships for the training of experts and research workers in agriculture, business administration, ceramics, chemical engineering, dairying, insurance, textiles, and other subjects.

Governmental Agencies Have Promoted Graduate Study

The federal government has also greatly increased and intensified its program of research in various fields in the South. The experiment stations of the land-grant colleges and special laboratories of the U. S. Department of Agriculture have undertaken the solution of many problems in the various branches of agriculture and forestry, and the U. S. Public Health Service has promoted an extensive program of professional study including fellowships for study and research in the field of public health and public health education. At one university alone, which has been designated as the center for the Southeast, a total of 1300 fellowships have been furnished in the past 10 years for graduate training for sanitary engineers, public health educators, nurses, and doctors. They have been provided by a wide variety of organizations, such as state departments of public health, the U. S. Public Health Service, and the Kellogg and Rockefeller Foundations, and the Commonwealth Fund.

Of even greater importance, possibly, is the influence that the Oak Ridge Institute of Nuclear Studies and the Tennessee Valley Authority—two of the greatest research laboratories developed in any country—have exerted in centering attention upon research as a means of increasing the wealth and general well-being of the citizenry of the region. The Institute of Nuclear Studies has worked out a cooperative program of training and research for prospective scholars and research workers. Fourteen higher institutions have been included in the program and unusually well qualified students from them are enabled to go to Oak Ridge and work under the direction of some of the most notable scientists of the world. The special laboratories and other facilities of the Institute are available to the fellows, and training of the most specialized kind is provided. The fellows also have the opportunity of consulting with the faculties of their own institutions and using their laboratories and facilities. The Tennessee Valley Authority has from its beginning in 1933 carried on a vast program of experimentation and research. It has tied this program in closely with the land-grant colleges and universities with the result that research has been stimulated on every campus it has touched.

The Status of Libraries Has Been Clarified

Not only has the tempo of graduate study and research in the region been stepped up. The understanding of the status of libraries and of their role in higher education has also been clarified. The region knows far better than it ever did before what the condition of its libraries is and what it must do to make them more effective educational instruments. This is evidenced in a number of ways.

First of all, more is known of their actual status as compared with that of the libraries of institutions in other parts of the country. The recent survey by the libraries of the Southeast carried out under the direction of the Tennessee Valley Library Council revealed a number of significant facts concerning them. No university library in the region, for example, contained in 1946–47 as many as one million volumes, although there are 12 universities within the nation having collections of more than one million volumes, with one exceeding five million. No university library in the region added more than 27,698 volumes or subscribed for more than 3558 periodicals in 1946–47, whereas there were 10 university libraries in the United States that added from 50,000 to 128,000 volumes in 1948–49 and received thousands of journals and transactions of learned societies through subscription and exchange. In 1938, in making a survey of the University of Georgia Library, the library of the first chartered state university in America, I found that in the entire course of its history it had built up a collection of only 117,808 volumes. At the same time I found that Harvard, in the decade 1928–38, had added an average of 117,810 volumes for each of the ten years, or two more per year than Georgia had added in its entire history! And the University of California Library regularly receives 18,000 periodicals of which 6956 are exchanges.

Of even greater significance the region has discovered that it does not possess many of the publications that are absolutely essential to basic work in the sciences, particularly for the land-grant institutions, and that it is confronted with great difficulty in securing them on account of their rarity even if funds were available for their purchase.

The region has also been impressed with the relationship which exists between the total number of volumes held by libraries and the amount spent annually for current materials on the one hand, and, on the other, the number of fields in which the universities and land-grant colleges can successfully carry on work leading to the doctorate or advanced professional degrees. It is a significant fact that institutions with libraries having one million volumes or more and spending over $150,000 annually for books and periodicals, usually award the doctorate in from 20 to 30 fields, whereas those that have only 500,000 volumes or less and spend $100,000 or less annually for materials usually award the doctorate in less than 20 fields. In 1948–49, 17 institutions outside the region spent from $150,000 to $457,330 for books and periodicals, whereas only five in the Southeast spent from $100,000 to $140,000. As a matter of fact, from 1944–45 to 1947–48, only eight institutions in the region awarded a total of 296 doctorates, there being four of the nine states in which no doctorates were awarded for the four-year period.

This point should not be labored. But it is obvious that the libraries of the universities, land-grant colleges, and professional schools of the region constitute a serious brake on graduate study, a situation which the Southern Association and the Conference of Deans of Southern Graduate Schools have considered and the Commission on Graduate Study of the Board of Control for Regional Education in the South was confronted at its meeting at Savannah last October, and about which the Board is now doing some constructive thinking. In the humanities, the social sciences, the physical and biological sciences, and the professional fields and industry, the Southeast's lack of library resources stands as a road block, second only to the lack of graduate personnel, to the most successful prosecution of graduate study.

The functions of the university library have likewise become clearer. Obviously, the library is not an end in itself, but it finds the reasons for its support in promoting the purposes of the college or university.

Sometimes it is important to remind ourselves what the functions of the college and university are, particularly of those institutions which are concerned with the development of graduate programs. As I understand them, they are five:

1. The first function of the university is the conservation of knowledge. This is basic. The university, therefore, must possess the essential knowledge and ideas of the past as they have been set down in books and journals. This function of the university imposes upon the libraries the obligation of securing such materials as have been found to be of the greatest importance in the past and to secure from the stream of current publications those materials that are likewise essential in the study of the fields embraced by the institution in carrying out its program. It also imposes upon the library the obligation to facilitate the cooperative activities of libraries which contribute to furthering these two ends, but which the library could not achieve through its efforts single-handed.

2. The university shares with the college the duty of teaching, of revitalizing the best that men have discovered, and of transmitting it to the oncoming generation. The library participates in this activity by making library materials available through library catalogs, indexes, and other library apparatus, by the organization of its resources in appropriate reading rooms, studies, and carrels, and by the assistance of an expert library staff.

3. The distinctive function of the university that differentiates the university from the college is that it discovers new knowledge and presents former ideas in new combinations that will insure their being understood under new conditions. The university also serves

as the principal trainer of research workers for all fields. The role of the library becomes particularly important at this point, since the first step in undertaking any investigation is to discover through indexes and bibliographies what has been written upon the subject. The great tragedy for the Southeast has been that it has lacked the personnel and library facilities essential for this training and the funds for research assistantships, fellowships, and scholarships to insure the training of the experts required for its well-rounded development.

4. Publication and interpretation of the findings of research supplement the function of teaching. They, too, have not been sufficiently developed in the region and await further cultivation. The whole program of research-use-education is based upon these functions. The establishment of university presses, of university studies, and of various institutes for research in the past quarter century has contributed to this end, but the findings of research have barely begun to find their way into the curricula of the schools and colleges of the Southeast much less into the daily living of the region's citizenry. At this point the aid of the library at all levels of education is tremendously important since it should furnish the channels through which such publications and findings should reach their intended users.

5. Extension and public service have come to be recognized as the proper functions in varying degrees, of all land-grant colleges and state universities. These institutions have, in many instances, become the fourth arm of government. Through their staffs, their experiment stations, their extension services, both agricultural and general, they serve the entire public, not in order to secure a kind of protective insurance for themselves, but to improve and enrich the heritage of all the citizenry. Here again, the library should serve as the principle distributing agency through which materials to support such public service can most effectively be provided.

How Are the Libraries to Perform These Functions Effectively?

This is the situation which confronts the libraries of the institutions of higher education of the Southeast today. The remainder of this paper may be devoted to answering the questions: What is the place of the library in the developing graduate programs of these institutions in the Southeast? How are the libraries of the region to perform these functions most effectively?

During my experience of nearly 50 years as a librarian or teacher dealing with the subject of university libraries, I have frequently been called in as a surveyor to discover from what disorders certain libraries have been suffering and to prescribe for their restoration to sound health and effective performance. As a result I have discovered that there are certain requirements which the institution and the library must meet to enable the library to perform its functions properly in building up its collections and serving its patrons effectively at the graduate level. Five of these requirements or prescriptions are as follows:

1. The first is that the institution shall have a well-defined policy concerning the administration and support of the library. Beginning with the university administration, the policy should be thoroughly understood by the entire institution and it should be complied with at all times. Such a policy defines what constitutes the library, who is responsible for its direction and administration, what support it shall receive, and how it may be kept in the full stream of developing and carrying out the institution's program of instruction, research, and extension. This calls for full understanding of the relations which exist between the administration of the institution and the administration of the library, the function of the faculty committee on the library, the teamwork of the library and the faculty committees on curriculum, graduate study, and publications, and all that relates to the steady maintenance and support of a library program that is de-signed to serve every university interest.

2. The second requirement is that the library must possess or must be able to secure library materials necessary in achieving the objectives of the institution.

It is at this point that the libraries of the region exhibit their greatest weakness. They do not have the accumulated resources, and they are not adding materials both old and new at a sufficiently rapid rate to make up their deplorable deficiencies. The most sustained program of acquisition in the region has been that of the library of Duke University which has increased the number of its volumes from 72,000 at the end of 1924, when Trinity College became the present University, to 960,859 in 1948–49—a gain of

888,859 volumes in 25 years, or an average of 35,547 volumes per year. In 1948–49 the libraries of the Universities of Alabama, Florida, Virginia, and Miami University, in addition to Duke, added between 31,000 and 37,000 volumes. But they were late in beginning such comparatively extensive acquisitions and they will have to maintain or increase this rate to measure up fully to the requirements that may reasonably be made of them. The libraries of Emory, Kentucky, North Carolina, and Tennessee, and the Joint Libraries at Nashville added between 20,000 and 30,000 in 1948–49. At this rate it will require from 15 to 20 years to build up to the million mark, and in the meantime the distance between their acquisitions and those of other major libraries will be still further increased.

This is the situation concerning the holdings of the university libraries. Libraries of other types of Southern institutions show even more limited holdings and slower acquisition rates. The total number of volumes held by the separate land-grant colleges and the Georgia School of Technology ranged from a high of 139,346 held by Alabama Polytechnic Institute to a low of 102,419 at North Carolina State, with additions for 1948–49 ranging from 10,193 at Alabama Polytechnic Institute to 4,864 at Mississippi State. For 1947–48 the largest collections for institutions for Negroes were held by Atlanta and Fisk Universities and Tuskegee Institute, with from 100,186 at Atlanta to 85,000 at Tuskegee, and the numbers added for these institutions ranged from 2964 at Atlanta to 5000 at Tuskegee. The largest single addition by any Negro institution in the region was 5,502 at Virginia State.

The number of journals, newspapers, proceedings of learned societies, documents, films, maps, and recordings are not indicated in these statistics but such materials are essential if a sustained graduate program is to be carried out. Obviously they have not been added in quantities sufficiently large to maintain such a program adequately.

At this point the question may be asked: How is a library to proceed in building up its materials so that the graduate program can be properly supported?

The answer is not far to seek. During World War II we became familiar with the idea of priorities. Materials were allocated for purposes for which they were most needed. The institutions and their libraries must likewise decide what subject or subjects shall receive attention first. This answer must be made by the administration, by the graduate school and professional departments, and by the library, and must be consciously supported by all combined. This constitutes one of the principal features of the library policy mentioned above. At Cornell University such a policy was steadily maintained by the Library Board, of which the President of the University and the Librarian were members, from its very beginning, and to its steadfastness of purpose is attributable the building up of one of the most substantial collections for the support of exacting graduate work to be found in the country. While there were many other phases of the administration of the library that were not effectively handled, there was seldom a meeting of the Board at which serious consideration was not given to securing material held to be fundamentally essential to graduate and professional work.

At North Carolina this procedure was decided on as early as 1905. The first two subjects chosen for work at the doctorate level were English language and literature and chemistry. Back files of the essential journals and transactions of learned societies and the standard reference and bibliographical apparatus were secured and subscriptions for current periodicals were placed. *Studies in Philology* was established by the Philological Club and the Graduate School, files of which were offered in exchange for publications of other learned societies in the fields of language and literature. In the case of chemistry, *The Journal* of the Elisha Mitchell Scientific Society was exchanged for the transactions of scientific societies, back files of fundamental sets were secured, and subscriptions for important continuations were placed.

In due course the same procedure was followed in the case of the Germanic and Romance languages and literatures and of the biological sciences. In the latter, two very narrow subjects were selected, sponges in zoology, and fungi in botany. These specializations were well established before other aspects of the two fields were considered.

In the field of Southern history, and later in sociology, when the Institute for Research in the Social Sciences and the *Journal of Social Forces* were established, similar methods were employed. In both instances a journal was utilized in securing exchanges, and the already-established collection of printed materials concerning slavery and the Confederacy was considerably extended. And, in addition, a comprehensive program of collecting historical manuscripts concerning the South wherever they could be found was organized and has been continued until the collection now contains more than 2,000,000 manuscripts.

This pattern, or one somewhat similar to it, has been followed by other institutions which now offer the doctorate. Duke has supplemented the pattern by buying *en bloc* a number of the private libraries of distinguished scholars. It has also cooperated with the Library of the University of North Carolina in building up its collection of state documents and its publications in the fields of Hispanic American history and literature. In both instances each institution has assumed responsibility for securing documents and publications from specific states and countries, thereby insuring greater resources for scholars in both institutions. Virginia has added to the pattern through its cooperation with other libraries of the State and the State Library in organizing and making available the historical archives and newspapers of the cities, counties, and industries of the State. In the Atlanta-Athens and Nashville areas the libraries have collaborated in developing bibliographical apparatus for scholarly use.

Underlying and supporting this kind of program, it is necessary for the library to establish an acquisition department to which responsibility is assigned for handling the acquisition of books, periodicals, serials, gifts, and exchanges and for utilizing the library staff and the library representatives of every department, school, and institute of the institution in the constant search for essential materials.

The necessity for employing such procedures, however, has only within the past decade been fully realized by a number of universities, land-grant colleges, and technological institutes in the region. In fact, it may be going too far to say that such recognition has been general. Nevertheless, such procedures must be followed at the master's degree level, and they need to be applied by every library that is being called upon to support graduate, professional, and technical work beyond the level of the first professional degrees.

Here, then, is a point at which the administration, the graduate faculty, and the library must set up its objectives and work for them incessantly over a period of years. The gratifying reward is that programs of this character, carefully set up and steadily maintained, result sooner or later in attaining the desired ends. This is the kind of goal every Southeastern university library should set for itself.

Two further observations may be made on this point. The first is that this goal cannot be achieved by complying with the minimum standards of support for libraries of different types of institutions provided for in the standards for the Southern Association of Colleges and Secondary Schools. For junior colleges the total number of volumes required is 4000 and the annual per student expenditure for library purposes is $5.00. For four-year colleges the book collection must support the curricula offered and the per student expenditure for books and salaries must be $15.00. And for the university libraries there are no specifications that differentiate them from the libraries of the four-year colleges, except that when graduate courses are offered the per student expenditure should be greater. Yet in the very nature of things they must offer graduate and advanced professional degrees in a much greater number of subjects than are taught in the four-year colleges. Obviously adequate library facilities cannot be acquired with so little support, a fact which the universities have by and large considerably exceeded. In 1946–47 the university libraries of the Southeast spent as a group five per cent of the total educational budgets of the universities for library purposes, and 269 of the colleges and universities of the region reporting spent $4,901,355, or $18.73 per student. In 1948–49 21 four-year colleges and universities for whites in North Carolina spent $1,109,041, or $33.74 per student for library purposes, the University of North Carolina and Duke University spending $40.59 and $68.08 per student respectively. Expenditures of this character must of necessity require more than five per cent of the educational budget. In fact, it will be impossible for the institutions of the region contemplating graduate work upon a firm basis, to build up the resources required unless they spend considerably more. This is a situation that should receive particular consideration by the separate land-grant colleges and professional schools of the region, which, during 1946–47, spent only 2.3 per cent for library purposes. Institutions for Negroes likewise are confronted with a similar situation in that their present collections are relatively small. Materials for the support of graduate work have been secured by them for only a comparatively short time, and their income is more dependent upon gifts and endowment than upon annual appropriations. For libraries of all of these different types of institutions larger legislative appropriations, greater income from endowment and generous gifts, and more extensive support of friends of the library organizations must be secured if they are to perform their graduate function properly.

The second observation is that constructive measures are being considered on a regional basis that should, if carried into effect, greatly improve the situation.

The Commission on Graduate Studies of the Board of Control for Regional Education in the South is considering a survey of the resources of Southern libraries for the support of the doctorate, and the Board, various library groups, the Conference of Deans of Southern Graduate Schools, and a Committee of the Southern Association Commission on Higher Education have conferred concerning ways and means of carrying out the survey and developing a remedial program of acquisition. From these joint deliberations it is to be expected that plans for sound development will come.

3. The third requirement the University must meet in order to play its part properly in carrying out such a policy of university library development as has been sketched and in integrating the library in the program of teaching, research, and extension obviously is to staff the library with personnel in greater number and with more extensive education, both general and professional, than has been characteristic of the library staffs of the region in the past. To achieve these objectives several steps will have to be taken. The director of libraries will have to be able to assist the principal administrators and shapers of policies in the university in formulating the administrative and educational policies of the institution. He will also have to be a skilled administrator of the libraries under his control. The members of the library staff will have to be able not only to carry out the purely technical details of administration effectively, but they should also be able, through their special knowledge of subjects and familiarity with reference and bibliographical materials to provide expert assistance for graduate students, and members of the faculty and research staffs in carrying on their work.

The expert reference librarian, the bibliographer, the subject-librarian specialist in charge of special collections, and the translator of important publications in foreign languages will have to be employed far more frequently in the libraries of the region if the libraries are to play their full part in support of the graduate program.

Assistance of a high order can also be provided by the library through cooperation with other libraries and research organizations. The effectiveness of this kind of cooperation has been demonstrated effectively in the university centers of the South, and the principle is especially applicable to other cooperative enterprises such as the description of library resources in the region, the preparation of union lists and bibliographical aids, the provision of photographic reproduction laboratories, and the designation of rare materials for the acquisition of which given libraries will hold themselves responsible, in order that library funds may be applied in securing for scholarly use the maximum amount of materials and services.

The three requirements which I have considered thus far are not all that must be met in bringing the libraries up to their proper support of a sound program of graduate performance. There must be adequate space in properly designed buildings to accommodate the library clientele—reading rooms, reference rooms, periodical rooms, carrels, studies, and special rooms for reading films and using other special materials. And the library materials must be organized and serviced in accord with essential administrative and technical detail. But if the universities and libraries formulate and adhere to sound policies, if they make available fundamental materials in greater abundance, if they increase considerably their annual expenditures and the effectiveness of their staff, they can place the graduate, professional, and technical training of the region on a sound graduate basis from which the region and the nation will greatly profit.

Education for Librarianship

Training for Librarianship in the South

IN THIS PAPER ON TRAINING for librarianship in the south, it seems important to me to present the following aspects of the subject: (1) The part which the library is to play in raising the level of general educational attainment in the south in the next decade; (2) the necessity for the professional training of the, to the south, comparatively new type of educational teacher and leader, the librarian, who affects the general educational program through books and other library resources rather than by means of lecture, text-book, blackboard, scientific laboratory or other formal educational processes; (3) the character of the training agencies will be required; (4) the kinds of training to be provided; (5) the number and distribution of such agencies, and (6) the financial support, physical and technical equipment and personnel which will be required to insure their successful operation.

I. Part to be Played by Libraries

No thoughtful person who contrasts the educational scene of today with that of the year 1900 can fail to discover that the level of general educational attainment in the south is far higher now than then. Length of school terms, capital outlays for buildings and equipment, largely increased operating funds and endowments, the establishment of summer schools, practice schools and schools of education for the professional training of teachers, perfected systems of certification and general administration bear testimony that the graduate of the southern high school or college of today goes out into life better equipped to meet its high adventure than this predecessor of thirty years ago. The expenditure of thirty million dollars annually upon the maintenance of the public schools in North Carolina today as

Reprinted from *Proceedings*, Second Conference for Education in the South, October, 1929, pp. 60–71, University of North Carolina Press, by permission of the publisher. Also published in *School and Society*, 31: 719–727, May 31, 1930.

against one million dollars in 1900, the enrollment of 110,000 pupils in the high schools last year as against 7,144 in 1907–08, the offering of professional courses for teachers on every college campus in the state, the consolidation of schools and transportation of school children in all save one of the hundred counties, the increase in the state's maintenance funds to its university from $25,000 in 1900 to $860,000 in 1928 and the bringing into existence within a five-year period of such an institution as Duke University through private means are but typical of what has been happening educationally throughout the entire south during this period.

Nevertheless, while the rise of the level of general educational attainment has been notable, it is none the less true that southern educational leaders have had to deal first with the quantitative aspects of education rather than the qualitative. In thinking about the future of education in the south, it would seem that the time has come when the qualitative as well as the quantitative should receive increasing consideration.

I make bold to predict that the next decade will witness a distinctive rise of the level of general educational attainment in the south, and that its nature will be qualitative as well as quantitative. I go further and say that the agency which will contribute to this rise as much as any other will be the library in its various forms.

I base this prediction upon five significant facts. Sir Francis Bacon stated the first of these in his essay "Of Studies" three centuries ago when he said, "Reading maketh a full man." Unfortunately, Sir Francis simply stated his observation and let it go at that. Science, as we know it today, was in its infancy, and such scientific tests and measurements as are applied to educational processes today could not be utilized to demonstrate the validity of his statement. But in the papers presented here yesterday by Dean Gray, of the school of education of the University of Chicago, and Mr. Koos, of the Winston-Salem schools, the validity of his observations has been attested in the scientific terms of the present-day educational experts. They have shown conclusively that the pupil in the grades or the student in college who makes intelligent and extensive use of library materials, in addition to the use of lecture and text-book, sees the subject under investigation more clearly and comprehends its total relationship more fully than the pupil or student who fails to use such materials. They are fully convinced that the per cent of promotions of such students to the next higher grade or class is definitely higher than that of students who do not make extensive use of library materials.

It is this fact which, in other sections of the country, has placed the library in the heart of the school and sends every pupil enrolled to the library for specific study for a fixed number of periods per day or week. It is this fact which has made necessary in such libraries as those of the University of Illinois and the University of North Carolina, which have been dedicated within the last few days, the provision of seats for three times as many students per thousand as were required ten years ago. It is this fact which has caused the Association of Colleges and Secondary Schools of the Southern States to adopt its present thoroughgoing high-school library standards and start a committee to work upon the upward revision of its college library standards. It is this fact which has influenced one of the great foundations to start an investigation of library resources of the small colleges of the country, because it is convinced that teaching, unsupported by library resources, falls far short of being the best sort of teaching. And it is this fact which, if fully understood and acted upon by state, county and city superintendents of schools in the south, can bring about, as much as the lengthening of the school term, the professional training of teachers or any other single thing, the lifting of the per cent of promotions among the white and colored school children alike throughout the south. It can assist in reducing the tragic waste of educational effort in a state educational system such as North Carolina's in which only two white children out of every three succeed in passing from one grade to the next higher, and only one out of two colored children. In this way the purposes of the school can be more perfectly realized qualitatively, and the level of educational attainment raised.

The second fact on which I base the prediction is that the educational expert has recently taught us that the old adage, "You can't teach an old dog new tricks," is untrue. Or, if it is true for old dogs, it is untrue in the case of mature men. The dictum of William James, the acknowledged leader in the field of educational psychology in the past generation, that for the majority of us the learning process stops at the age of twenty-five, has been sharply contradicted, and it has been scientifically demonstrated by Professor Edward Thorndike that the period after twenty-five, if properly utilized, can be made one of the most fruitful in intellectual accumulation and accomplishment in the whole life span.

The third fact which underlies my prediction is so obvious that it scarcely needs stating. Life has become so complex for the vast majority of men that even if they wished they could not cease to study the work they have in hand. This has not always been true in the south. Life in the ante-bellum, slave-owning era was simple. But even in the field of agriculture the scene is far more complicated today than it was before 1860. The boll-weevil alone has made necessary knowledge of insecticides and rotation of crops. Scientific breeding of long-lint cotton has been required to take the place of the almost extinct sea-island staple. The fruit-fly in Florida likewise has temporarily confronted a state with a serious economic puzzle and the housewives and mothers of the nation with problems in household economy and infant feeding.

Complexity of modern civilization has made itself not only in law, medicine, engineering and the various learned and scientific professions, but in business and industry as well. It is because of this new complexity that thousands of men and women of maturity were enrolled in extension and correspondence courses last year for which they paid well up into the millions. It accounts for the presence in such great industries as the American Telephone and Telegraph Company, General Motors, Metropolitan Life Insurance Company, Bankers Trust Company, Pennsylvania Railroad Company and many others of highly specialized business libraries which are considered as indispensable as the experiment staff and scientific laboratories of all such industrial institutions. This being true for the nation as a whole, it is inconceivable that the area stretching from Lynchburg to Birmingham, rich beyond measure in coal and iron and water-power, and in those respects potentially able to support as varied an industrial civilization as that of Pennsylvania and New York, will continue to overlook this keen-edged tool of industry as well as sol-vent of the social and economic ills by which industry in other sections has been splendidly served.

It is more than barely possible—it is highly probable—that south-ern merchants who have felt the adverse effects of the chain store, that southern tobacco and cotton farmers who are experiencing the blighting disaster of low prices, that southern state, county and city governments which are struggling with the intricate problems of taxation could remedy somewhat the distressing plight in which they find themselves, if for the rule of thumb the rule of exact information might be substituted. Knowledge is power, and the sort of knowledge which has been essential in the south to maintain a civilization based hitherto on an agricultural foundation will not give men power to win increasing economic freedom where it must be won from narrow margins under highly competitive conditions. Stated concretely, the south, with 24 per cent of the nation's population but only 5 per cent of the nation's business and industrial libraries, stands handicapped in this respect as it toes the starting-line in the industrial race. In this same connection, I go further and say that it is not inconceivable that the south could have escaped some of the industrial loss and tragedy which the press has recently been reporting daily, particularly in North Carolina, had it been more familiar with the history of industrial and social progress as it has been slowly and painfully worked out in other times and places. In this instance, knowledge might give power over social bitterness and stay the footsteps of tragedy.

The fourth basis for my prediction is that the proper utilization of leisure, as well as the complexity of life and the keenness of industrial competition, will make an increasingly heavy demand upon the library resources of the south. From 1860 to 1910, the south, economically speaking, could think only in the terms of bread and butter, as it was not until 1910 that its per capita wealth equaled that of 1860. Since 1920, however, the economic burden has been lifted from the shoulders of thousands with the result that hundreds of individuals are pursuing special studies today where dozens were formerly involved. The University of North Carolina, whose participation in the adult education and university extension movements of today may be considered as typical of libraries and universities in general, enrolls as many students in correspondence courses and extension classes as are now present on the campus and successfully directs the informal study of more than ten thousand women in special reading courses.

The final basis for my prediction is the increasing faith of southern individuals, school, college and university administrators, educational foundations and city, county and state governing bodies in the library as an agency for promoting education. The setting up of high-school library standards by the Association of Colleges and Secondary Schools of the Southern States, the entrance of the Rosenwald Fund into the field of county library development and the matching of Rosenwald Fund allotments by the city and county administrations of Davidson and Mecklenburg counties bear eloquent testimony to its ability to raise the level of the south's general educational level to a new height.

II. *The Necessity for Training for Librarianship in the South*

If the foregoing conclusions are correct, it inevitably follows that the south must give serious and immediate attention to the task of training those who shall direct and make generally effective this educational force. It must not make the mistake of thinking that the men and women who are to organize and direct and make effectively available library materials on this increased scale can be secured without providing thoroughly equipped and competently staffed library schools for their technical training. It must think of librarianship somewhat as the charter members of the Institution of Civil Engineers of London one hundred years ago thought of civil engineering when they conceived of it as the "art of directing the great sources of power in nature for the use and convenience of man." It must conceive of librarianship as the "art of directing the great sources of power in books for the use and convenience of man." The south must realize that librarianship "fulfills its function through mastery of the science and art of making, building or using collections of books and library tools, buildings, equipment and the like," and that it requires special knowledge, not only of books and other library materials, but of the laws of economics, sociology and psychology as well. It must be understood that the modern public has no greater justification for expecting adequate service from librarians without adequate library schools than it has for expecting expert service in the fields of education, law and medicine without adequate facilities for training therein. The fact that only one librarian is needed to every ten teachers, if the public schools are to be properly manned, does not lessen one whit the necessity of having that one as thoroughly grounded in his specialty as the other ten are in theirs.

III. *The Character of Training Agencies*

The character of the agencies which will be entrusted with this important task, therefore, is a matter of major educational importance. If the experience of the library profession can be relied upon for guidance, it is clear that the most effective agency is the fully equipped, adequately staffed library school, located preferably upon the campus along with the other undergraduate, professional and graduate schools of a modern American university. Other types, such as special departments in connection with teacher-training institutions for the training of school librarians, or the training classes of large public libraries where training for the routing of the individual library is concerned, and summer schools, will be required.

IV. *The Kinds of Training to be Provided*

The kinds of training to be provided in such schools have already been suggested, if not specifically stated, in this paper. The training of the school librarian is unquestionably a matter of first importance at present. The standards of the Southern Association which go into effect in 1930 will require 488 partly trained and 445 trained librarians, if the requirements are fully complied with. Standards not so high have also been set up by the state departments of education in Virginia, North Carolina, Florida, and others of the eleven southern states. The inevitable result has been that hundreds of students have been seeking library instruction during the past summer and that institutions which never offered courses before have had significant enrolments the first year. During the summer sessions recently concluded, the following enrolments have been recorded: Alabama, seventeen at one institution; Florida, twenty-three at one institution; Georgia, twenty-nine at one institution; Kentucky, eighty-nine at two institutions; Louisiana, twenty-seven at one institution; Mississippi, six at one institution; North Carolina, 144 at two institutions; South Carolina, six at one institution; Tennessee, 201 at two institutions; Texas, ninety at four institutions; Virginia, 268 at two insti-

tutions—a total of 900. And within the past three years, in addition
to the existing schools at Atlanta for whites and Hampton for Negroes, the following institutions have established formal schools or
departments for their regular terms: Florida State College for Wom-
en, North Carolina College for Women, Eastern Kentucky Teachers College, University of Tennessee, Peabody College, Southwest
Texas Teachers College, Texas College for Women, West Texas
Teachers College and the University of Virginia (by extension in
Charlottesville).

Training for public and county library work stands next in order
of importance, and the recent entry of the Rosenwald Fund into this
field will greatly quicken this type of library development. Recent
campaigns, such as that conducted by the citizens' library movement
in North Carolina, and surveys of library conditions, such as that
being undertaken by Tennessee librarians, and demonstrations such
as those afforded by county libraries at Greenville, South Carolina,
Charlotte, Chattanooga and Birmingham have focused the attention
of the public upon the advantages which the county library has to
offer the sparsely settled agricultural, as well as the thickly settled
industrial, areas of the south.

The demand for thoroughly equipped college and university librarians may not be as apparent as that for the schools, cities and counties, but it is none the less persistent. Only so recently as 1912, it was
a fixed rule in two of the major universities of the south that the
rank of the librarian could not exceed that of an associate professorship. At that time, with the exception of the University of Texas, no
southern university library maintained a regular annual budget of
over $15,000. Book funds ranged under $10,000, and cataloguing
staffs were three or less. The total enrolment of the largest graduate
schools was not in excess of fifty. Highly complex collections, such
as the North Carolina Collection and that of the department of rural
social economics in this university, were unknown or at their beginning. And no southern university library east of the Mississippi had
as many as 100,000 volumes. But recently this picture has radically
changed. Last year Mr. McMillen, librarian of Louisiana State University, published the statistics of twelve southern university libraries
east of the Mississippi. Of these, six spent between $15,000 and
$52,000 for books, while six had salary budgets ranging from

$17,000 to $53,000. One reported a staff of twenty-two members, and in 1928–29 another has built up a cataloguing staff of ten and added over 22,000 volumes. The total increase in volumes for North Carolina colleges and universities for 1928–29 was 55,043, and at the beginning of the present fall term the University of North Carolina had a total of 210,000 volumes and during the summer and winter quarters had enrolled 628 students in its graduate school. Situations such as these, the handling of highly specialized collections and the administration of such plants as are rapidly spreading throughout the south call for a type of training of which the south is sorely in need and without which its libraries of research and investigation cannot be properly manned.

What the demand for the business librarian will be is not so clear. "Book larnin'" as applied to agriculture in particular has been strongly resisted in the south. The fact that North Carolina reports only two special libraries out of the 975 in the country speaks rather eloquently of the ascendancy of the rule of thumb over the rule of exact information in the realm of industry—and that too in the face of the fact that in 1927 it produced a total of $205,000,000 in cotton and tobacco crops, $425,000,000 in textiles and $415,000,000 in manufactured tobacco products. But within the past two years the state has spent approximately $50,000 in assembling data on its tax problem, and it is inevitable that, as competition becomes keener, the special library and scientific laboratory will become more and more in demand. And along with the demand for librarians for these positions will come the demand for the trained archivist, the art librarian, the public health librarian and special librarians in other fields which comprise a unified and highly complex modern civilization.

V.   The Number and Distribution of Training Agencies

The fifth aspect of the general subject of training for librarianship in the south is that of the number and distribution of the proposed training agencies. What this number shall be and where they shall be located no one can definitely say. There are, however, several suggestions which might well be considered. First of all, it would seem to me that while the demand for additional agencies is real, institutions considering their establishment should proceed only after the most careful investigation of what is involved. Quick decisions to enter the field and institutional rivalry should be avoided. During the past academic year 1,347 students were enrolled in library schools in the United States and Canada. Of these only forty were in the south—thirty-two white students at Atlanta and eight colored students at Hampton. The other 1,307 were in library schools in the highly developed library areas of New England, the Middle Atlantic, the middle west and Pacific slope states—states in which library schools have appeared slowly and at points where they were essential to the service of well-defined library areas. Something of the same thoughtful consideration should be given the establishment of southern library schools, especially those which undertake to train for all the types of service mentioned above, and, if possible, groups of states should provide the constituency for certain general regional schools.

In the case of teacher-training institutions which are confronted with the necessity of training teachers and school librarians, only one or two per state should undertake the task, as, at most, the ratio of librarians to teachers cannot soon be expected to exceed one to ten, and the multiplication of agencies can consequently only reduce the effectiveness of all offering instruction. Provision for summer school courses should also be thought through carefully upon this same basis, and, as far as possible, all agencies should attempt to work out their curricula in such ways as to effect the highest degree of coordination and consequent saving of a student's time, training and arrangement of academic and professional credits. An accord should also be sought as to entrance requirements and transfer of credits, as whatever is done now should be soundly based and in the interest of the largest and most permanent good.

These suggestions for schools for whites are equally applicable to training agencies for Negroes. The school at Hampton has made an excellent beginning, and with the completion of the addition to the main library will be able to take care of an increased enrolment. It is inevitable, however, that with the increased demand for service to Negroes through school, college, public and county libraries, and with the multiplication of college and university resources for Negroes such as are being provided through proposed new libraries at

Fisk University and the University of Atlanta, other schools will be required. Here again, location upon college or university campuses will be highly desirable, and provision for summer courses and special institutes will be necessary. Apprentice classes in connection with colored branches of large public libraries will also prove of decided worth in the preparation of local workers.

VI. *Financial Support, Physical and Technical Equipment and Personnel*

In undertaking the establishment of a general library school which will measure up to the standards of the American Library Association, it should be clearly understood what physical and technical equipment and personnel will be required and what their adequate provision will cost. The American Library Association, through its board of education for librarianship, has worked out tentative model budgets for such schools from which it is apparent that the task should be undertaken with due regard for all the elements involved. Study of the operating budgets of training agencies now in existence also points conclusively to the fact that American library education today is costing well up with the most expensive type of special training, medical training being included. The tentative budget for a model school calls for the expenditure for all purposes of a minimum of $35,000 annually, for a school enrolling fifty pupils, and data taken from the operating budgets of the more successful schools with such enrolment show that actual expenditures ranged well up towards this amount. A director, four full-time instructors, part-time instructors and special lecturers, a secretary and readers or revisers are essential by way of staff. Desks, chairs, typewriters and other furniture for staff and fifty students run into rather high figures, and the initial cost of general reference and bibliographical materials and special technical practice materials can easily run well up toward $25,000. In these respects the initial expense for a library school in a southern institution like the University of North Carolina or the expense distributed over the first five years will be far greater than that incurred by such institutions as the University of Michigan and the University of Minnesota where extensive bibliographical holdings formed a part of their libraries before their library schools were organized. The expense for staff will also be proportionately higher because, unlike professors of English or history or mathematics who are largely drawn from the south at comparatively low salaries, the professor in the library schools will have to be drawn from the more highly competitive library areas of the east, the middle west and the Pacific coast. Travel, printing, subscriptions to current journals, new books, provision for loan funds and scholarships, practice collections and equipment for special types of libraries complete the picture.

I have not spoken in detail of a number of other matters which have to be omitted for lack of time or are to be discussed by others at this conference. I have taken it for granted that in projecting schools or providing training of any character the standards and ideals of training maintained by the American Library Association will be constantly kept in mind. I have also taken it for granted that each institution which enters the field will have to decide for itself whether it shall be a junior undergraduate, a senior undergraduate or a graduate school. In the case of schools for school librarians I have also taken it for granted that due consideration will be given the place in the curriculum for courses in psychology and education. I have also not spoken of the part which national foundations might take in assisting southern institutions in placing library training on such a sound basis as to insure the greatest possible effectiveness. I am strongly convinced, however, that the same methods which have been employed with such signal success in the south during the past twenty years by several of the foundations in providing buildings for public libraries and schools of education, in establishing professorships of secondary education and inspectors of high schools, in encouraging study in the fine arts and investigation in the fields of the social sciences can be applied to training for librarianship in equally helpful ways.

Others who follow me on the program will speak of these and other matters. It has been my purpose to point out some of the more general aspects of the subject in the hope that here in the south we may thoughtfully and effectively meet the challenge of the hour for the training of a steadily increasing group of librarians who are masters of the "art of directing the great sources of power in books for the use and convenience of man," and thereby contribute in a large and significant way to the qualitative enrichment of the south's educational and cultural life.

Research in the Field of Library Science

RESEARCH IN THE SCIENCES, medicine, education, the social sciences in general, and the business world, is universally recognized as a primary necessity and constitutes one of the major activities in these and related fields. The amount spent upon research in the United States alone runs high into the millions and involves thousands of the nation's most competent scholars, scientists, engineers, statisticians, and other research workers.

Research in the field of the library has been very limited and is not organized on an adequate basis. The American Library Association has been organized fifty-five years and contains more than 12,000 members. More than nine thousand public, college, and scientific libraries serve the population of the United States, and, in this respect, constitute one of the nation's chief educational and social agencies; yet there do not exist today bureaus or divisions in connection with libraries or educational or research foundations engaged extensively and exclusively in research, either as to the abstract principles of library service or the common procedures by which such service is made available to the public. Considerable study has been devoted by educators to the art of reading and the reading interests of various groups, but the statement by Lord Bacon three centuries ago that "reading maketh a full man" still lacks exact scientific verification. Only here and there have beginnings been made in discovering the effect of what is learned through reading upon the development of traits, interests, habits, and mental and social attitudes, and but slight study has been devoted to the social and governmental significance of the library as a social institution. The library profes-

An unpublished paper read before the American Library Institute, New Haven, Connecticut, June, 1931.

sion has produced no body of scientific data bearing upon these and other related library subjects comparable to the body of data on education contained in Teachers College Contributions to Knowledge, on economics contained in the Harvard Economic Studies, or on social sciences contained in the University of Chicago Sociological Series. No major university has perfected an organization completely staffed with research professors, associates, fellows, and other essential personnel able to promote such investigation, and where investigation has been undertaken it has depended largely upon individual effort, as in the case of the special studies of Williamson, Gray, Works, Waples, Learned, Charters, Brown, and the College Advisory Group now considering the problems of the college library.

Library service in its most significant aspects will profit greatly from such investigation. Although extensive investigation has not been carried on in this field, it has resulted in great good in those instances where it has been carried on. The Williamson report, dealing with library schools, pointed out their weaknesses and has resulted in the closer integration of library training agencies with major universities. The Works report on university libraries fixed the attention of university administrations upon what constitutes proper financial support for adequate university library service. The present study of the College Advisory Group on the place of the college library in teaching is already centering the attention of faculties upon the enrichment of the teaching process through the utilization of library resources.

From the facts set forth above, it may be confidently expected that a thoroughgoing, comprehensive program of investigation in the field of library science, embracing both service studies and fundamental abstract research, will yield the same sort of results as those derived from investigation in other fields and from the limited investigations in the library field. Among these results the following may be achieved:

(1) The practical improvement of library service growing out of service studies; (2) the extension of knowledge as to the increase in power of comprehension and the cross fertilization of ideas through reading and the effect of what is learned through reading upon the development of traits, interests, habits, and mental and social attitudes; (3) the extension of knowledge of the social and govern-

mental significance of the library as a social institution; (4) the development of the scientific spirit in the library profession by means of which librarians will be brought to a better understanding of the ideals and procedures of their colleagues in other disciplines and in the business world; and (5) the enrichment of library school curricula by virtue of the fact that the teaching of yesterday is vitalized by the scientific practices and discoveries of today.

The South today is probably undergoing more fundamental changes than any other section of the country. Agriculture, industry, education—in fact every phase of its civilization—is experiencing this change. The library, hitherto less extensively developed than in the East and Far West, is emerging in this civilization as an important educational and social agency. On account of the rural background of the South, the presence of two races for whom a dual system of library service must be provided, and the high percentages of farm tenancy and adult illiteracy, the Southern library problem is, in many respects, quite different from that of the New England town or the Pacific Coast county. This difference is further accentuated in that the South has the mill village, the isolated mountain settlement; the child whose reading has been limited to the Bible, the almanac, the farm paper; the senior in the high school whose ability to understand and define words in the Thorndike vocabulary contest equals that of the freshmen of the high schools of the nation as a whole; a school system for which standards of library service have only recently been set up, and a public and county library service which embraces only 30 per cent of the total population.

Exact information on these subjects is needed in order to wage a successful campaign for library extension. If facts could be presented instead of assumptions, county boards of finance would listen; whereas, at present, they turn deaf ears to library proposals.

The Development of a Program of Research in Library Science in the Graduate Library School

IN AN ARTICLE IN THE LIBRARY JOURNAL for October 15, 1933, entitled "The Development of Research in Relation to Library Schools",[1] I undertook to show how development in research in library science had accompanied the development of library schools. This growth was evident in the better organization of library schools as integral parts of universities, the greater training of library school faculties, the extension of curricula, the increased opportunities for library school students to pursue advanced studies in related fields, the establishment of fellowships for the benefit of research students, the provision of grants for the support of investigation, the addition to library school faculties of research associates and assistants, the establishment of the Graduate Library School of the University of Chicago with the express purpose of furthering research and advanced study in library science through it, and the founding of the *Library Quarterly* as a medium through which the results of investigation might be published. Reference was also made to the work of the Advisory Board for the Study of Special Projects which had summarized, in an article in the *Library Quarterly* for October, 1933,[2] the suggestions made by practicing librarians concerning problems which they wished studied, and the list of theses submitted by graduate students in library schools for the five year period 1928–32 also published in the *Library Quarterly* in July, 1933.[3]

In a paper in *The Library Journal* for April 15, 1934, entitled "Research in Progress in Library Science",[4] investigations then engaged in by members of the staff and students of the Graduate Library School of the University of Chicago were briefly described. It is my purpose in this paper to describe the way in which the program of

Reprinted from *Library Journal*, 59:742–746, October 1, 1934, by permission of the publisher. A paper read before the Professional Training Section, American Library Association, June 25, 1934.

[1]For notes see page 237.

investigation has been developed by the Graduate Library School, and to show what further means should be provided to insure the continued development of the program.

1. *Development of Staff.* The composition of the staff of a given library school necessarily largely determines the nature of investigation in which the school can properly engage. For this reason the organization of the staff of the Graduate Library School was carefully considered by the University, and the staff first chosen was selected in keeping with the University's emphasis upon the social as well as the technical and historical aspects of librarianship. Any additions which may be made to it in the future will be made in line with what the School thinks may be most profitably undertaken by it in conjunction with the University as a whole. Two fields of investigation which at present seem of particular importance to the School, but which it has been unable to cultivate as extensively as desired, are those of public library and school library administration. The resources of the University of Chicago in personnel and equipment in the departments of political science and education would seem to justify the exploration of these fields by the Graduate Library School, either through additions to its own staff or through members of the staffs of the other departments concerned.

2. *Definition of Fields.* Since its organization, the Graduate Library School has gone carefully about the organization of the fields of investigation which it has felt able to cultivate successfully. So far these may be said to be: Reading interests, including book selection and the reading interests of children and college students; college and university library administration, community analysis, classification and cataloguing, bibliography, and the history of libraries and printing. An analysis of the theses submitted in the School for the M.A. and Ph.D. degrees and the recently listed studies now under way would show these subjects had been dealt with in the main. The actual work of investigation in these subjects has also been accompanied by an accumulation not only of library resources to support these subjects, but of extensive collections of raw data as well. Inasmuch as the social significance of the library has been emphasized by the School, thousands of forms and questionnaires have been secured and filed in the library and statistical laboratory of the School.

3. *Integration with Work in other Fields.* Definite effort has been made to integrate all of the work of the School, both in instruction and in investigation, with that of other departments and schools of the University. In this respect the School has taken full advantage of its connection with the University, and in every way possible has enabled its students to pursue courses offered by other departments in the University. In the case of studies dealing with college and university administration, for example, individual curricula have been followed by students. These curricula have embraced courses in the department of education in college and university administration and, in a number of instances, students have participated in, or have been kept in close touch with, studies in the field of college and university administration, notably in such studies as the recent twelve-volume Survey of the University of Chicago[5] and the revision of standards, including college library standards, of the North Central Association. A thesis[6] recently completed by a student in the Graduate Library School was based largely upon data secured by the Committee of the North Central Association charged with the revision of college library standards. It deals with the measurement of college library efficiency in relation to the efficiency of the college of which it is a part, and the soundness of its conclusions has been carefully considered by the committee in question. Two other theses[7] dealing with the character of books printed and of the contents of private libraries in the Colonial period have in turn grown out of courses in the Graduate Library School on the one hand, and departments of literature and history respectively on the other. The courses in these departments dealt specifically with the history of Colonial literature and culture, respectively. Studies in classification, as in the case of special subjects in the field of religion, have been closely integrated with work in the Divinity School, and students working on varied aspects of reading and reading interest are kept in touch with such studies as those on readability by Gray of the department of education, and on the development of attitudes in children by means of movies by Thurstone of the department of psychology. Training and experience in the use of statistics are acquired through courses and laboratory work in that field through a number of departments such as education, sociology, economics, psychology, commerce, and mathematics, depending upon the nature of the study concerned.

Studies carried on in this manner result in a broadening of the student's range of experience and contribute to the value of the investigations concerned.

4. *Development of Methods and Procedures.* The task of developing methods and procedures of investigation engaged the staff as soon as it was organized. Not only were other departments drawn upon for suggestions, but two special courses, similar to introductory courses in graduate study and investigation in many fields such as sociology, economies, education, history, and literature, were organized, dealing specifically with library science. The effort in both has been to acquaint the student with the spirit and methods of science. The first course has dealt primarily with procedures followed in recognizing, defining, and limiting problems in library science which may be investigated profitably. All members of the School staff participate in the conduct of this course and present problems from their respective fields. Problems of local or general application are differentiated and methods of recognizing what problems may be successfully studied are indicated. The second course has dealt with the method or methods which may be employed successfully in solving problems thus discovered and defined. For the solution of any given problem one or more methods may be employed. In certain instances the historical method may be indicated, in others, schedules or questionnaires may be necessary, in another the case study, in still another the survey. Problem solution, in this respect, is not unlike golf. Different clubs or methods are used for different purposes. Students must be familiar with many methods, such as those employed in the social and physical sciences, if satisfactory answers are to be found to problems of varying character. In carrying out a successful study, it is as necessary for the students to be able to choose the right methods as it is for the golfer to use the correct club.

In acquainting students with methods and procedures, two means have been extensively employed. The first, as stated above, has been through cooperation by students with members of the staff of the School and with the staffs of other departments in the carrying on of some specific investigation. The second has been through the careful analysis and criticism of a number of studies in related fields. In the course in methods referred to above, a dozen or more of such studies are selected for consideration in detail. Among them are such titles as:[8] Lundberg—*Social Research*, Odum and Jocher—*Introduction to Social Science*, Waples and Tyler—*Research Methods and Teachers' Problems*, Cheney—*Economic Survey of the Book Industry*, Jordan —*Children's Interests in Reading*, Judd and Buswell—*Silent Reading*, Waples and Tyler—*What People Want to Read About*, Thurstone and Chave—*The Measurement of Attitude*, Pearson—*The Grammar of Science*. These may be added to or others may be substituted for them as the occasion may demand. They are all studied, however, in the light of such questions as these: "Which of the studies read in connection with this course do you consider most important from the three standpoints: (a) Purpose, (b) Technical structure, (c) Completeness or relevance of the data? Why? Redraft or criticize the study constructively, i.e., plan it in considerable detail, as you might if you were given time and funds to repeat the study in order to accomplish the original purpose more fully. This should include checking important assumptions, securing more adequate samples, experimental checks on conclusions, *et al.* Take particular pains to confine your discussion to the practicabilities of the problem in hand."

5. *Studies Become Bases of Other Studies.* One of the characteristics of investigation is that the results of one study become the bases for other studies. In the field of science major discoveries of years ago are constantly being applied in new ways. Through the procedures indicated above, studies have been developed in the Graduate Library School which in turn have become the bases or starting points from which other studies in library science have been begun. The study by Waples and Tyler—*What People Want to Read About*[9]—is a case in point. Before studies could be begun dealing with the reading interests of special groups, it was essential that certain basic facts about the interests in reading of people in general should be established. While such a general study might or might not prove interesting to the general public, or even to librarians, it was essential that such a study should be made and along scientific lines before, for example, the reading interests of college students could be investigated successfully. In order to compare the reading interests of senior men and senior women in a given college upon given subjects—athletics, or how to achieve a successful marriage, for example—it was necessary to determine first of all that sex and edu-

cational attainment are among the five or six most important factors in determining interest. The more recent studies by Carnovsky[10] and Gerberich,[11] in which extensive comparisons of student reading interests are made, could not have been successfully undertaken had not the foundation been laid in this earlier study. The Shaw[12] and Hilton[13] lists for college and junior college libraries have, in turn, become the bases for comparisons of the holdings of various college libraries. The study by Akers[14] of the differentiation between professional and clerical procedures in the catalog department can easily be used as a guide for studies dealing with similar procedures in other departments.

6. *Data Become Bases for New Combinations.* Equally important has been the building up of data for future studies. Examples of subjects in which such data have been secured include: Reading interests, college libraries, college library standards, classification and cataloging, the library in relation to public administration, county library development in the South, distribution of library resources in cities, counties, and the nation, statistics of circulation, registration, and population in relation to library use. Such data are available not only for the specific purpose for which they were first selected, but are available for use for different purposes and different combinations. Data recently secured through twenty-two studies carried on by the University of Chicago under the Federal Office of Education furnish an illustration of this important fact. Although they dealt with specific aspects of education at the pre-school, elementary, secondary, college, and adult levels in the Chicago metropolitan area, they are now available for use in new combinations which will increase the scope and significance of the original studies for which they were secured. Combined with other data from the Tennessee Valley Authority, Frazer Valley library demonstration, and the Rosenwald county library demonstrations in the Southern states, they may yield further information of significance.

7. *Administrative and Financial Procedure Established.* In carrying out this program, the School has been guided by the general plan of the University. The present basis of work of a professor in the University of Chicago is three courses per quarter for three quarters of the year. This work may be allotted to administration, teaching, or research as the interests of a department or school may de-

mand. In order that the members of the staff of the Graduate Library School may have opportunity to carry on individual research, their programs are arranged in such way that one-third of their time can be devoted to investigation and two-thirds to teaching, and the fourth quarter can be utilized as vacation or devoted to research, as the instructor may desire. During 1934–35 the time devoted to meeting classes will be further curtailed by general legislation passed by the University to make possible greater opportunity for investigation and the direction of student work. Three fellowships have been awarded annually to students who have demonstrated ability in research, and grants-in-aid and research assistantships, in varying numbers, have been provided for research purposes. The School has also been fortunate in receiving a number of grants for the conduct of such studies as the revision of the standards of college libraries of colleges having membership in the North Central Association, and the public administration and Rosenwald county library studies.

In developing further its work in the field of investigation, the Graduate Library School will be confronted with a number of problems. Among them the following are worthy of mention here:

1. *Additions to Staff.* It will be necessary to make new additions to the staff. Such additions should be made in the light of the fields which the School and the University of Chicago combined can cultivate to the best advantage. As indicated earlier, it would seem that special consideration should be given to public and school library administration as the resources of the University of Chicago in these fields are such as to insure sustained programs in these subjects.

2. *Additional Funds Required.* As the program of investigation has been gotten under way it has become increasingly apparent that the expense of carrying on such work is high. So far the expenditures which the School has been able to make have been very modest and in no sense are comparable to the more extensive funds which have been provided for investigation in education, political science, and other of the social sciences. As a matter of fact, the library profession and investigators in the social sciences have largely thought of all investigation dealing with librarianship as technical, bibliographical, or historical. The social significance of reading as a common behavior of many aspects has largely been overlooked. The

schools have taught pupils to read and libraries have organized reading materials and made them available. But the importance and meaning to society of their use is yet to receive the consideration that crime or delinquency or a number of other behaviors have received. Librarians, foundations, and research councils have been interested in great bibliographical undertakings, such as the publication of the *Union List of Serials*, the development of the Union Catalog in the Library of Congress, and the reprinting of the *Catalog of the British Museum*. They have provided financial support for them. If investigation in the field of library science is to be effectively developed, and reading as a social behavior is to be studied in its broader aspects, funds for this purpose will have to be materially increased. Foundations and national research organizations will also have to realize that funds over which they have control may be appropriately made available for the employment of personnel and for the collection of important data. As yet no library school has been provided with personnel and funds for teaching and investigation in any sense comparable to those regularly required in the establishment and conduct of a medical school, and a number of institutes for research in social science spend annually far more for research alone than any library school spends for all purposes.

3. *Funds for Fellowships, Grants-in-aid, Research Assistantships, and Part-time Positions Essential.* The Graduate Library School is conscious of the fact that if it is to develop and maintain a successful program of investigation, funds for fellowships, grants-in-aid, research assistantships, and part-time positions will have to be increased. Graduate study in the main is not paid for by the students who are going through graduate schools. It is largely supported by subsidies of one kind or another, and this is particularly true in the field of librarianship where salaries are low and where the opportunity for advanced study has been too brief for the development of a compelling tradition. It is our conviction at the Graduate Library School that the best form of support is that which is provided through research assistantships, part-time positions, and grants-in-aid. Better trained investigators can be secured in this way than through fellowships which meet the entire student expense. The latter method seems to be the more effective for promoting study leading to higher degrees and should be supported generously in order to in-

crease the number of librarians whose training is comparable to that of leaders in educational and scientific fields.

4. *Closer Integration with Other Departments and Fields of Specialization is Desired.* The Graduate Library School is also aware of the necessity of securing closer integration with other departments and fields of specialization. It will be necesary for it to develop the closest possible contacts with other departments and have its students participate not only in courses offered by them but in investigation carried on through them. Until more basic studies in the specific field of library science have been developed, it will be necessary to draw largely upon courses and studies in other fields for guidance.

5. *More Cooperation with Practicing Librarians Must be Secured.* One of the greatest difficulties with which the School has been confronted to date has been that of securing raw data concerning library problems. Such data are obviously indispensable and they cannot be secured outside of libraries. They are not produced in a vacuum. To secure these the School has to make provision for the keeping of records which busy librarians ordinarily do not maintain. If analyses of library procedures are to be worked out, for example, in the matter of cost accounting, it will be necessary for a number of libraries of different kinds to maintain records which at present are not kept. This will require an expenditure of both money and time on the part of the libraries maintaining them. The School can work out forms and indicate the nature of the information to be sought, but it is only through cooperation with librarians that it can secure the essential raw data for studies of this nature. It will also be necessary for those who are charged with the responsibility of defining library terms to perform this highly important service as comparisons cannot be made until common bases are available.

6. *Better Methods for Selecting Research Students are Desirable.* As the work of the School has developed it has become increasingly clear that it must improve its means of selecting persons who are likely to become effective research students. The fact that a student has done acceptable work in academic and library subjects is not sufficient to indicate that he will be able to carry on successful work in a highly specialized piece of investigation.

7. *Methods of Keeping Informed about Research in Progress.* In carrying on its work, the Graduate Library School is confronted

as are other schools with the desirability of having a more complete annual record of research in progress in library science. A program of cooperation on the part of the Association of American Library Schools, the Advisory Board for the Study of Special Projects, the Editorial Board of the *Library Quarterly*, the Editorial Committee of the A.L.A., the Association of Research Librarians, and cooperating research councils in other fields, could help the staff keep informed as to subjects and fields of interest and studies being carried on.

8. *More Money for Publication is Required.* A fundamental incentive to investigation is the expectation of seeing the results of such work published. The Graduate Library School would look more confidently toward the carrying out of its program if it had additional funds for the publication of the results of important investigations. It is only through such publication or the provision of additional copies of theses that the results of investigation can be made available and work in progress influenced accordingly.

9. *A Clearer Understanding of the Methods and Objectives of Research is Desired.* The program outlined in this paper has been gotten under way with what it is hoped may be considered some degree of success. A greater degree of success, however, can be achieved if the difficulties suggested can be overcome, and if the profession by and large will accord the problems presented more critical consideration. The service which the library is rendering the public is being subjected to greater question today than it has ever been before. Greater knowledge of the nature of the service rendered, of the groups served, and the benefits flowing from such service are demanded. It is the hope of the Graduate Library School that through the cooperation of the profession, other library schools, and investigators in other fields, it may conrtibute to the increase of this essential knowledge. Investigation is, after all, not an end in itself. In the case of library science, it is a means by which it is hoped that the service of libraries may be improved and the value of the library as an educational and cultural institution of society may be multiplied many fold.

NOTES:
[1]Louis R. Wilson, "The Development of Research in Relation to Library Schools." *Library Journal*, 58:817–821. October 15, 1933.

[2]Louis R. Wilson, et. al, "Proposals Submitted to the American Library Association for Study and Investigation." *Library Quarterly*, 3:390–407. October 1933.

[3]Douglas Waples, "Graduate Theses Accepted by Library Schools in the United States from June 1928, to June 1932." *Library Quarterly*, 3:267–291. July 1933.

[4]Louis R. Wilson, "Research in Progress in Library Science." *Library Journal*, 59:337–341. April 15, 1934.

[5]*University of Chicago Survey*, Volumes I–XII (Chicago: University of Chicago Press, 1933).

[6]Errett Weir McDiarmid, Jr., "Conditions Affecting Use of the College Library," Unpublished doctor's thesis, Graduate Library School, June, 1934.

[7]Arthur Berthold, "American Colonial Printing as Determined by Contemporary Cultural Forces," and Thomas Keys, "Private and Semi-Private Libraries in the American Colonies, an Analysis of Their Contents." Unpublished Master's theses, Graduate Library School, University of Chicago, June, 1934.

[8]G. A. Lundberg, *Social Research* (New York: Longmans, Green and Company, 1929).

H. W. Odum and Katherine Jocher, *Introduction to Social Research* (New York: H. Holt and Company, 1929).

Douglas Waples and Ralph Tyler, *Research Methods and Teachers' Problems* (New York: The Macmillan Company, 1930).

O. H. Cheney, *Economic Survey of the Book Industry, 1930–31* (New York: National Association of Book Publishers, 1931).

A. M. Jordan, *Children's Interests in Reading* (Chapel Hill: University of North Carolina Press, 1926).

C. H. Judd and G. T. Buswell, *Silent Reading* (Chicago: University of Chicago Press, 1924).

Douglas Waples and Ralph Tyler, *What People Want to Read About* (Chicago: A. L. A. and University of Chicago Press, 1931).

L. L. Thurstone and E. J. Chave, *The Measurement of Attitude* (Chicago: University of Chicago Press, 1929).

Karl Pearson, *The Grammar of Science* (3rd ed., London: A. and C. Black, 1911).

[9]Waples and Tyler, *Op. cit.*

[10]Leon Carnovsky, "A Study of the Relationship between Reading Interest and Actual Reading." *Library Quarterly*, 4:76–110. January, 1934.

[11]J. R. Gerberich, "The Optional and Required Reading of College Students." *School and Society*, 38:1–4. July 15, 1933.

[12]C. B. Shaw, *A List of Books for College Libraries* (Chicago: American Library Association, 1931).

[13]Eugene Hilton, *Junior College Book List* (Berkeley: University of California Press, 1930).

[14]Susan G. Akers, "The Reading Needs of Typical Student Groups: With Special Attention to Factors Contributing to the Satisfaction of Reading Interests." Unpublished Doctor's thesis, Graduate Library School, University of Chicago, August, 1932.

Essentials in the Training of University Librarians

IN CONSIDERING THE ESSENTIAL training of the future university librarian, I wish to deal with the subject from three points of view. First, the nature and complexity of the position for which the university librarian is to be trained; second, the character and extent of the demands which the university administration may make upon the university librarian and library staff; third, the appropriate preparation of the librarian and library staff for the effective discharge of their duties.

The modern American university had its beginning in the establishment of Johns Hopkins University in 1876, the year of the founding of the American Library Association. Even though it grew out of a colonial college or early state university, it has assumed its present organization, characteristics, and functions within the period of the lifetime of some of us who are participating in this program. And, just as the activities of the university have become infinitely more diverse and complex since 1876, the demands which the university makes upon the university library have become correspondingly diverse and complex.

These variations may be readily illustrated. In 1900, Harvard led in enrollment with 4062 students. Today California leads the state universities with 25,530 and New York the private universities with 37,677. The physical plants required to house such universities are so immense and so complicated that special maps and organized tours are necessary to enable new students to find their way about. Curriculum offerings have multiplied many fold, and departments, schools, and institutes have similarly increased in number. Funds for

Reprinted from *College and Research Libraries*, 1:13–21, December, 1939, by permission of the publisher. This paper was contributed *in absentia* to a symposium of the Association of College and Reference Librarians, San Francisco, California, June, 1939.

endowment and research have likewise greatly expanded. Johns
Hopkins had $3,000,000 for endowment in 1900. It has approxi-
mately $31,000,000 today. Harvard had approximately $14,000,000
in 1900. Today it has over ten times this amount.

Each of these developments has had an indirect effect upon the
university library. Certain changes within the library itself have also
contributed to its complexity. In 1900 the Harvard book collection
numbered 525,000 volumes. Today it numbers approximately
4,000,000, and for the past ten years it has added an average of
117,000 volumes annually. Universities in each of the six major regions of the country have book collections of more than 500,000 volumes, as well as special collections of pamphlets, manuscripts, prints,
films, and other highly specialized materials.

Research Work Increasing

Though the American university has always served undergraduate as well as graduate students, it has encountered the most serious
challenge to its service at the graduate level. In 1900, graduate
schools awarded approximately 2000 Master's degrees. In 1938, the
number was 20,000. The number of Ph.D. degrees showed an even
more spectacular proportional rise. From 200 in 1900, the number
rose to 3000 in 1938. The demand upon libraries for research materials and for staff members to organize and administer them increased in similar proportion. Chinese collections at Harvard, Hispanic American materials at Tulane, western history at California,
Near East objects and materials in the Oriental Institute at the University of Chicago, and the seemingly endless variety of materials
available today through microphotography and other forms of reproduction suggest the range and complexity of these materials.

Card distribution by the Library of Congress and other libraries;
the publication of union lists of serials, manuscripts, newspapers,
and catalogs of major world-famed libraries; the development of
local, regional, and national union catalogs have likewise placed responsibilities upon university libraries which were all but unknown
in 1900.

Recently the American university library has been called upon to
organize and direct significant programs of cooperation. These programs have taken the forms of mutual agreement, as at North Caro-

lina and Duke; contractual agreement, as at Vanderbilt and Peabody; and state legislative action, as at Oregon, Oregon state, and other state institutions in Oregon. In the southeast, the responsibility for the description of the holdings of the research libraries of a whole region has fallen largely upon the shoulders of a group of university librarians. Such cooperative undertakings are not limited to local situations, but operate also upon an international front. The demonstration of microfilm apparatus in Paris in1937, participation in international conferences, and recent cooperation with Hispanic-American libraries and scholars serve as illustrations.

Other Responsibilities

Not only has the library been pressed into service on these different fronts, but in the past twenty-five years it has in many instances become responsible for training students in bibliographical method and the use of libraries, and for the direction of library schools with curriculums covering all phases of library work leading to the A.B., M.A., and Ph.D. degrees. All of these developments have profound implications for the university librarian. They clearly reveal situations with which he must deal, the kind of imagination and leadership he must exhibit, and the character and extent of the subject matter with which his training must be concerned.

In 1865, Daniel Coit Gilman resigned from the librarianship of Yale because the university did not pay him an adequate salary and did not support the library well enough to carry into effect his recommendations for the development of an effective library program. Later, at Johns Hopkins, he could say:

> The librarian's office should rank with that of a professor. He will be the better administrator if he cultivates his own special branch of study, for thus he will have a sympathetic relation with other investigators, and he will be the better investigator if he is also a teacher. . . . The profession of a Librarian should be distinctly recognized. Men and women should be encouraged to enter it, should be trained to discharge its duties, and should be rewarded, promoted, and honored in proportion to the services they render.[1]

But he could point to few universities which had developed their library staffs in accordance with several principles set forth by him.

[1]For notes, see page 251.

In 1901, in my first annual report as librarian at the University of North Carolina, I was confronted with the fact that the library had no well-defined policy. The concluding recommendation of my report read as follows:

> That the University make the position of Librarian such that he, from a financial point of view, can remain in it for several years at least. Within the past thirty months, four men have filled the position. . . . If the present system of low salary and frequent change continues, I am unable to see how a policy can be devised and carried out which will result in the steady up-building of the library. . . .[2]

Although some of my then-colleagues saw in the statement not an indictment of the inadequate conception which the university held of the library, but certain Scotch traits which they attributed to me, it is the one recommendation in the thirty-one annual reports written by me in which I now take most pride.

Role of University Library Today

In contrast with the situations described in these two instances, many university administrators today have a clear, informed conception of the role which the library should play in the university. Such administrators know (1) that the library must aid the university in conserving knowledge through the conservation of materials; (2) that the library must assist it in the transfer and extension of knowledge through the acquisition of materials for instruction and research; (3) that the library must make its services available to student and teacher by means of appropriate quarters, adequate bibliographical resources, and trained staff. If the university engages in extension service, the library must also participate in that service.

If the library is to meet these varied and complex demands, the librarian and his staff will have to possess correspondingly varied and high qualifications. Fundamentally the librarian should have a broad general understanding of the objectives of the university as a whole as opposed to a narrower departmental view; he should possess a scholarly knowledge of library science and related fields of scholarship; he should have a thorough understanding of the functional relationships which exist among the various departments of the library, and ability to organize and direct library personnel.

These demands upon the librarian, however, go a step farther. He should be able to participate effectively in formulating the administrative and educational policies of the university and to administer the library upon a sound function basis. This is fundamental as there are few aspects of teaching or investigation that are unaffected by library performance. Through his training in scientific investigation and mastery of his special field, he should understand and promote the scholarly activities of every department of the university, and at the same time enrich librarianship through administration, investigation, and writing in the library field. He should also be able, through his personality and interest in books, his knowledge of materials for instruction and research, and his cooperation with students, faculty, and other librarians and scholarly organizations, to bring the library into a closer relationship with the educational and scholarly activities of the university and of the scholarly world.

Staff Has Its Part to Play

The librarian will not be called upon to achieve these results single-handed. The staff has its part to play. The university administrator will naturally expect the professional staff and experts in charge of special collections to possess the technical and bibliographical knowledge essential to carry on the normal process of administration, to be conversant with both the subject matter and the literature of the department or school with which they are associated, and to be skilled in working effectively with students and faculty.

So much for the nature and complexity of the position of the librarian of the modern university and the demands which the administration may make upon the librarian and his staff. What should be the nature and extent of the training necessary to prepare them for the effective performance of their duties?

In discussing this question, I wish to refer to "Libraries and Scholarship," by Mitchell; "The Librarian of the Future," by Rush; and "College and University Libraries," by Wriston, which recently appeared in *The Library of Tomorrow*.[3] They may well be supplemented by "Staff Specialization: A Possible Substitute for Departmentalization," by Hurt; "A Look Ahead for Library Schools," by Reece; "Why Graduate Study in Librarianship?" by Carnovsky; and the "Report of the School of Library Service for 1931," by Williamson.[4] All of these papers bear upon this subject and serve as excellent background for its consideration.

Let me say at once that university librarians have been successfully trained in the past in a variety of ways. No single way has been chosen to the exclusion of all others. In the light of the development of universities, however, and of the consequent demands made upon university libraries, the training of the university librarian must necessarily fit him more exactly for his duties than it has in the past. In European universities, where the major objectives of students and scholars have been more narrowly formulated and where student bodies have included only students above the junior college level, more precise patterns of training for librarians have long been prescribed. And the training will be recognized as a more professional pattern than it has been in the past. Furthermore, it will differ from that of the public or school or other type of librarian, who is confronted with different conditions and duties. Not only this, but the differentiation will begin in the pre-professional period, including general undergraduate training and will continue through the first-year professional and graduate professional periods.

Basic Training

Fundamentally, the pre-professional training should consist of a broad general education. The present new plan of the University of Chicago illustrates what I mean by broad education. Through a connected, well-ordered course in the humanities, running throughout an entire year, this plan provides a splendid introduction to all the subjects embraced within this general field. It provides similar introductions through three other courses organized in similar fashion to the subjects embraced within the social sciences, the biological sciences, and the physical sciences. And accompanying these courses, which require two-thirds of the time of the student during the first two years, are other courses which lay the foundation for specialization in the junior and senior years and lead to the A.B. degree. Other institutions offer comparable undergraduate courses upon which later study leading to the A.B. and higher degrees or professional training may be appropriately based.

Such a basic training seems to me indispensable to the university librarian. Students who have come up through such studies should be recruited by library schools, and those whose specialization has been in the fields of the social, biological, and physical sciences, should be sought as well as those in the field of humanities from which they have been so largely drawn in the past.

Final Desired Element

The value of such undergraduate training for the later professional training of the university librarian would be enhanced if it included courses which would give the student command of tool subjects such as French, German, and statistics; courses which would acquaint him with the general principles of administration and personnel management and the educational aims and administrative practices of universities; and courses in the use of reference materials and the library in general. Part-time assistantships in actual library activities would constitute a final desired element in such undergraduate preparation.

Some Major Objectives

The major objectives of the first year of professional training should be: (1) to give the student a broad overview of librarianship; (2) to acquaint him with the library's role in an educational institution; (3) to set forth for him in their appropriate relationships the theories and principles underlying the major subjects within the field; (4) to acquaint him with the body of literature pertinent to these subjects; and (5) to give him, through course assignments and observation, the command of library procedures which will be foundational for future professional performance.

Upon such a basic foundation, followed by a period of service, if possible, specialization in the university library field may be begun. The student should begin work leading to the Ph.D. degree in library science. If he wishes, he should be able to do this in two stages. He might first work for the M.A. and then for the Ph.D. In either instance, he should know definitely what is expected of him at these levels. At the M.A. level he should be expected (1) to become acquainted with the methods and spirit of graduate study and research in the fields of library science; (2) to extend his knowledge of library science generally; (3) to increase considerably his knowledge

of the special field of university librarianship and related subject
fields; and (4) to demonstrate his ability to use research methods in
the preparation of a report or thesis in the field of his specialization.

At Ph.D. Level

At the Ph.D. level, the student should be expected (1) to extend
greatly his general knowledge of the various fields of library science;
(2) to master the particular field of university and scholarly libraries; (3) to supplement his knowledge of this field with that of other
subjects related to it; and (4) to carry out an original investigation
within it. At both the M.A. and Ph.D. levels, he should be free to
take courses in the library school and other departments which
would extend his undergraduate and earlier graduate interests and
give him a firm foundation in subject specialization as well as mastery of his special field. In this way he should become thoroughly
acquainted with the methods and spirit of graduate instruction. The
thesis should grow out of research carried on independently and
should make some new contribution to the subject chosen.

For some of the professional members of the university library
staff, the B.S. in L.S. and the M.A. programs may be sufficient; for
others, the Ph.D. is clearly desirable.

The question may now be raised whether individuals drawn from
the teaching, legal, or other professions or fields are preferable as
university librarians to the type of librarian trained in the manner
above indicated. I should like to cite two commentaries which are at
least partially relevant to this point.

Fifteen years ago the Commission of the University of Chicago on
the Future Policy of the University Libraries declared that the library existed solely for the facilitation and encouragement of research, and therefore that it must be directed by a member of the
faculty who had demonstrated such interest in his work.[5] In short,
the librarian should be a teacher-investigator. The second commentary comes from President Henry M. Wriston of Brown University.[6]
He argues that the least important qualification of the librarian is
his training; furthermore, that the individual with ideas and appreciation of problems, with resourcefulness and energy, can learn many
of the technical details as he administers the library, but all the

courses in the world will not supply imagination or tact, industry or a feeling for scholarship.

Overlook a Fundamental Fact

It is true that these statements were made without reference to the type of preparation for librarianship which I have outlined; nevertheless they merit careful consideration, as much for what they include as for what they omit. They clearly fail to recognize that librarianship, instead of being concerned with mere technical routines, is a many-sided, far-ranging subject in which an individual possessing tact, imagination, and resourcefulness in dealing with problems may achieve scholarly distinction as well as in other fields of learning. They overlook the fundamental fact that the education of the university librarian is designed to give him not only a scholarly command of his field, but a knowledge of the functional organization and administration of the materials and personnel under his control with which the scholar or specialist trained in another field is wholly unacquainted. Though a scholar may be quite profound in his own field, this carries no guaranty of particular competence in any other field, and, in fact, it is at least conceivable that a too narrow subject specialization may lead to a parochial rather than a universal point of view.

My major quarrel with these statements is that they do not go far enough. They mistake the indispensable for the possibly sufficient. Because it is vital that the university librarian have an appreciation of research and an understanding of research needs, it does not follow that this is all he must have. When one argues, as I do, in favor of an individual with library training, he is not pleading for this *to the exclusion* of research training; he is simply saying that both are indispensable and that neither one by itself is enough. I would even say that in the light of the changes which are taking place in student selection by library schools, and in the nature of the training which is now available, the prospective librarian should possess an enthusiasm for research and the capacity to carry it on himself—and all this without sacrificing an interest in and an ability to look after the administrative and routine processes of the university library.

Regarding Untrained Librarians

This answer, however, should not close the door to persons of ability and scholarship in other fields to entrance into university library positions. A director drawn from the ranks of the faculty or a subject specialist may bring rare ability and knowledge to the administration of the library or to the handling of materials in a special collection or subject field. The probabilities that he can do this successfully are attended by considerable risk unless several precautions are taken. First of all, he should be caught young enough to make new adjustments easily. It should be demonstrated that his tact, scholarship, and imagination will concern themselves with the major considerations of librarianship rather than with the narrow aspects of his former specialization. And before he begins to make important decisions concerning the administration of the library, he should acquire, through systematic study, an understanding of the principles upon which successful functional administration is based. Thus equipped, he should be able to conceive of the library as a major functional unit of the university or the special collection as an integrated part of the library as a whole. Provided he bring his entire abilities to bear upon his work as librarian, his accomplishments in the field of administration and his professional writings may contribute significantly to the advancement of librarianship.

Four other aspects of the training of the university librarian may now be briefly considered. I refer (1) to certain desired characteristics of library schools which provide the training; (2) to the training of staff members; (3) to internship; and (4) to recruiting.

Library School Policies

The policies of the library schools concerning admission, curriculums, and degrees are largely controlled, for the first year of study leading to the B.S. in L.S. degree, by the schools themselves. But at the M.A. and the Ph.D. levels, although library science is usually selected as the field of specialization of library school students, the programs of the schools conform more strictly to the regulations of the graduate school and of the various departments involved. The rigidity of departmental requirements frequently makes it difficult for the student to select those courses in the library school and the university as a whole from which he would profit most. In the case of the Graduate Library School of the University of Chicago this difficulty is obviated, as the school has complete control over the student's program of work and can have him take such courses in other departments as may be most suited to his needs without subjecting him to departmental degree requirements.

A similar difficulty in securing the kind of training which would be of most value to him is also encountered by the professor or subject specialist who wishes to enter the library profession. Questions of admission, of required elementary courses, and of conformity to regulations for duplicate degrees frequently prove too difficult for appropriate solution. They also support the conviction of many critics of the graduate school in the American university that it should re-study (as it is now doing in a number of institutions) the pattern which Johns Hopkins gave it in 1876 and which, so far as the Ph.D. requirements are concerned, has not been seriously modified since. For librarians, a less departmentalized and more flexible type of training seems to me particularly desirable.

What the training of professional staff members should be has, in a sense, already been indicated. Obviously, the majority of staff members will come up through the colleges and library schools. Many of them will complete work at the level of the Master's degree, and others will go on to the Ph.D. Others not interested in degrees but with sound basic training and an understanding of professional requirements and subject fields will take advantage of the freedom which library schools and graduate departments will increasingly provide for the pursuit of studies to fit the student's individual needs.

Internship has yet to make its place as an integral part of training for librarianship. The case for it has been argued on the basis of the analogy of internship in medicine, but this argument has not as yet carried great conviction because of the fundamental differences in the responsibilities of the young librarian and physician. Here and there, particularly in those university libraries where close connection is maintained between the library school and the library administration and where adequate supervision of the work of the intern may be combined with his training, internship gives promise of greatly aiding in the professional and administrative equipment of the student of university librarianship. However, the opportunities for such close cooperation must be considerably extended if it is materially to affect present conditions of training.

Recruiting Personnel

Many indications lead me to believe that the question of recruiting suitable personnel, while not answered satisfactorily in the past, will be answered more satisfactorily in the future. One of the most significant influences operating in this direction has been the action of the North Central Association of Colleges and Secondary Schools in setting up qualitative standards for determining excellence of college and university library performance. College presidents have begun to seek intelligently for librarians who understand the educational objectives of the college, the relation of the library to their achievement, and who have acquired an understanding of investigation and its place in the work of higher institutions. They seek such librarians, not because of their "academic respectability," but for what they can contribute to the formulation of general administrative and educational policies, and for their ability to administer libraries effectively.

The grants of the Carnegie Corporation of New York to libraries of liberal arts, junior, and teachers colleges have likewise contributed to this end. College presidents have had to study carefully the problems of library and institutional relationships in securing and administering these grants. As a result, many of them have gained a realistic conception of the function of the library in the college program. The same end has been achieved in other ways at the university level. The survey by Brown of land-grant college libraries, and the surveys by Raney, Works, Carlson, and Wilson-Branscomb-Dunbar and Lyle, of university libraries, and numerous articles dealing with various aspects of university library administration, have played their part. And recently, the cooperative arrangements for increasing library resources have brought the attention of leaders in higher education in general to a new appreciation of the part which the university library is to play in the cooperative enterprises which are getting under way and will multiply in the field of higher education.

These influences have had a bearing on the placement and salaries of students who have fitted themselves through advanced study and investigation for college and university library positions. In spite of the depression, there have not been enough qualified graduates to meet the demand and at salaries frequently above those of associates who have become college or university teachers.

All the foregoing influences have been indirect. They are, nonetheless, powerful. A direct influence may now be cited. A survey conducted last year of admission practices of the accredited library schools revealed the fact that tests of varying kinds are being given by a number of schools to determine the fitness of applicants for admission. This is in addition to the personal interview, testimonials, and academic records previously required. The recent experimentation with tests devised by the Social Science Research Council for the selection of its graduate fellows, the experimentation with tests now being carried out in four large eastern universities to determine the abilities of graduate students, and the proposed study of the Association of American Library Schools of tests specifically designed for prospective librarians, similarly point in the direction of sounder bases of selection for those who will become the future librarians of American universities.

In summary, I wish to point out again the tremendous expansion which the American university library has undergone. University administrators have become perceptibly clearer in their conception of the role the library should play in university life, they have accorded the librarian an increasingly more important field of activity in the university's affairs, and the rewards of the librarian compare favorably with those of other members of university staffs.

Finally, let me say to the prospective university librarian that a rigorous period of training, undergraduate, professional, and scholarly, will be required of him in the future, but that if he meets the requirements adequately, he will create for himself an opportunity for service comparable in extent, nature, and satisfaction to that open to anyone with whom he may be associated in the modern American university.

NOTES:

[1] Daniel C. Gilman, *Development of the Public Library in America.* Ithaca, New York, 1891, p. 10.

[2] Louis R. Wilson, "Annual Report of the Librarian." (typewritten manuscript), 1901.

[3]Sydney B. Mitchell, "Libraries and Scholarship;" Charles E. Rush, "The Librarian of the Future;" and Henry M. Wriston, "College and University Libraries:" in Emily Miller Danton, ed., *The Library of Tomorrow*. American Library Association, 1939.

[4]Peyton Hurt, "Staff Specialization: A Possible Substitute for Departmentalization," A. L. A. *Bulletin*, 29:417–421, July, 1935; Ernest J. Reece, "A Look Ahead for Library Schools," A. L. A. *Bulletin*, 32:32, January, 1938; Leon Carnovsky, "Why Graduate Study in Librarianship?" *Library Quarterly*, 7:246–261, April, 1937; C. C. Williamson, "Report of the Director of the School of Library Service for the Period Ending June 30, 1931," Columbia University *Bulletin of Information*, January 2, 1932.

[5]Commission on the Future Policy of the University Libraries, *Tentative Report*, January, 1924. University of Chicago Press, 1924, p. 47.

[6]*Op. cit.*, p. 147.

Historical Development of Education for Librarianship in the United States

EDUCATION FOR LIBRARIANSHIP has maintained a prominent place in the thought of American librarians from the first meeting of the American Library Association in 1876. It took concrete form in 1883 when Melvil Dewey outlined his proposal for a school of library economy at Columbia. A committee was appointed to consider the subject of education for librarianship in general as well as the specific proposal made by Dewey.

From that date to the present, the American Library Association has not been without a committee on library training. At first it was a special committee. In 1903 it became a standing committee and was required to submit a report annually. In 1923, upon the recommendation of this committee, a Temporary Library Training Board was appointed. The Temporary Training Board was succeeded in 1924 by the Board of Education for Librarianship, which was charged with the responsibility of considering all problems incident to the professional training of the men and women who were to ad-

Reprinted from *Education for Librarianship*, edited by Bernard Berrelson, Papers presented at the Library Conference, University of Chicago, August 16–21, 1948, Pp. 44–59. Copyright ©1948, American Library Association, by permission of the publisher.

minister the libraries of the nation. That Board still operates today on the major concerns of library education.

During 1947–48 the subject of "Education for Librarianship" has been considered at conferences held on the Pacific Coast, in the South, in the Midwest, and in the East. Now the Graduate Library School renews consideration of this topic. My assignment in this discussion is to comment upon what I consider the most important movements, events, and influences that have characterized the development of this field. I have selected ten of these factors for consideration here.

The First School At Columbia

The first important step in this development was the establishment of a School of Library Economy at Columbia in 1887. Melvil Dewey presented the proposal for such a school at the meeting of the American Library Association in 1883, and spent four years in developing the plan for it and in overcoming the opposition of the faculty and trustees of Columbia to it.

Two significant decisions were involved in the establishment of this first school. American librarians, after full and careful consideration, decided in favor of educating librarians through a professional school in preference to apprenticeship in libraries; and they approved a thoroughly practical curriculum embodying best practice, with little consideration of theoretical studies.

Both of these decisions have had important consequences, the effects of which are still evident. As a result of the first decision, the foundation for the present system of library schools was firmly established, as contrasted with the English system of apprenticeship which continued unbroken until 1919 and is still preferred by many English librarians. Even though the curriculum was severely practical and limited, it was developed systematically, and afforded the student an opportunity of mastering in a minimum of time the various subjects embraced in the curriculum and of seeing them through an over-all and unified perspective impossible through apprenticeship in a single library. To this decision, more than to any other one thing, may be attributed America's acknowledged leadership in the field of modern library procedures.

This Conference, like the conferences at Berkeley, Urbana, Atlanta, Chicago, and New York during the past year, is concerned with the second decision. It is confronted with the problem of developing curricula not conceived of in the framework of the scheme adopted by Dewey, and largely followed until the late 1920's. It is attempting to formulate, outside that framework, programs of study that will be truly professional and will be nicely articulated in their entire structure, from undergraduate and preprofessional studies through the strictly professional and graduate levels.

The Association of American Library Schools

The second important step was the establishment in 1915 of the Association of American Library Schools. This organization, following the example of similar professional schools in other fields, was set up with the expectation of shaping educational policy in librarianship. It deepened the professional consciousness of those engaged in the administration of the schools and it established certain standards which other schools were expected to meet and to maintain in order to become members. Its effectiveness, however, was severely limited, and continues to be limited, although its membership now includes all schools accredited by the American Library Association, some of whose faculties are demonstrating marked ability in the development of significant programs of study.

The importance of the organization derives from its potentialities rather than its past accomplishments. What it may accomplish in the future will depend upon whether it will bring its collective thinking to bear seriously upon its problems, work out appropriate solutions, and adopt new procedures which will insure a sound program of professional training. Failure to do this in the past may be largely attributed to lack of funds to insure meetings of the Association and its committees apart from the meetings of the American Library Association; absorption of the interest of the directors (who were also directors of libraries) in the programs of the American Library Association; lack of familiarity of the faculties, particularly in the early period, with the procedures of other faculties and of other professional educational associations in dealing with the problems of formulating and enforcing standards; and since 1926, the automatic admission of all schools accredited by the Board of Education for Librarianship to membership in the Association without the stimulating experience of re-examining standards and applying them in the accreditation of new schools and of assuming responsibility for constantly exploring the field. The Association has also been a closed organization and has lacked the infiltration of points of view which stem from contacts with other bodies and individuals. For these reasons, the Association has been largely unable to exercise influence in the development of professional objectives and standards with anything like the comparable results secured by other professional associations such as those in the fields of medicine, law, engineering, commerce, and social work. Perhaps the future will witness a strengthening of its role in library education.

Next Steps in the 1920's

Education for librarianship underwent extensive professional reorganization and experienced a new degree of financial support in the 1920's. Several movements contributed to this end. Three stand out as particularly important and constitute the third, fourth, and fifth events to which attention will now be directed.

The first grew out of a paper read by C. C. Williamson at the Asbury Park meeting of the American Library Association in 1919 on "Some Present-Day Aspects of Library Training." In this paper Williamson proposed a better-organized system of library training agencies under the supervision of a library training board which would adopt standards and regulate the certification of librarians. This was the central idea which he carried into his studies of all types of library training for the Carnegie Corporation from 1919 to 1921, and elaborated in September, 1923, in his famous report on "Training for Library Service."[1]

The second grew out of two related actions taken by the American Library Association in 1920 and 1923 before the Williamson Report was published. In fact, they largely prepared the way for the discussion and acceptance of this report. They were the appointment in 1920 of a National Board of Certification for Librarians and the discussion of its studies and reports during the next two years; and the adoption of a recommendation of the Committee on Library Training in April 1923 that a Temporary Board on Library Training be appointed "to investigate the field of library training, to formulate tentative standards for all forms of library training agencies, to devise a plan for accrediting such agencies, and to report to the Council."

[1] For notes, see page 268.

The third movement grew out of the decision made in the first half of the 1920's by the Carnegie Corporation of New York to project a comprehensive program of library development, including education for librarianship, which assumed the form of what came to be known as the "Ten-Year Program of Library Service," and which resulted in the expenditure of approximately five million dollars, much of which was for the support of various aspects of education for librarianship.

These three movements were so far reaching in their influence that they merit separate consideration.

The Williamson Report

The Williamson Report was the first to make itself felt. Williamson spent considerable time visiting the existing library schools and carefully studying all aspects of education for librarianship. Trained in the field of political science, and experienced as a municipal reference librarian and director of the information service of the Rockefeller Foundation, he was able to view the schools objectively and critically. His analysis of the status of library school faculties, budgets, curricula, and students revealed a situation wholly unflattering. His prescription for the improvement of the condition of the schools included recommendations that they become integral parts of universities; that their staffs contain a high percentage of full-time instructors chosen for distinction in ability and training; that the first year of study be general and basic; that there be a sharp differentiation between professional and clerical studies, with the latter largely eliminated; that specialization be reserved for the second and third years; that financial support be substantially increased; and that a national examining board be created to formulate requirements concerning library training in general and to pass upon the credentials of library school graduates.

Here was a bold, penetrating analysis that defined the professional field, described the serious limitations within it, pointed out the possibilities of improvement through advanced study and investigation, and, in a very real sense, charted the possible course for a sound development within the field. The report was widely discussed, and, as a result in part of the preceding studies and discussions by the American Library Association of certification and training, many of the recommendations were carried out later at Columbia, under Dr. Williamson's direction, and at many other library schools.

The Board of Education for Librarianship

The importance of the work of the Temporary Library Training Board and its successor, the Board of Education for Librarianship, from 1923 to 1933, is probably less generally recognized and understood by the present generation of librarians than that of the Board during the past fifteen years. In this recent period, due to reduced personnel and more limited funds, the Board has concerned itself largely with routine; only occasionally has it undertaken special studies of large-scale operations like those carried on during its first decade. Among the accomplishments of the Board were: the visiting of each school by several of its members, with an over-all discussion of the school's administrative organization, staff, financial support, and curriculum; the preparation of minimum standards for different types of schools and their accreditation; the publication of textbooks prepared under its direction for the use of library school students and librarians generally; the encouragement of the establishment of schools in certain areas and the discouragement of others that seemed ill-advised; the allocation of funds made available by the Carnegie Corporation for the support of existing schools; the recommendation of endowment for new schools; the establishment of the American Library School in Paris; the provision of fellowships for librarians and prospective librarians; and, in 1933, the changing of its standards from a quantitative to a qualitative basis.

In this work the Board brought the schools face to face with the meeting of standards imposed by an outside agency. It discussed conditions affecting the schools with administrative officers of the universities with which the schools were connected. It recommended budgets to be provided by institutions contemplating the establishment of schools. It conferred with the Association of American Universities concerning degrees to be awarded upon the completion of the various curricula. And in 1933 it changed its standards from a quantitative to a qualitative basis in order to give greater flexibility to the schools in setting up special objectives and engaging more generally in experimental programs.

Naturally this kind of activity evoked criticism and opposition. The Second Activities Committee in 1930 reported that the work of the Board had elicited more criticism, mostly adverse, than any other organization within the Association. The Board responded spiritedly. It stated that the inspection and the accreditation or nonaccreditation of schools was a difficult task to perform; and that measuring the effectiveness of the schools and classifying them accordingly naturally led to differences of opinion and, in some instances, to pointed resentment. In general, the profession rallied to the Board's support, some of the critics reversing themselves to the extent of suggesting that greater financial support be given the Board in order that it might carry on its work more effectively.

This kind of activity involved the Board in certain mistakes. At the beginning, it lacked some of the familiarity that present library-school faculties have with admission requirements; university organization and procedures; undergraduate, graduate, and professional curricula; and the attitude of graduate faculties concerning professional studies and degrees. A case in point is to be noted in the Board's dealing with the Association of American Universities concerning the degree to be awarded upon the completion of the fifth year, devoted to professional study. The Board accepted the ruling of the Association that a certificate or a second Bachelor's degree be awarded instead of a professional or Master's degree. Acceptance of this ruling in 1926 has been responsible for much of the confusion concerning the proper content of the preprofessional, professional, and graduate-professional curriculum and for salary discrimination against holders of second Bachelor's degrees, since it was not clear what the degree stood for. Nevertheless, the Board set up a program to the effectiveness of which the Williamsport Report and the grants of the Carnegie Corporation greatly contributed. In fact, it largely provided the framework within which the schools have carried on for the past quarter century.

The Ten-Year Program of Library Service of the Carnegie Corporation

The Ten-Year Program of the Carnegie Corporation helped make possible the implementation of the recommendations of Williamson and of the Board of Education for Librarianship. The Corporation provided funds for the Williamson study and it financed in large measure the program of the Board of Education for Librarianship during its most active period. It aided in merging the library schools of the New York State and the New York Public libraries at Columbia in 1925, and contributed $25,000 annually to the support of that school from 1925 to 1935. During the same period it contributed a similar amount annually to other then-established schools upon recommendations made by the Board, and at the end of the ten-year period it distributed the million-dollar principal among them in the form of endowments. It likewise provided for the establishment of the library school for Negroes at Hampton Institute and the School of Library Science at the University of North Carolina. And in 1926, upon the recommendation of the Board and the Chicago Library Club, it made available funds for the establishment and endowment of the Graduate Library School at the University of Chicago. In 1929, after the re-establishment of the School of Library Service at Columbia and the provision for advanced study there, at Chicago, and at the Universities of California, Illinois, and Michigan, it established a number of fellowships from which in the following decade 93 librarians benefited.

The Establishment of the Graduate Library School

The establishment of the Graduate Library School at the University of Chicago may be considered as the sixth event in the historical sequence. In 1925 the Carnegie Corporation issued its famous Office Memo called the "Ten-Year Program in Library Service." This memorandum followed the report of Williamson, the report of the Temporary Library Training Board, the appointment of the Board of Education for Librarianship, and the publication of Learned's *The American Public Library and the Diffusion of Knowledge* in 1924. This program involved the expenditure of $5,000,000. One of the items included in it was, as President Keppel phrased it, "an allotment of one million dollars to make possible a graduate library school of a new type which could occupy for the librarian's profession a position analogous to that of the Harvard Law School or the Johns Hopkins Medical School."

Wheeler, in his *Progress and Problems in Education for Librar-ianship*, says: "The founding of the Graduate Library School ... may well turn out to be of greater influence on library training and on librarianship than the publishing of the Williamsport Report in 1923 or the establishment of the Board of Education for Librarianship in 1924." Miss Howe, in her *Two Decades of Education for Librarian-ship*, remarks that the School fully met the criterion that it was to be "an integral part of a university which meets the standards for grad-uate study laid down by the Association of American Universities."

Whether the statements made in the Office Memo by President Keppel or these statements by Mr. Wheeler or Miss Howe have been realized, it is probably too soon to say. Nevertheless, its establishment stands out as one of the most significant developments in the history of education for librarianship in America and may be commented on at some length, since the conclusion of the twentieth year of its operation is being celebrated at this meeting.

This significance is to be seen in several facts. The first was the composition of its initial faculty. Contrary to the expectation of the profession, it was drawn in large measure from disciplines other than that of librarianship. Its head was drawn from the fields of higher and rural education. His principal contact with libraries had come through a survey of college and university libraries. A second mem-ber was an expert educational investigator, with a special penchant for investigation of the sociological and psychological aspects of reading. A third was a historian with a brilliant record in the field of medieval scholarship, one of whose major works deals with medieval libraries. A fourth, with a special interest in Arabic manu-scripts, had grown up in the University of Michigan library, had taken his Doctor's degree in a theological seminary, and had come to the School via service in the reorganization of the Vatican Li-brary and the study of American college libraries for the Carnegie Corporation. Of the three other members of the staff prior to 1932, one had come from library school and extensive graduate training, another had long and varied library experience, and another held a Doctor's degree from a theological seminary and had served as an expert on rare books in the Newberry Library. When I came to the headship of the School in 1932, only one member of the then existing staff had come up through the regular channels of library schools and work in a public library. The "irregularity" of the group was seemingly so glaring to the strictly library-minded members of the profession that it was not until the Board of Education had changed from quantitative to qualitative standards in 1933 that I dared submit the application of the School to it for inspection and accreditation!

The value inherent in this unusual situation was fourfold. Here was a staff, several of whose members were familiar with the curricula and procedures of professional schools in other fields; it was untrammeled by the crystallized form of the prevailing curriculum of education for librarianship; it was acquainted with the fields of bibliography, history, education, psychology, and sociology upon which librarianship could and must draw for its enrichment; and it was extensively trained in scientific methods of graduate study and research. The effect produced upon the library profession was similar to that of shock which is sometimes essential in bringing back to reality the sufferer from amnesia and other mental disorders. In this instance, the shock was desirable to jar the profession out of its prolonged devotion to the practical techniques set up by Dewey and at no time thereafter wholly satisfactorily departed from.

A second value was the separation of the head of the School from the administration of the university library. A program of advanced study, investigation, and publication had to be set up. An effective staff had to be organized, and leadership and guidance had to be provided for graduate students in a new and undeveloped field. This called for the full time, energy, and thought of the head, and for freedom from the innumerable decisions which the administrator of a large university library must make daily. Freedom from such interruptions was essential in order that the dean could devote such time as was necessary to the consideration of the "changing needs of librarianship" and to the formulation of a program suitable to meet them.

These were initial values. Others have accrued throughout the years. At the head of the latter may be placed the development of a critical, scientific attitude in the School's students. They have been taught to challenge unproven assumptions, to devise experimental techniques for the solution of unsolved problems, and to reach conclusions only after thorough examination and testing.

The School has also developed an extended series of important library publications. Its series, *Studies in Library Science*, now contains more than thirty volumes, many of which have been notable in
the advancement of various phases of librarianship. *The Library
Quarterly* has regularly published the results of extensive investigations and its reviews have critically appraised the important literature of librarianship and related subjects.

Through its teaching and publications the School has likewise contributed to the development of a philosophy of librarianship, the
lack of which had long been decried. Munthe, in writing of Butler's
An Introduction to Library Science, published in 1933,[2] said: "Dr.
Butler employs a universally valid process of philosophical reasoning
in an attempt to show it is impossible to understand a social institution like the library without scientific investigation of the social,
psychological, and historical problems that attach themselves to it.
. . . Butler's little book is the first attempt at a scientific synthesis of
library science in its various aspects, and a step on the road toward
a philosophy of librarianship. Some day it may rank among the
classics of the library profession."

This was a first step in the formulation of a philosophy of librarianship. J. H. Wellard, in his *Book Selection, Its Principles and Practice*[3] and *The Public Library Comes of Age*,[4] has taken a second step.
He set the library in its relation to the fields of history, literature,
bibliography, psychology, and sociology. He gathered up the results
of many of the studies of the School and worked them into a sustained synthesis that may well be studied by all students who would
understand the bases upon which the public library movement in
America and England rests.

The School's publications have contributed another factor of importance to the acceptance of librarianship as a scholarly professional discipline. They have clarified the field of librarianship and
have made it understandable to scholars in other fields. Munthe, in
writing of Joeckel's *The Government of the American Public Library*,[5] said: "One might be tempted to say this treatise alone is suf-
cient documentary evidence in justifying the existence of the School."
A Metropolitan Library in Action, by Joeckel and Carnovsky,[6] and
The Chicago Public Library, Origins and Background, by Spencer,[7]
evoked the interest and commendation of the historian and political

scientist as well as of the student of American social institutions. Illustrations might be drawn of the impact of other publications and studies upon other fields, particularly of the publications growing out of previous conferences like this one, but these are sufficient for the purpose of showing how librarianship has been enriched, and how other disciplines have profited from this activity of the School.

Skepticism as to the value of the Doctorate in librarianship has also been reduced, certainly in university and research libraries if not in public libraries, owing to the leadership and accomplishments of graduates of the School. Wheeler bears testimony to this fact; and Munn, who in his *Conditions and Trends in Education for Librarianship* (1936)[8] maintained that library schools were not training for leadership and that comparatively few librarians with advanced training were required in cities like Pittsburgh, somewhat modified this statement in his American Library Association presidential address, "Fact versus Folklore," in 1940.[9] There he stressed the point that if libraries were to respond effectively to changing needs, they must have objective studies of every kind, particularly concerning the reading interests and abilities of their patrons. Through its graduates who hold Ph.D. degrees, the School has demonstrated that extended training in advanced studies and research not only tends to insure such competence, but that it does so more quickly than prolonged experience.

These influences may be thought of as having been tangential to education for librarianship. Three that have affected the subject directly will now be pointed out.

The first is the contribution the School has made to the upbuilding of the staffs of other schools. At the very outset the School held conferences for the training of teachers in library schools. In the two decades since its establishment, it has steadily supplied directors and staff members to the faculties of other schools. The number of holders of advanced degrees in faculties of other schools has steadily increased since 1929, and several schools which began offering work leading to the Master's degree and the Doctorate in librarianship in 1948 or have strengthened their work at the graduate level, will be staffed in considerable measure from the School's graduates with higher degrees.

The second direct contribution has been the example the School has set in formulating a professional curriculum that proceeds logically through the various stages of general, preprofessional, professional, and graduate-professional education. It first undertook this step in 1941–42. That it was able to do this was due in part to the organization of the School as an integral part of the University of Chicago. Without reference to a general graduate school, it has been able to work out a program in keeping with the spirit and structure of the University that breaks away from the excessive techniques of the Dewey tradition and that prescribes the nature of the preprofessional and professional fields. It has done this not in the old framework, but in a new framework in close cooperation with other departments and schools. This development holds promise of the highest order.

The third direct contribution has been the steady provision during the past two decades of fellowships, scholarships, grants-in-aid, and research assistantships for graduate students in librarianship, from which a hundred or more librarians have benefited. Many of the beneficiaries have been employed in surveys and studies conducted by the School, have published the results of their investigations in the *Library Quarterly* and the series of *Studies in Library Science*, and have gained experience in attacking library problems from which the profession generally has profited.

This activity has by no means been limited to the School. On the contrary, the Carnegie Corporation provided a series of generous fellowships from 1929 to 1942 in which 93 librarians participated, and library schools in general have offered scholarships, fellowships, and assistantships to a growing number of students throughout the nation. This activity has emphasized, however, the fundamental importance of such assistance for graduate study and the enrichment of library service.

The Contribution of Practicing Librarians

The influence exerted by practicing librarians constitutes the seventh aspect of the development of education for librarianship. This has been in the main of a conservative nature. However, there have been notable exceptions. Perhaps the two most notable have been the approval by the leaders of the American Library Association in 1883 of a library school as preferable to apprenticeship for the training of librarians, and the constructive work of the Temporary Library Training Board and the Board of Education for Librarianship from 1923 through 1933.

Against these significant developments is the tendency for many practicing librarians to insist that graduates of library schools joining their staffs should be able to render the kind of service normally expected of apprentices in their own library systems. Placement of advanced students at higher than beginning levels, particularly by public libraries, has been fairly difficult; and opportunities provided by libraries for leaves of absence with pay for advanced study and for assignments to tasks involving extensive specialization, experimentation, and research, have been comparatively few. Part-time positions have been more generously provided, particularly by the New York Public Library and the libraries of universities whose library schools have formerly awarded the Master's degree.

The Role of Certification Agencies

Education for librarianship has likewise felt the impact of accrediting agencies within and outside the field of librarianship. The adverse effect of the ruling of the Association of American Universities upon the degree awarded for the completion of the one-year professional program has already been noted. The role of graduate faculties in determining the conditions under which graduate programs of the schools are to be carried out has also been suggested. The part played by school accrediting agencies and state certification boards has also been extremely important.

The point does not require elaboration. The example in the states served by the Southern Association of Colleges and Secondary Schools will suffice to show the extent of this influence. Before the Southern Association adopted its standards for the training of high school librarians in 1927, there were only two library schools in the area. The establishment of the standards stimulated the organization of schools at William and Mary, the University of North Carolina, George Peabody College, and Louisiana State University; and of departments of library science for the training of school librarians in a score of additional institutions. State aid for public libraries has likewise made it possible for state library agencies to set up definite professional requirements to be met by county and regional librarians. All these requirements have had to be considered by the schools and have been reflected in the programs of study offered by them.

Studies of the Past Decade

The ninth influence to be considered in the development of education for librarianship has been that of related studies which have proliferated during the past decade. I shall not undertake to single these out by name. Some of them were related to the fiftieth anniversaries of the schools at Columbia and Illinois. Others have been undertaken for the Carnegie Corporation. Still others have been developed by members of library school staffs. All have dealt with various phases of the subject. They have analyzed conditions, pointed out limitations, and prescribed remedies. Fortunately they have been projected against the background of from fifteen to twenty-five years of experience of library schools as parts of American universities. They reflect the influences described in the foregoing sections of this paper, and provide in large measure the foundation of the new curricula recently put into effect. This new development will be looked back to in the future as marking a significant advance in education for librarianship.

New Curricula

Finally, passing consideration must be given to the new curricula that are emerging from these studies. They represent something more than individual opinions. They are the outgrowth of studies which have preceded them and they embrace programs of action which will markedly affect the future of education for librarianship.

The most obvious change in the new programs is the change in the degree to be awarded at the conclusion of what has usually been considered the fifth year of undergraduate and professional study. The second Bachelor's degree is to be dropped by a number of schools and the A.M. or the M.S. is to be awarded.

The change in the degree, however, is not the most fundamental change. It is only superficial. The most significant change is to be found in the nature of the curricula leading to the new Master's degree. Requirements for this degree have been restated and represent an attempt at placing preprofessional, professional, and graduate-professional studies in a logical order in keeping with the spirit of professional and graduate study. The pressures exerted by undergraduates colleges and graduate schools have been relaxed to such an extent that a more realistic approach to the professional requirements of librarianship has been made possible.

The content of the curricula also exhibits extensive change. A glance at the courses offered at Chicago, Illinois, and Columbia, for example, reveals a sharp break from the titles of courses contained in the minimum standards adopted by the American Library Association upon the recommendation of the Board of Education in 1926. A core curriculum introduced at the undergraduate level replaces much of the former curriculum. New courses such as The Library and Society, Books and Libraries in the Cultural Process, Communication and Libraries, Readers and Reading Interests, The Resources of Libraries, The History of Scholarship, and Methods of Investigation are combined with other professional courses and seminars as well as graduate courses from other disciplines. In two new instances they are continued beyond the fifth-year level with advanced courses and seminars leading to the Doctorate. Closer integration with other schools and departments has been effected, with consequent enrichment throughout the entire professional curriculum. The total result is the provision of a program of professional and intellectual content that should go far in giving the future librarian the background, competence, and scholarly understandings that will better fit him for the exacting demands of American librarianship.

It is upon this kind of foundation that education for librarianship is being placed today. After sixty years, the framework established by Dewey and only partly modified by Williamson and the Board of Education for Librarianship has, in considerable measure, given place to the framework fashioned by the needs of modern librarianship. From these changes, generally long overdue, librarianship stands to profit greatly.

NOTES:

[1]Carnegie Corporation of New York, *Training for Library Service* (New York: Updike, 1923).

[2]University of Chicago Press.

[3]London: Grafton, 1937.

[4]*Ibid.*, 1940.

[5]University of Chicago Press, 1935.

[6]*Ibid.*, 1940.

[7]*Ibid.*, 1943.

[8]Carnegie Corporation of New York.

[9]In A. L. A. *Bulletin*, 34 (1940) 38–84, 402.

The Impact of the Graduate Library School Upon American Librarianship

To ATTEMPT TO APPRAISE the impact of an institution upon any phase of American culture is at best hazardous. Disassociation, objectivity, and long perspective are fundamental to the success of such an undertaking. In my effort to evaluate the impact of librarianship of the Graduate Library School of the University of Chicago, whose twenty-fifth anniversary we are celebrating, I find that these essentials are almost completely wanting. I was intimately associated with the School for ten years as its dean. My point of view, therefore, is necessarily somewhat personal and partial rather than objective. And the perspective through which I view the work of the School is very limited. Seemingly, it was only yesterday that I moved from my office in the Social Science Building on the Midway to the Li-

Reprinted from *Addresses by Vice-President R. Wendell Harrison and Dean Emeritus Louis R. Wilson*, On the Occasion of the 25th Anniversary of the Establishment of the Graduate Library School, July 12, 1951, pp. 5–12, University of Chicago, by permission of the publisher.

brary at Chapel Hill. Nevertheless, the Graduate Library School has affected American librarianship in seven important particulars which I think should be set down in a permanent record.

I. *Broadened the Concept of Librarianship*

First of all, the School has greatly broadened the limited concept of librarianship that generally prevailed in 1926. In May of that year, I was invited by the special committee of the University of Chicago charged with the establishment of the School to come to Chicago to confer with it concerning the nature of the program of study and re-search in which the School should engage. Upon my arrival, I was handed a copy of a tentative curriculum that represented the think-ing of the Chicago Library Club, that had formally proposed the es-tablishment of the School "for the development of the cultural, liter-ary, bibliographical, and social aspects of librarianship as a learned profession"; of the A.L.A. Board of Education for Librarianship, which had submitted a tentative list of theses subjects for considera-tion; of several librarians from important libraries of the country, who had likewise been called in for consultation; and of the special committee of the University of Chicago.

The proposed curriculum reflected much of the then-current prac-tice of the two schools that offered work for two years leading to the B.L.S. degree. Book selection, classification and cataloging, adminis-tration of different types of libraries, reference work and bibliogra-phy, the history of books and libraries, and research in those fields were included. To these subjects were added manuscripts, paleogra-phy, and the literature of several fields, particularly of the humani-ties. But many aspects of librarianship that are taken for granted today were not mentioned. In fact, the adult education movement had been formally inaugurated only two years before; the Library Extension Board of the A.L.A. was just completing its publication on library extension; and the Board of Education for Librarianship was putting into final form its Minimum Standards for the accredita-tion of library schools.

In considering the proposed curriculum with the special commit-tee, I commented as follows: "The curriculum outlined by your com-mittee seems to me to include, in the academic field, subjects that are quite appropriate and essential. It would seem to me, however, that a fourth division should be added in which the handling of statistics and methods of research and investigation would receive specific consideration. By way of differentiation from the work done at Illinois and Columbia in the second year, it is hoped that specialization may be emphasized rather than adding more of the same kind of subject material. In the case of students going on for the Ph.D. degree, specialization of a high order, with investigation and field work, is desired."[1] I further recommended that training should be provided for "investigators and conductors of surveys in the library field." "This," I added, (was) 'in recognition of the fact that the American public library (was) a great social and educational institution whose functions, practices, and effectiveness had not in any sense been subjected to close, scientific scrutiny."

Obviously, the School cannot claim credit for all the expansion that the concept of librarianship has undergone in the past 25 years. But it can claim with complete propriety that it pioneered in treating the library as a social institution, and in insisting that advanced study of librarianship should be carried on in accord with scientific measures just as advanced study of other institutions was carried on.

II. *Developed Librarianship as a Field for Scientific Study and Research*

The School did not stop with a mere declaration that the library was a social institution to be studied scientifically. It broke with the tradition of treating librarianship altogether as an art and took the second step of developing it as a field for scientific study and research. Those whose memories go back as far as the meeting of the American Library Institute at Yale in 1931 will remember the clever advocacy by Seymour Thompson of librarianship as an art; his scathing attack upon the methods used by Waples and Tyler in their *What People Want to Read About,* in which interest in reading as an aspect of librarianship was treated scientifically; and the improvised defense of the scientific point of view made by C. C. Williamson, of Columbia, and myself. In spite of widespread misunderstanding and opposition, the School dealt with the subject as a science and employed all related scientific methods applicable to it.

[1]For notes, see page 277.

The School stressed research methodology, not only in solving general problems of librarianship, but as a means of attacking local and special problems. It likewise emphasized the importance of library surveys, and sent its graduates out prepared to undertake the solution of problems of which other librarians were afraid because they had not been trained to deal with them. For example, *Who Uses the Public Library*, by Haygood, represents the completion of a project that others started but could not finish; and Chancellor Hutchins had to wait until a new group of midwest university librarians came along, many of whom had been trained by the Graduate Library School, before the complex concept of the Midwest Inter-Library Center could become a reality. The erection of library buildings embodying the principles of modular construction and including divisional reading rooms was likewise boldly advocated by Graduate Library School students; and the research projects in librarianship which the A.L.A. will soon submit to the Ford Foundation reflect the handwork of other students of the School.

III. *Introduced a Critical, Objective Point of View*

The third contribution the School has made to librarianship was the introduction of a critical and objective point of view. From the outset, the School took nothing for granted. It challenged every assumption dear to the hearts of practicing librarians and constantly insisted on objectivity in observation and statement.

Two examples of how imbued the early members of the faculty were with these points of view may be cited. In the summer of 1933 during the Century of Progress Exposition, sight-seeing busses brought thousands of visitors to the Midway to see the University and especially the Rockefeller Memorial Chapel. One day as I was walking in front of the Chapel with Carnovsky, one of the first Ph.D.'s of the School then finishing his first year as a member of the Faculty, several busses rolled up and the Midway vendors of ice cream and other articles began to hawk their wares. One of the vendors, who was selling some sort of inexpensive cigaret lighter, spied us as we approached, and called out: "Right this way, gents; get your everlasting match; one for fifty cents, three for a dollar!" Surcharged with the spirit of letting nothing go unchallenged, Carnovsky stopped in his tracks and said: "See here, Mister, there's something fundamentally wrong with that assumption. If one match is everlasting, why get three?"

A few years later the present dean entered the School from the Library School of the University of Washington. Early in the autumn quarter he exhibited special interest in library staff unions and wrote a term paper on the subject for my course on library trends. When his paper was returned to him, he found it rather heavily blue pencilled. Later, he came to the office and asked why the blue pencilling. I suggested that he read the blue pencilled statements carefully and see whether he had written as an objective, scientific student or as a special advocate. The present dean instantly saw the point and has lived an exemplary objective life ever since, but I have yet to discover what reform Carnovsky's observation wrought in the hawker's career!

IV. *Related Librarianship to Other Disciplines*

Prior to the establishment of the School, librarianship was, as I indicated earlier, a self-contained subject narrowly limited to technical procedures, the administration of various types of libraries, reference work and bibliography, and the history of books and libraries. It was almost completely divorced from other disciplines and lacked their range and depth. Even after library schools became incorporated in universities, they remained, as President Keppel, of the Carnegie Corporation, phrased it, largely outside the blood stream of the institutions of which they were parts. The School sharply broke with that tradition, intimately integrated its work with that of other departments and schools, and undertook to extend and enrich librarianship as a field of learning. It had its students take related courses in economics, education, history, political science, statistics, and business and public administration, as well as in the humanities and the physical and biological sciences generally, thereby gaining for librarianship a breadth and depth and sense of relationship and direction that it previously had lacked. It likewise opened its courses to anyone in other departments who could profit from them, and when it developed the subject of communication, one of its instructors organized a seminar in that field that was widely attended by representatives from the entire University. As a result, students of the School have gone out with a broadened outlook that has enabled them to relate their work effectively to that of associates in other fields, an outlook, by the way, which is less frequently acquired by students in subject fields. In this way it has won for librarianship a wider acceptance than it previously enjoyed both as an academic subject of study and as a profession.

V.   Greatly Affected Education for Librarianship

The fifth impact the School has made upon librarianship has been in the field of education for librarianship. In proposing the establishment of the School, President Keppel expressed the hope that it might play a role in education for librarianship comparable to that played by the Johns Hopkins Medical School in medical education or by the Harvard Law School in legal education. Wheeler, in commenting on the School's work, said that its establishment "may well turn out to be of even greater influence on library training and on librarianship than the publishing of the Williamson report in 1923, or the establishment of the Board of Education for Librarianship in 1924."[2] And Wilhelm Munthe, writing in his *American Librarianship from a European Angle* in 1939, said: "In the space of seven or eight years the limited staff of the School and a few of its graduates have managed to translate into action the program which the 100 esteemed members of the exalted American Library Institute had brooded over for about a generation: To direct their efforts toward the more scholarly aspects of librarianship, hitherto neglected, and toward a careful and scientific study and discussion of the more important problems of library service."[3]

The nature of this contribution has been many fold. Four aspects may be selected as of special importance:

(1) Its early faculty, drawn largely from fields other than librarianship, and experienced in graduate study and research, introduced new ideas from non-library fields, and related librarianship to other enriching disciplines. In fact, the School postponed asking for accreditation by the Board of Education for Librarianship until the Board had adopted qualitative instead of quantitative standards in 1933, because only one member of the school's faculty had had what

might be considered regular library school training and there was some question how the accrediting board at the time would react to that situation. The School held back until more propitious signals were sighted!

It was such an irregular, unusual group that when I think of it, I am reminded of an incident in the life of a German wood carver who carved the figures in the rapidly-becoming famous circus in the soft drinks bar of the Monogram Club at Chapel Hill. The wood carver, an anti-Hitler refugee, was living happily in a small North Carolina town until World War II broke out. Then, when they met him on the street, some of the children of the community began lifting their eyebrows and saying, "Nat-zi, Nat-zi." This distressed him beyond measure. So he went to his friend, the postmaster, and told him he and his wife just couldn't take it, and asked the postmaster if he knew of any place to which he could go where he would not be taken for an objectionable oddity. The Postmaster thought a minute, then suggested that he go to Chapel Hill, the seat of the University of North Carolina where, he said, there were so many odd characters that the addition of one more would make no difference, and he would be lost in the crowd!

(2) The School has developed a curriculum that has greatly influenced education for librarianship at all levels. It included basic courses essential to librarianship in the undergraduate program, and provided at the graduate level courses and seminars that led to the Master's degree and the doctorate on a basis comparable to that upon which the degrees were awarded by other departments and schools of the University. In fact, the type of curriculum which the Board of Education for Librarianship is now submitting for approval by the Council of the A.L.A., is largely patterned after the program adopted by the School almost a decade ago, a program which the School has every reason to believe is producing better *educated* rather than better *trained* librarians than heretofore.

(3) Through its institutes begun in 1936, the School has provided in-service training not only for the one or two hundred librarians who have attended them annually, but for the thousands to whom the papers and discussions have been available through the published proceedings. Few undertakings have been more fruitful in keeping a profession abreast of current ideas and problems than these annual

conferences in which librarians and leaders in related fields have come to common grips with matters of large professional import.

(4) Since its establishment, the School has awarded 209 bachelor's degrees, 150 M.A.'s, and 69 Ph.D.'s. How many of its students have become teachers in library schools is unknown to me. But I do know that staff members of the schools at California, Columbia, and Illinois have been heavily recruited from the group, and that others from it fill many important positions throughout the country as directors and teachers. Through these individuals the point of view, the mental ferment, and insistence upon solid training, which have characterized the School from the beginning, have been transmitted to other campuses and have profoundly influenced teaching and research wherever they have gone.

VI. Contributed Through Publication to the Development of a Philosophy of Librarianship

Librarians have long deplored the lack of a philosophy of librarianship to give unity and meaning to their work. It would be claiming far too much to say that the School has furnished such a philosophy. But it is not too much to point out that through its teaching, through the *Library Quarterly*, through its publications, and through the theses and publications prepared by its students, the School has developed a scholarly, critical, and scientific attitude toward libraries and library problems and has produced an extensive literature concerning the operations and purposes of libraries that have magnified and enriched librarianship as a learned profession. After the appearance of *An Introduction to Library Science*, by Butler, and *Book Selection*, by Wellard, librarians could better understand the relationship of librarianship to bibliography, literature, history, and sociology than they had been able to formerly. The studies by Joeckel, Spencer, and Shera clearly revealed the reasons why the American people established and supported the public library as a governmental institution for the enlightenment of a free democratic society. Since the publication of *The College Library* and the two volumes on the administration of college and university libraries, librarians and administrators of institutions of higher education have had at hand statements that analyze clearly the function of the library in teaching and research. Through its publications dealing with the psychology of reading and communication, the School has opened up a subject about which librarians have had a better opportunity to be informed than most of their colleagues in other professional and academic subject fields. Today, as the A.L.A. focuses the attention of its members on the American heritage, and as the nation steps up the Voice of America and organizes a new board on Psychological War Strategy, this School well knows that its pioneering in this field should greatly aid in promoting the national welfare.

VII. *Furnished Leaders in the Field of Librarianship*

Finally, through its alumni, the School has contributed heavily to leadership in American librarianship. Many of them came to the School with native intellectual drive and extensive training. They responded enthusiastically to its stimulation. When they went out from it, many of them did so with a confidence that springs from an understanding of principles and from the ability to analyze complex problems. One has only to glance at the library map of the nation to see how responsibly many of them are placed and how effectively they are maintaining the point of view and expressing the spirit of their *Alma Mater* in the work to which they have put their hands. I congratulate them and the School alike on what they have accomplished in this quarter century, and I urge them and their *Alma Mater* to press forward to higher attainment in the next, since the door of opportunity swings even wider open today than it did in 1926.

This is, as I see it, a part of the record of the impact on American librarianship of the Graduate Library School whose original endowment fund President Hutchins told me in 1931 he was going to give back to the Indians, whoever they were, unless I would come and be its dean. This statement that he would return good money to the Indians, coming from a University president, was such an unheard-of pronouncement that it left me shocked into open-mouthed attention. Then President Hutchins described what he considered to be the possibilities of the School in spite of the ups and downs, mostly the latter, through which it had been passing. He impressed me as being either a very unusual university president, or a very bold flatterer, or an individual who was terribly worried over the future of the School and wanted to do something about it. His worry over it reminded me of a story Senator Z. B. Vance, the popular Civil War Governor of North Carolina, told of one of his clients who had inherited from his father a fairly extensive tract of western North Carolina mountain land. His brothers and sisters had been excluded by their father's will from sharing in the tract, and they got mad and brought suit to set the will aside. The client became greatly distressed at the unexpected rancor and bitterness the suit occasioned in the family. In fact, he became so worried that, in discussing the strategy of the final stage of the litigation, he said to the Senator, "You know, Senator, this situation is so terrible I sometimes almost wish that Pa hadn't died!"

NOTES:

[1] Louis R. Wilson, Typescript Memorandum Concerning Advanced Graduate Library School, May, 1926.

[2] Joseph L. Wheeler, *Progress and Problems in Education for Librarianship.* Carnegie Corporation of New York, 1946. P. 74.

[3] Wilhelm Munthe, *American Librarianship from a European Angle.* Chicago: American Library Association, 1939. P. 152.

The Challenge of Library Literature to Education for Librarianship, 1923 - 1953

I.

IN DEALING WITH THE CHALLENGE of the literature of librarianship to modern librarianship, my major purposes are to show: (1) what the status of library literature was in 1923; (2) how it limited the education for librarianship programs of that day; (3) what the na-

Reprinted from *Challenges to Librarianship,* edited by Louis Shores, Florida State University Studies, Number Twelve, pp. 125–140, Florida State University, Tallahassee, 1953, by permission of the publisher. This lecture was the seventh of a series to which eight individuals contributed.

ture and extent of its growth in the past three decades have been; (4) what its present status is; and (5) how it inevitably affects the preparation of librarians of the future. In considering the subject I shall not undertake to treat it exhaustively, but on the contrary, what I shall say will be in the nature of a commentary on certain of its most significant aspects.

II.

The present day library school student may well take with a grain of salt the statement that his predecessor in 1923 could almost count on the fingers of his two hands the number of titles of important professional library textbooks and journals which he would have to master in order to qualify for a successful career as a professional librarian. His skepticism would be altogether natural. Today with all of his hours crowded with constant reading not only about books in the humanities, the social sciences, and technology and science, but especially in books and journals in the field of librarianship, he certainly has little in his present experience to justify him in giving full credence to such a pronouncement.

The facts, however, are against him, or largely so as far as the date 1923 is concerned. That year definitely marked a turning point, and since then the amount of time the student has had to spend upon the literature of librarianship has steadily grown until now it is seemingly impossible for him to read everything that has appeared and is appearing in the field.

The American Library Association was well aware of the situation in 1923. Its members had recently studied carefully the Williamson *Report* on the library schools of the day and knew that among the many limitations they were confronted with was that of adequate materials upon which to base a sound educational program. The appointment of a Temporary Library Training Board in 1923 to survey the general field of education for librarianship and of a permanent Board of Education for Librarianship in the year following was aimed at the stimulation of better teaching materials as well as at the establishment of higher standards, the employment of better trained faculty members, the provision of greater financial support for library schools, and the association of library schools with degree-granting universities.

Mudge's *Guide to Reference Books*, the *Dewey Classification*, parts of the *Library of Congress Classification*, the *Library Journal*, *Public Libraries*, the *Wilson Bulletin*, the *A.L.A. Bulletin*, a number of the H. W. Wilson Company indexes and catalogs, *Publishers Weekly*, and *The New York Times Book Review*—these titles, with national bibliographies and the publications of the Library Bureau, the R. R. Bowker Company, and the office of the U.S. Office of Education, constituted the core of professional literature with which the library school student had to deal.

Such a limited literature, devoted almost exclusively to the housekeeping aspects of librarianship, provided a correspondingly limited foundation for a broadly based curriculum. Consequently, when in 1926 the Board of Education for Librarianship requested the Association of American Universities to indicate the type of degree it would recognize as an appropriate credential for the completion of a one-year library curriculum imposed upon a bachelor's degree, the Association replied that a second bachelor's degree was all that it could allow, and that its actual preference was a certificate in library economy. The inadequacy of the degree was thus made to match the inadequacy of the literature of the subject, the poor administrative organization and financial support of the schools, and the limited qualifications of their faculties.

III.

Nineteen twenty-four witnessed a decisive change in library interest and a corresponding growth in library publications. Three organizations were principally responsible for this. They were the American Library Association, the American Association for Adult Education, which was established in 1924, and the Carnegie Corporation of New York, which in 1925 embarked upon a dynamic program of library stimulation.

The American Library Association, responding in 1925–26 to the stimulation of extensive grants from the Carnegie Corporation for education for librarianship, for library extension, and for adult education, established boards to develop those interests and set them to preparing a series of publications in those fields for its fiftieth anniversary in 1926. For that occasion, it carried out a national survey of all types of libraries, and reported the results in two notable volumes. Its Board of Adult Education projected a series of *Reading with a Purpose* publications and produced a major report entitled *Libraries and Adult Education.* The Board of Library Extension likewise issued a detailed statistical report entitled *Library Extension,* and the Board of Education for Librarianship completed its first comprehensive study of the library schools and published its first codification of *Minimum Standards.* The *A.L.A. Catalog,* revised and enlarged for the occasion, was also published and widely distributed and rounded out an important addition to the professional resources of the day.

The American Library Association, through the Board of Education for Librarianship, also undertook to improve teaching in library schools through the preparation of a series of texts in the fundamental subjects of the curriculum. It placed a specialist in the field of curriculum revision in charge of this undertaking and set a number of experienced librarians to work in the preparation of texts to take the place of the notes which individual teachers had previously been required to prepare for themselves. Texts on circulation work, by Flexner; reference work, by Wyer; book selection and book ordering, by Drury and cataloging, by Miss Mann were issued in rapid order, each covering a specific field systematically, thereby making it possible for library school instructors to dispense largely with detailed lectures from notes and to emphasize special aspects of subject matter which required special consideration. While some of the texts proved somewhat unsatisfactory and have been superseded in recent years, they appeared at a time when on account of the limited number of students in library schools it was impossible for librarians to produce texts unaided.

The second event which stimulated library interest and brought into being a new series of publications which demanded consideration by librarians was the establishment of the American Association of Adult Education in 1924. This Association inaugurated a vigorous program of publication. It established *The Journal of the American Association of Adult Education,* projected a series of *Studies in Adult Education* featuring the results of research in adult reading, and prepared handbooks for the guidance of adult education workers in thirty or more fields, including libraries. *The Public Library: The People's University,* by Johnson, pointed up the role of the public library in the movement, stimulated the American Library Association to step up the tempo of its *Reading with a Purpose* series, and promoted the provision of reader's advisory services in libraries. The publication by the Association of the results of research in different aspects of reading also threw new light upon the role of print in the continuing education of adults.

Waples and Tyler, in *What People Want to Read About*, devoted their attention to the subjects about which different elements in the population were interested in reading. Through careful research they identified the reading interests of the public library's varied clientele. Gray and Monroe undertook to discover the actual reading ability of the average American and came up in *Reading Interests and Habits of Adults* with the disconcerting fact that reading was a very difficult undertaking for the average citizen because he possessed the reading ability of only a sixth-grader. Then Gray and Leary, in their work *What Makes A Book Readable*, went on to discover what elements in writing make for ease or difficulty in reading, their work leading ultimately through the studies of Lorge and of the Readability Laboratory of Columbia University to the preparation of a series of volumes published in *The People's Library* which librarians hoped would lessen the difficulty of the poor reader in comprehending what he read. Thorndike, of Columbia, was put to work investigating the truth or falsity of the adage that an old dog couldn't be taught new tricks, or, that as an individual became older, his ability to learn decreased almost to the vanishing point. The results of his study, published under the title *Adult Learning*, showed that while the period in which it was easiest for an individual to learn was when he was from 16 to 24 years of age, it was possible for him to continue to learn throughout his entire life though with increasing difficulty.

These publications furnished a sound foundation for work in the field of adult education, thereby contributing to the conviction that the library, whether school, college, university, or public, was an educational agency in its own right altogether capable of contributing to the diffusion of knowledge and therefore fully entitled to public support as a significant educational institution.

The role of the Carnegie Corporation in this development was four-fold. It aided the American Library Association financially in greatly extending its work in adult education, in library extension, in education for librarianship, and in publication. It provided the stimulus and financial support for the establishment of the Graduate Library School of the University of Chicago and for the support of the School of Library Service of Columbia University and other library schools. And in the late 1920's it set up the College Library Advisory Committee for the stimulation of interest in the four-year liberal arts college libraries, thereby initiating work for the next ten years in the improvement of college libraries generally. Its activities in this field resulted in the publication of *College Libraries*, by Randall; *Principles of College Library Administration*, by Randall and Goodrich; *The College Library Building*, by Gerrould; *A List of Books for College Libraries*, by Shaw; *A List of Books for Junior College Libraries*, by Mohrhardt, and a number of booklets and articles by Bishop and other members or associates of the College Library Advisory Committees on various aspects of college library administration.

IV.

While the publications mentioned above covered a wider range of interest than library publications did prior to 1923, they nevertheless dealt primarily with the activities of libraries. Their scope was broader, but they remained library centered and were little concerned with educational and social movements in general. Beginning in 1930, however, publications in other fields began to influence librarianship profoundly. This was strikingly true of publications in the fields of education and the social sciences. In 1933 under the editorship of Ogburn and Odum, the President's Research Committee on Social Trends issued the highly important work *Recent Social Trends in the United States*. This two-volume survey of the social forces at work in the nation and the special monographs on education, on inventions, on government, on population changes, and similar subjects, by which it was accompanied, focused the attention of librarians upon the role of the library as a social institution. Library schools began to list courses in their curricula on the library in the community or the library as a social institution, and the Graduate Library School of the University of Chicago went so far as to offer a course on library trends. The library schools sensed for example, as they had not previously, that the study of such a subject as population had implications for libraries; that the composition of the population in states such as South Carolina and California, in which the ratio of children of school age to adults varied greatly, might have a direct effect upon library practice. For example, in South Carolina the ratio of children of school age to adults was one to one, whereas in California it was one to two. In the light of such simple ratios, it was clear that when the public librarian in South Carolina selected books for his clientele, he should be an expert on books for children and that a comparatively large number of persons should be trained in that State to administer school libraries. This is because there are as many school children as there are adults. Furthermore, one-third of the children use the public library once a month, whereas only one-tenth of the adults use it that often. In California, on the contrary, books and adult education programs for grown-ups would call for principal consideration since the adult population is twice as large as the school population. From a careful examination of *Recent Social Trends* and other social studies, it became apparent that the multiplication of subjects in the school curriculum, the size of governmental units, the invention of the automobile and radio and other developments of this nature had a direct bearing upon the library, and that if the library attempted to adjust itself properly to the changes effected, it would be compelled to understand clearly what the implications of the situations were.

Three examples of social movements in the early 1930's which greatly stimulated thinking concerning the library in the social order were (1) the depression, (2) the setting up of the National Resources Planning Board, and (3) the establishment of schools and departments of public administration in American universities.

The depression, spreading its scourge over the nation in the early 1930's brought the public library into a prominence it had never known before as an educational and recreational agency and as an emergency employer of persons on relief. It sent throngs of the unemployed to library reading rooms everywhere, and it rapidly brought into being a type of library service that in some sections of the country greatly contributed to the subsequent establishment of public libraries and evoked a considerable number of reports and publications on public library development. It emphasized the importance of the equalization of service whether in schools or libraries and led to increased activity in library extension and publication through state aid.

The establishment of the National Resources Planning Board by the Federal Government set off a nation-wide chain-reaction in planning. State planning boards sprang up everywhere and began to study intensively the development of their physical resources and to publish the results of their investigations in numerous reports. Library planning at the national and state levels followed, the American Library Association issuing its *National Plan for Libraries* in 1935, with librarians in 45 states issuing state plans by the end of 1936. Post war planning for all types of libraries followed as a natural step after World War II, bringing into being such notable titles among others as *National Plan for Public Library Service*, by Joeckel and Winslow, and *School Libraries for Today and Tomorrow*, by Douglas.

The general provision in the 1930's of courses in educational administration, public administration, and industrial management in departments or schools of education and public and business administration in the universities of the nation, led to the close scrutiny of theory of administration and its application in those fields. Numerous treatises appeared on the elements and principles of administration in these subjects and were studied in turn by librarians and were applied to all phases of librarianship. Thus the writings of Cubberly and Strayer in educational administration, of Merriam, Gulick, White, and others in the field of public administration, and Keynes and Slichter in industrial administration, were followed by Joeckel and the McDiarmids, by Miles and Martin, by Wilson and Tauber, by Randall and Goodrich, by Lyle, Miss Herbert, Wight, and many other librarians on various phases of library administration. In fact, the subject of library administration profited tremendously from contributors from within and without the profession and can be studied by the prospective librarian with the assurance that it will meet his major needs if it is constantly added to through research and current publications.

V.

Investigation in public, industrial, and educational administration

not only influenced publication in library administration but stimulated studies and publications in other aspects of librarianship. The
library schools which offered graduate work leading to the M.A. and
Ph.D. degrees in librarianship have responded to this challenge and
in the past two decades have produced an extensive body of literature in which the results of investigations, surveys, and critical
studies have been recorded. This development has, from many points
of view, been especially important and salutary, since library situations and practices have been subjected to careful observation and
evaluated in accord with approved standards.

Three types of publication may be attributed to this development.
Of these, the most obvious and, from the practical standpoint of library administration, the most important, have been the reports of
surveys of college, university, and public libraries. The studies of
college libraries by Randall and Mohrhardt; of university libraries
by Wilson, Kuhlman, Coney, Tauber, Jesse, Orr, and others associated with them; of public libraries by Joeckel, Carnovsky, Wight,
and their associates; of regional libraries in the Pacific Northwest
and the Southeast; and of public libraries throughout the nation
by Leigh and his collaborators, have dealt with many phases of librarianship and have supplied specific illustrations of how actual
practice may be made to conform to approved standards. The reports
growing out of these studies have not only acquainted librarians and
library school students with actual library practice, but they have
also shown how standards can be applied and procedures can be recommended to insure improved administration. These publications
have greatly aided university and city administrators in establishing
proper administrative financial policies for libraries at a time when
such administrators were being confronted with staffs and book collections which had doubled in a relatively short period of time.

The publications growing out of the Public Library Inquiry have
had an additional value. They have dealt comprehensively with the
whole public library movement in the United States from its incep-
tion to the present, and they make clear the nature of the contribution of the public library to American democracy. They show that
the public library, while not patronized by a majority of American
citizenry, has stood for a century as a symbol of democracy and has
helped shape the democratic ideals of hundreds of thousands of

leaders of public opinion—an accomplishment of the greatest significance to the Nation. Like the press, the school, and the church, it has fought for the freedom of the individual and has insisted upon his right to share in the Nation's cultural and spiritual heritage.

The publication of articles embodying the results of research in the *Library Quarterly*, in *College and Reference Libraries*, and to a less extent, in other library periodicals, has likewise been highly salutary. Its effect has been four-fold. It has familiarized librarians with the methods of research; it has stimulated investigation by practicing librarians and graduate students; it has helped convince scholars in other fields of the breadth and soundness of graduate study in librarianship; and it has filled the need which librarianship has long felt of reshaping and revitalizing its theory and practice in the light of new methods and discoveries.

The publication of long critical essays and carefully considered book reviews has exerted a comparable influence upon library literature. Criticism reflects a knowledge of standards and an ability to apply them, for the lack of which library literature long suffered to the detriment of its standing in the eyes of librarians generally and of members of other disciplines and professions. The ability to criticize intelligently gives proof of maturity in point of view and poise in judgment; when criticism is constructively applied, it insures not only a finer type of training for librarians, but improvement in performance and in the advancement of librarianship as a profession.

VI.

Contributions to library literature from four other sources merit comment: (1) library schools (2) libraries which issue significant bulletins and occasional monographs (3) organizations which have established journals in related subject fields, and (4) individuals or organizations which have published compilations of resources for research or indexes or catalogs of special materials and collections.

The Graduate Library School of the University of Chicago has played a distinctive role as a library publisher. Reference has already been made to research studies in reading by Waples and Tyler and Gray and Monroe, and in other fields by other members of the School's staff which it has published. Comment has also been made on the part played by the *Library Quarterly* in stimulating research and criticism. In 1933, however, the School began the publication through the University of Chicago Press of *The University of Chicago Studies in Library Science*. To date it has issued 40 volumes in this series, 16 of which have contained the papers presented at its annual institutes which have been held since 1936. In all of the volumes, whether by members of its staff and alumni or by scholars and experts in other subjects, the School has undertaken to apply, when dealing with problems of librarianship, standards and methods of treatment similar to those applied to studies in other disciplines. The subjects treated have ranged from the history of mediaeval libraries and printing through the beginnings of libraries in New England, the South, and the Mid-West, down to the latest developments in the new but rapidly growing and tremendously important subject of communication. Certain titles stand out as landmarks in library study. Butler's *An Introduction to Library Science* and Joeckel's *The Government of the American Public Library* have attained the status of classics; and the volumes by Randall and Goodrich, in college library administration; of Joeckel and Carnovsky, in public library administration; and by Fussler, in microphotography, to mention three as representative, are constantly referred to by librarians everywhere.

The Columbia School of Library Service has likewise contributed notably through its syllabi on the subjects within its curriculum. *Living with Books*, by Haines, has become a classic in book selection, as has the *Guide to Reference Books* by Mudge and her successor, Winchell, all at one time of the Columbia School of Library Service or Library. Reece's works on education for librarianship have brought down to date the important developments since the Williamson *Report* of 1923, and the recent publications by Leigh, Bryan, and their associates growing out of the nation-wide Public Library Inquiry, have become *must* reading for all alert present and prospective librarians.

The Library School of the University of Illinois and the School of Librarianship of the University of California have published less extensively, but their publications in the field of education for librarianship have been challenging. *Library Trends*, a journal recently established at the University of Illinois and featuring the publication in a single issue of a number of articles on different aspects of a specific subject, and *The University of Illinois Contributions to Librarianship* have already established a significant place for themselves among library periodicals and monographs.

Publications by libraries throughout the Nation fall into different categories, though they are predominantly bibliographical or descriptive of special collections. They are indispensable for their humanistic content and supplement the subjects treated by the library schools concerned largely with phases of administration or education.

The *American Archivist* and the *Journal of American Documentation*, to mention two journals in special fields, are representations of new titles by fairly recent organizations, and, with the major surveys of library resources, with various union lists and catalogs, and with publication-wide indexes and catalogs, round out the field of library publication in the United States.

The impact of the study of these various publications from the social sciences and librarianship upon education for librarianship is vividly illustrated by two outlines I have developed over the years. The first was developed in the 1930's when I began offering a course on university library administration at the Graduate Library School of the University of Chicago which later grew into the volume by Wilson and Tauber entitled *The University Library*. In that course, by drawing upon the writings of Henri Fayol, Gulick and Urwick, and others, I developed a statement concerning the theory of administration in which the elements and principles of administration were set forth with brief definitions. The whole statement barely filled four typed pages, and all of it was drawn from fields other than the field of librarianship, and it was in a sense incidental or at most introductory to the course, the main body of which dealt with library practice. As I recall it, I devoted only one or two class periods to its consideration. Last week I concluded a course on the theory of library administration, the outline for which began with approximately the original four pages, but the body of which was drawn largely from publications written by librarians, which dealt theoretically and practically with elements and principles. Each publication presented a full-length study of organization, or planning, or staffing, or budgeting, or some other phase of administration, with practical situations and problems drawn from recent surveys of public and university libraries to give the subjects a specific basis of reality.

The outline had grown from less than four pages to twenty-five, and the number of class periods from two to fifty, and the individual topics had acquired a range and comprehensiveness that was undreamed of by librarians a decade and a half earlier.

VII.

The impact of the humanities upon the literature of librarianship during the past three decades, while less obvious than that of the social sciences, has nevertheless been significant. Just how significant, I cannot say. I cannot give a similar illustration showing the relation of cause and effect in the case of the humanities. I am not sufficiently familiar with literary criticism and the history of the arts and the literatures to see clearly what the relationship is between them and book selection and the book arts, nor am I able to trace the relationship between publications that deal with standards of value and appreciation on the one hand, and publications by librarians on the other, that apply their underlying principles to librarianship. But I am sure there is such a relationship, and that it is significant. James Harvey Robinson's *The Humanizing of Knowledge* (1923) written for scientists, and W. S. Learned's *The American Public Library and the Diffusion of Knowledge* (1924) pointed up the possibilities of contributions from the main stream of humanistic publications from which man has gained mental stimulation and aesthetic and spiritual insight. Books such as Butler's *An Introduction to Library Science* and Wellard's *Book Selection* showed how librarianship and book selection derived much of their motivation and standards of value from literature, the arts, philosophy, history, and the sciences as well as from the social sciences. This motivation and these standards have contributed to the broadening and deepening of the philosophy of librarianship upon which library service and adult education in America are firmly based. They emphasize the importance and dignity of the individual in a democratic society, an importance and dignity which must be maintained at all cost if men are to remain free.

Practical applications of this theory or philosophy have eventuated in a class of publications of great significance to librarians. *Living with Books*, by Haines; *How to Read a Book*, by Adler; *The Literature of Adult Education*, by Beals and Brody; *Books that Have*

Shaped the World, by Eastman; *Classics of the Western World*, by
Brown; and the "outlines" of history and literature and philosophy
are but representative of the many titles of books about books, of
bibliographies, and of special bulletins, handbooks, and treatises
that enable librarians and library patrons to avail themselves of the
ministry of the arts, philosophy, and literature. Publications of art-
ists and musicians, of art museums and musical organizations, and
of library associations in those fields, facilitate this work and lay
open an inviting field of librarianship. The Great Books and to a
less extent the American Heritage programs stem from this basic concept, as do those of libraries that loan reproductions from the fine
arts and musical recordings or provide facilities for viewing notable
pictures and listening to music reproduced by means of recordings or
radio.

VIII.

The American Library School student cannot limit his professional
reading to American publications since librarianship knows no national bounds. Like scholarship, it transcends national limitations
and must concern itself with publications originating in other countries and dealing with foreign cultures. This fact I hardly need to
emphasize here where you have only recently welcomed the return
of your Dean after a year's study and association with European librarians. You have undoubtedly read this statement in the January
1953 A.L.A. *Bulletin* in which he wrote: "In areas of classification,
cooperation, union catalog, documentation, library education, citizens advisory service, rural and urban public library service, and
special library development, British librarianship compares very
favorably with American librarianship." He might well have said
the same of British library publications since they and the library
publications of other countries likewise challenge the attention of the
American library school student today. A half-dozen titles of major
works in English, French, and German will illustrate this point: *The
Library Association Record, the Year's Work in Librarianship, Bibli-
otheque de l'Ecole des Chartes, Handbuch der Bibliothekswissen-
schaft, Jahrbuch der deutschen Bibliotheken,* and *Zentralblatt für
Bibliothekswesen.* Whether French, or German, or Italian, or Scan-
dinavian, or Indian, or Japanese, they too are extensive and can

broaden and deepen his understanding of the role librarianship has played down through the centuries in conserving and transmitting the written record of man's priceless cultural heritage.

IX.

This is the library literature, the library book shelf in outline upon which you as prospective librarians must draw for your professional preparation. These are the materials which you must master if you are to be fully informed about how the graphic records of man's past and present can be made to minister effectively to his present and future. This is the field in which you must carry on research and publish. You have already sensed how this material has broadened the scope of our training and laid the foundation for work leading to the M.A. and Ph.D. degrees. The library book shelf of 1923 could not support such curricula. But the book shelf of today, lengthened and enriched to a degree undreamed of three decades ago, makes such attainment possible. If it is supplemented and enriched by knowledge of related fields, it brings within your reach means by which you can prepare yourselves to enter upon a rich and significantly fruitful service to your fellow men.

Publishing in the South

Print in the Service of the South

FOR THE PAST TWENTY-FIVE YEARS speakers and writers who have sought to direct the South's collective thinking have steadily held up before the public a half dozen specific objectives or ideals looking to the development of the section, with the happy result of seeing the public united in a program of common action through which these ideals have been in part realized. Larger educational opportunities, improved highways, better standards of sanitation and health, a greater interest in the welfare of the public, and the development of agricultural and natural resources are the evidences of the increasingly successful accomplishment of these common tasks.

An objective which has not been generally held up before the South, however, but which is essential to the development of a South that is more articulate and more capable of realizing fully all of its ideals, is the greater need of books and libraries and magazines and publishing houses which I shall consider under the somewhat ambiguous title, Print in the Service of the South.

At the outset there are several explanations which are essential to this consideration. First, the title, as has been indicated, is ambiguous. I shall speak of libraries and books and magazines and publishing houses and bookstores instead of mere print. Second, it is too inclusive, as I have in mind only the section south of Washington and east of Texas. Third, I shall find it necessary to refer more frequently to North Carolina than I should if my knowledge of conditions in other states were more extensive; and finally, the discussion may reveal certain situations which should be considered frankly if they are to be changed for the better, even if consideration of them is not altogether pleasant.

With the subject limited in this way, I wish first of all to show that while we have been working to secure equality and universality of

Reprinted from *Virginia Alumni Bulletin*, Vol. 17, No. 3, July, 1924, by permission of the publisher. An address delivered as Visiting Exchange Lecturer, May, 1924.

educational opportunity, the improvement of our roads, the protection of our health, the safeguarding of our common welfare, and the development of our agricultural and natural resources, we have failed, and are now failing, to make the fullest use of print in the sense in which I have defined it. In the second place, I wish to make clear what some of the results of our failure are; and in the third place, I wish to indicate how the ideal of greater use of print may be realized.

I. *The Evidences of Failure*

Our failure to use print as extensively as we should is indicated in at least seven ways. The first of these is we do not have our quota of books in public libraries. This conclusion is based on a table which appeared in *School and Society* in 1922, giving the number of volumes in public libraries per 1000 inhabitants in the respective states. New Hampshire, according to this table, had in her public libraries 1978 volumes per 1000 of her population, or practically two books per inhabitant. With New Hampshire at the head of the list stood, in order, Massachusetts second, Vermont third, Nevada fourth, Connecticut fifth, Rhode Island sixth, Maine seventh, California eighth, while at the other end were Georgia forty-second, Virginia forty-third, New Mexico forty-fourth, Mississippi forty-fifth, South Carolina forty-sixth, North Carolina forty-seventh, and Arkansas at the very bottom with 37 books in her public libraries for each 1000 of her people or one book to every 28 people.

This study did not take into consideration books in school or college libraries. Had these been considered, it would have been found, for example, that in North Carolina, whereas there were approximately 850,000 children in the common schools, the libraries of the common schools possessed only 500,000 volumes or five-eighths of a book per pupil, that the 40,000 high school students of the state possessed approximately 200,000 volumes, or 5 books per pupil, and that the 10,000 young men and women in the colleges and State University had only 500,000 volumes at their service, or 50 books per student. Studies of this sort, appearing in recent reports of Southern departments of education, library commissions, and in the *Library Journal* show that where this sort of measurement is consistently used we do not make the use of print in the form of public and school library books that citizens in other sections of the country do.

A second evidence of our failure is to be found in the fact that even where we have libraries, they are comparatively small and not highly specialized.

Cities like Winston–Salem and Norfolk and Charleston and Savannah and Knoxville have only from ten to forty thousand volumes to place before their respective populations; their average annual income per inhabitant for library purposes has been between twenty and forty cents instead of the standard of $1.00 set for the country at large by the American Library Association; and only in the more exceptional cases is there the wealth of material, the variety of manuscript, and picture, and rare book, and special edition, and map, and stereograph, and musical score or record such as thousands of other Americans find in their libraries which public and students use in performing the tasks of a highly complex civilization, or from which they derive concepts and standards of the fine and the beautiful in life.

The library resources of Salem, Massachusetts, illustrate the point I am making. With a population of 42,520, and therefore comparable with Southern cities like Roanoke, Raleigh, and Columbia, this city had in 1920 a public library of 70,000 volumes, an association or subscription library of 30,000 volumes, a scientific library of 120,000 books and 405,000 catalogued pamphlets, and a law library of 30,000 volumes. That is, Salem, with its 100,000 volumes in its public and association libraries, had 10,000 volumes more than the combined book collections of the public libraries of Asheville, Winston, Charlotte, Durham, Greensboro, Raleigh, and Wilmington and 5,000 volumes more than the combined public libraries of Charlottesville, Lynchburg, Norfolk, Roanoke, and Winchester had in 1923, three years later. Its law library of 30,000 volumes was the equal of the law libraries of the University of North Carolina Law School and the Supreme Court of North Carolina combined; and its scientific library (the library of the Essex Institute) contained as many volumes as the library of either the University of Virginia or North Carolina or Vanderbilt, with some 300,000 monographs and pamphlets to boot.

Someone has humorously suggested that 10,000 of these volumes were probably on witchcraft or codfish; but at all events the books were there, with other great libraries like those of Harvard, and Yale, within fairly easy access if recourse to them was necessary. On the other hand, Louisville is the only city between Washington and Austin, Texas, which possesses a library that contains more than 200,000 volumes, and the number exceeding 100,000, such as the state libraries at Richmond and Nashville, the public libraries at Atlanta and New Orleans, and the university libraries at Virginia and North Carolina and Vanderbilt, can be counted on the fingers of two hands.

A third evidence is to be found in the fact that the assembling of our largest book collections has required a much longer period than the assembling of similar or even much larger collections elsewhere. The Universities of Virginia and North Carolina this year attain the 125,000 volume mark after 100 and 138 years of existence, respectively, while the libraries of Wisconsin and Michigan, much younger than our own institutions, number 315,850 and 545,675 respectively. These latter institutions have not been ravaged by war or swept by fire, it is true, but their rapid development is due to the fact that they add annually from two to five times as many accessions as our own institutions do. The library of Louisville is the only one south of Washington that adds over 15,000 per year, whereas scores of libraries in other sections add that number and on up to 60,000 or more.

If the question were to be asked, "Does the south read?", I doubt not that with some show of resentment the press, representing general opinion, would answer, "Well, possibly we are not readers of books, but we read our quota of magazines and daily papers. But, by and large, in the South, do we read our quota of magazines and dailies? What is the evidence on this fourth point?

The answer is not far to seek. Publications such as *The Ladies Home Journal, The Saturday Evening Post, The Country Gentleman,* to mention Curtis publications, *The Literary Digest, The Outlook, The World's Work, The Review of Reviews, The American Magazine, McClures, The Red Book,* publish either through their advertising departments or audit bureaus, semi-annual or annual analyses of their total circulations by states, and frequently by counties and towns. If, for example, you wish to know how many copies of *The Literary Digest* or *The Saturday Evening Post* are taken in Berkeley,

California, or Charlottesville, or Chapel Hill, or in the counties and states in which these places are located, the matter is very simple.

Likewise, annual summaries in *The Editor and Publisher*, and Ayers' "American Newspaper Directory" include tables which assist in giving any state a cross section of its reading habits in the newspaper field. And according to these means of measurement we discover that we do not read our quota of these publications. The story runs about as follows:

One copy of one of three Curtis publications goes, on the average, to every group of 27 persons in the whole of the United States. California leads with a copy for every 10 of its citizens. Oregon and Washington follow with one copy for every 11, Nevada and Montana with one for every 13, Wyoming and Colorado with one for every 14, Idaho and Vermont with one for every 15. It is interesting to note that the Northwest, rather than the Northeast, is the leader in the field. The ten states standing at the bottom of the list, however, are all Southern states, as follows: Virginia with one copy to every 44 of her population, North Carolina and Tennessee with one to 46, Louisiana with one to 52, South Carolina with one to 55, Georgia with one to 58, Alabama with one to 70, and Mississippi with one to 74. In the case of *The Literary Digest*, California leads with one to 42, the average for the United States being one to 85. Nine Southern states with an average of one to 240 occupy the lowest fifth of the total list, and if averages for other national journals such as *The Outlook, The World's Work, The Cosmopolitan, McClure's The American Magazine*, and *Good Housekeeping* are worked out the record will not be materially changed.

In the field of daily newspapers the average circulation in 1922 throughout the United States was one copy to every 3.6 persons. Massachusetts led with one copy to every 1.9 persons. The five states standing at the top were Massachusetts, Washington, New York, California, and Oregon. The ten at the bottom were South Dakota, West Virginia, Georgia, Alabama, North Dakota, Arkansas, North Carolina, South Carolina, New Mexico, and Mississippi. Virginia, which had an average of one copy to every 8.2 persons, stood thirty-seventh; North Carolina, with one to every 13.5, stood forty-fifth; and Mississippi, with one to every 37, stood forty-eighth. The one notable exception in the case of the circulation of dailies, weeklies, and monthlies is furnished by Florida which ranks comparatively high. Judging, however, from the fact that the averages of resort cities such as Asheville and Southern Pines runs far in advance of adjoining non-resort places, the rather high averages of Florida are easily accounted for.

The fifth word of testimony is to be found in the low vitality of journals of opinion and comment and literary magazines published in the South. Someone recently asserted that the South was the graveyard of literary journals. Last August I undertook through a questionnaire to determine the truth of this assertion. I shall not give in detail the results of my investigation, but the truth of the statement is inescapable. Church journals, agricultural papers, fraternal organs, historical and genealogical quarterlies deriving their support from state or private sources or from special fees, have been successfully maintained. But with scarcely a half dozen exceptions, such as *The Sewanee Review, The South Atlantic Quarterly, The Texas Review, The Reviewer, The Double Dealer,* and *The Fugitive,* the record of Southern literary journals since 1865 has largely been one of failure. One publication after another has arisen to meet the fate of *The Southern Eclectic, The Sunny South, The Uncle Remus Magazine,* and *Trotwood's Monthly,* to mention a few of the most notable in the list. A recent inquiry concerning the status of *The Texas Review* and *The South Atlantic Quarterly* showed that these publications did not have sufficient subscribers to make them self-supporting. *The Sewanee Review* declined to furnish an analysis of its circulation, and the managers of *The Reviewer, The Double Dealer,* and *The Fugitive* did not answer the inquiry at all and statistics of their circulation were not available in any directories at hand. *The Southern Literary Magazine,* started in Atlanta last year, expired at the end of the third or fourth issue, to reappear recently at Nashville with seemingly a new lease on life. At no point in the South has a review achieved the success attained by *The Yale Review,* for example, which, in its present form, though considerably younger than *The Sewanee Review* and *The South Atlantic Quarterly,* has built up a circulation of 18,500 and a national reputation as well.

The fact that the section between Washington and New Orleans has sustained few great publishing businesses other than those of church and educational publications constitutes the sixth link in this chain of evidence. Of the 375 publishing houses whose catalogues appear in "The Publishers' Trade List Annual," for 1923, 21 are located between Baltimore and New Orleans, and of the 1692 publishers listed in "The American Book Trade Manual" for 1922 who bring out occasional books, 143 are located in the same territory, of which 47 are in the city of Washington. As yet only Johns Hopkins, the University of North Carolina, Trinity College, and the University of the South, among Southern institutions of higher learning, have established formal presses and entered fields comparable even in a very limited sense to those occupied by the presses of Princeton or Chicago or Yale. The Southern Presbyterian Publishing Board, in 1922, reported a business covering the publication of books and church and Sunday School literature of all kinds which totaled approximately $900,000. The Southern Baptist Publishing Concern reported similar sales amounting to $1,398,000; and the Methodist Episcopal Church South Publishing House $6,698,252. A few educational publishing houses such as B. F. Johnson, at Richmond, have extensive businesses, but at present the South has no press or publishing concern of which all of us instantly think when our attention is directed to the general field of book production.

The scarcity of well-established, effective bookstores, such as are listed in "The American Book Trade Manual," and of distinctive book-review pages in our dailies, constitutes the final evidence I shall offer of our failure to use print as fully as we should in the South. North Carolina, for example, with 279,000 automobiles in her garages and with auto sales agencies in all her hundred counties and along all her highways, has only 225,000 books on the shelves of her public libraries and 31 book stores distributed in 10 of her cities, according to the list furnished by "The American Book Trade Manual" for 1922. Her auto sales agencies are selling two automobiles to every book bought by her public libraries. Virginia, with 2,309,187 people, has 47 bookstores listed in 13 of her cities. Tennessee, with a population of 2,337,885 has 43 stores in 7 cities. Wisconsin and Iowa, with populations approximately equal to those of the states mentioned, have double the number of stores located in double the number of cities, while Rhode Island, Connecticut, and Vermont, with a combined population equal to that of any one of the Southern states mentioned, has 125 stores in 33 cities. These stores are the agencies through which books find their way into the homes of the people and make a public a reading public. This essential agency for the dissemination of books, together with the modern book-review page in the dailies, has not been fully developed even in the larger cities, not to mention the vast rural areas of the South, and a steady demand for its services is yet to be created.

II. *The Significance of Our Failure*

Without presenting other evidences of the non-use of printed material, and without attempting to determine the causes which have given rise to the situation set forth, I wish now to consider the significance of the facts presented. Various causes which in part account for the condition will at once suggest themselves. The presence of the negro in the South, the bankruptcy of the South following the Civil War, our vast rural areas, our delight in happy conversation rather than in reading and study, the inevitable and wholly natural concentration of the facilities of publishing in the metropolitan area —all these have had their effect in producing the situation, but they should not be allowed to obscure the real significance of it.

Reading, Sir Francis Bacon said, maketh a full man, the sort of man a democracy must rest upon if it is to survive.

If only one of us out of every 10 or 15 in the South reads a daily newspaper, if the average circulation of the national weeklies and monthlies is only a third or a fourth of that in other sections of the country, if general public library facilities are much more limited here than elsewhere, it is inevitable that we cannot hope to be as well informed concerning what is taking place and what is being thought of in the world as our fellow-citizens who read more. If, as a people, we cannot secure information from these sources which are provided more generously elsewhere for the instruction of men and women after the formal instruction of the schools is ended, we cannot become full men in the Baconian sense, nor can we co-operate quickly and fully with our fellows in those enterprises which look to the advancement of the common good. Coordinated, effective action in behalf of schools and roads and health and all the other major programs for further development has been greatly retarded because a common body of information could not be quickly conveyed to a public laboring under such a serious, all-inclusive handicap.

The absence in the South of highly specialized or unusually complete collections of books for the use of students or scholars or individuals who wish technical or complete information on any subject, also places us under a heavy handicap. Our life at the South is rapidly becoming more and more complex. Consequently, more exact information is required as a result of this increased complexity. New standards must be evolved, mistakes must be avoided, experiments made by others which have resulted in failure must not be repeated, and confidence and assurance which spring from knowledge, and spiritual power which comes from familiarity with the thought and achievement of others, must be secured from great central libraries or specialized libraries to which the South can have full access. Libraries, in this sense, are utilitarian, as well as inspirational. They are the indispensable tools not only of the lawyer, and doctor, and teacher, and minister, but of the banker and engineer and cotton manufacturer and farmer and of every man who has a task to perform and wishes to perform it in a more thorough going way tomorrow than he has performed it today. That, it seems to me, is a fundamental lesson that the South must learn. If we are to make all of our people continuously throughout their lives more effective workers, if we are to give them a fundamental knowledge of the world in which they live, if we are to bring them to a larger appreciation of science and literature and the arts, if more of them are to become able to express themselves in the various arts, the backgrounds of their lives must be enriched through schools and libraries and museums with which we surround them. A good teacher on one end of a log with a pupil on the other may, in many instances, have constituted a fine school. But if distinction of achievement and thought is to be attained not only by the occasional individual but by many men, the fullest opportunities for complete development must be placed within the reach of all.

I have already suggested the loss we experience through failure to handle new books in attractive, well-supplied bookstores. Have you ever stopped to think that it is from such shops that books, in the main, enter our homes and become the companions of our children, and a very intimate part of us? Books from libraries merely pay us brief visits. If bookstores do not exist, if they are cramped, if their offerings are not varied and do not stimulate our interest, if through them it is not easy for us to secure books on any subject we may desire, we fail to order them from a distance and our intellectual horizons necessarily reflect their limitations.

The loss which the South suffers from the lack of well-established, widely-circulating journals is two-fold. First, the immediate door of opportunity open to our youth for the further development of their talents either as editors or as contributors, is seriously restricted. Of course there are distant doors just as there are distant bookstores such as Scribner's or Brentano's or Wanamaker's. But they are not sufficiently immediate to challenge the interest of the student who has shown special aptitude a an undergraduate writer and who would advance further if the means were immediately at hand. Two illustrations of what I mean occur to me. A few days ago I heard one of my colleagues remark that he had received a check for a book-review contributed to a certain Southern historical journal and that it was the first pubilcation of its sort in the South, so far as he knew, to pay for contributions. At the same time I read in the press that *The Reviewer* of Richmond had announced that its contributors must take their pay in fame rather than in the coin of the realm. Lack of journals for which to write and from which to receive compensation, means that for many the impulse is chilled at the very start, and the road to excellence of thought or craftsmanship is suddenly terminated. But the lack of opportunity is not as grave as the lack of a steady contribution of pertinent, vital comment concerning the affairs of the South and Nation by men who know at first hand the situations to which their comments relate and whose opinions cannot be waived aside but must be considered even if they are not generally acceptable. Life in the South is becoming so highly specialized that it must be subjected to the most searching close-at-hand criticism to keep it sane and sound.

In the same way the absence of publishing houses in the cities and of well established presses at the leading universities has restricted the activities of Southern writers and scholars. Nowhere in the South have there been such agencies with which an author could easily place his work as the publishing houses of Houghton Mifflin for

New England, or the Macmillan Company for the Middle Atlantic States, or the presses of Harvard and Yale and Princeton and Chicago, for the constituencies of those institutions. Distance from publishing concerns, lack of acquaintance with their directors and the ways and means of placing manuscripts, have made the task of contributing to the thought and scholarship and literature of the Nation through monographs and sustained works most difficult if not well-nigh impossible.

For this reason, also, there has not been turned back into the life of the South from local sources a steady current of stimulating regenerating criticism. Books, like Walter Hines Page's "Rebuilding of Old Commonwealths," and E. Gardner Murphy's "The Present South," admirable though they were and written by men who knew the South as only Southern men could, failed to convey the message of which the South was sorely in need, because they were published outside the section to which they were applicable and because there were few bookstores or other agencies through which their contents could be generally made known to the people.

It may have occurred to you that the loss which we have been considering is not only two-fold, but three-fold. There has been the loss of opportunity for development, the loss of stimulating criticism, and there is unquestionably the loss of intellectual freedom which the present generation must endure, but which it should not pass on to be borne by the next. The proposal of the Kentucky legislature to limit state institutions in their teaching of science, the placing of the ban on certain text-books in biology by the governor of North Carolina, the theological controversies which fill the columns of the church press in the South, the attitude of Southern capital concerning the coming of the closed shop and of labor to capital—these and other like situations are inevitable in a community or a section where points of view are not steadily expanded through continuous study and the free exchange of opinions on the subjects under consideration. The hands of men are not as free to take up some of the tasks that look to the liberalization and broadening of our lives as they should be, because through our journals and publishing houses the habit of tolerance and cooperation and the consideration of the point of view of the other side has not been widely cultivated.

Furthermore, our conservatism and individualism have not at

times been things in which we could justly take pride. Failure to co-operate in a program which offered large community benefits has too frequently been due to lack of knowledge both of the certain benefits which were to result from the program and of methods to carry it out. Conservatism and individualism of this sort, which have retarded the improvement of schools and roads and other means of hastening the progress of the South, should not be set down as virtues but hindrances which they really are.

III. *Our Objective for the Future*

Thus far I have attempted to show the extent of our failure to use print, and what it has cost us in development and effectiveness. I now want to point out what should be our objective for the future.

This, it seems to me, is to build upon the foundations which are now being laid in the fields we have been considering. I have in mind the continuation of the sort of thing which has been begun throughout the South generally in recent years. In North Carolina, for example, the first public library was established in Durham in 1897. Today the number of public libraries has grown to 64. Twenty-six years ago the library of the University contained 25,000 volumes and had a total income of $1500. Today it has 125,000 volumes, it is adding from 10,000 to 12,000 volumes annually, and has a total annual income of $59,000. In 1897 there were no trained librarians in the State. The present number is well up towards the hundred mark. Two years ago no library had a circulation of over 100,000. Today two or three libraries are running a race to see which will reach the 150,000 mark first. In 1900 there were not 25,000 volumes all told in the public schools of the State. This number has grown to 500,000 in the elementary schools and 200,000 in the high schools, with requirements passed by the State Department of Education which look to the steady, intelligent upbuilding of all school collections. In 1909 there was no State Library Commission at Raleigh or library extension service at the University. After fifteen years of service the State Library Commission has an annual operating fund of $28,000 and is sending package and traveling libraries into every section of the State, and the extension service at the University is directing the special study of 9000 club women and is furnishing study outlines and reference materials to thousands of citizens. In

1920 there were no regular, well-conducted book-review pages in the leading dailies. Four dailies now conduct such pages of fair distinction; a journal of opinion and comment devoted to the consideration of social problems has been established and has built up a circulation of 2000; and presses at Trinity College and the University have brought out a total of a dozen worthwhile books during the current academic year.

Similarly library commissions, or state libraries with commission functions, are promoting library development in almost every Southern state. Traveling libraries are sent into rural districts from practically every state capital. A library school has been established at Atlanta, and library instruction is given at Charlottesville, Chapel Hill, Greensboro, Rock Hill, Athens, Nashville, Birmingham, Louisville, and other points throughout the South. Since 1900 books by the thousands have been placed in the grammar grades of the public schools and in 1922 the Southern Association of Colleges and Secondary Schools established library standards which are now being complied with by all accredited high schools. Country-wide library service with book-truck delivery has been established in a number of Southern counties and the habit of depending upon local donors for library buildings instead of the Carnegie Foundation has been firmly established. Appropriations for buildings and maintenance are more generous than ever before, and the necessity of developing an adult as well as juvenile reading public is becoming generally recognized.

Print, in the sense in which I have used the term, has not been used to the greatest possible advantage in the South. But the objective which is already being realized in part and which we must hold up as our future ideal is that libraries will more and more be enabled to operate with funds sufficient to provide complete information on subjects of importance to their patrons; that journals of opinion or literary excellence will increasingly exert their stimulating influence upon an alert, open-minded public; that bookstores will multiply; and that here and there at strategic points in the South, well-endowed and equipped presses and publishing houses will serve as the agencies through which a fuller, more articulate South will make permanent its contributions to the thought and scholarship and literature of the Nation.

It is possible that the ideal may not be immediately or perfectly realized. But we must remember that there is value in an ideal, in a plan, in a standard for the future. In some way such things are fertile. Like the mustard seed of biblical mention, they germinate, they take root, they grow. In what they become, men and women find happiness and fullness of life. This has been true in the development of schools and roads and agriculture and the forces which make for a better physical environment. In this instance the ideal, the plan, look to the day when the capital we invest in the making of men will more nearly equal that we invest in the making of things, when the wealth of our minds will more clearly match the wealth of our factories, and when the paths to learning and more perfect self-government and self-expression are made straight and accessible even unto the most under-privileged.

Publishing in the South

AN UNDERSTANDING OF THE ROLE of the university press in the development of graduate study and research in the South is important alike to those who are engaged in scholarly publishing in the universities of the nation and to all colleges and universities interested in this comparatively new and rapidly expanding phase of southern education.

The South today is experiencing a ground swell of interest in training experts essential to its economic and social development through advanced graduate and professional study and research. Belatedly, it is coming to the conclusion that it must provide graduate and professional schools and training at the doctoral and post-doctoral levels if it is to compete on an equal basis with other parts of the country. It has come to realize that it cannot do this upon the

Reprinted from *Journal of Higher Education*, 22:365–372, 399–400, October, 1951, by permission of the publisher. A paper read before the Association of American University Presses, Chapel Hill, North Carolina, April, 1951.

basis of the Bachelor's and the Master's degrees. To cite a specific example, although the South is predominantly agricultural, the region has grasped the fact that it cannot develop its agricultural program to the highest point if it fails to train the experts required. It cannot repeat its performance of the decade 1929–38 in which 547 doctorates in agriculture were given by the land-grant colleges and universities of the United States but not one by any institution in nine southeastern states.

The evidences of an increased interest in graduate and professional training are not far to seek. Several may be cited.

First of all, there is the Conference of Deans of Southern Graduate Schools. This hard-working, purposeful body has held numerous conferences and workshops dealing with various aspects of the problems of graduate study through which it has gained a clear understanding of what must be done to ensure their proper solution. The most concrete evidences of this understanding are the standards it set up for the Master's and Doctor's degrees in 1935 and 1947 respectively. These standards have clearly defined the qualifications of graduate faculty members, the nature of the curriculums to be offered, and the type of laboratories and library facilities required. Closely allied with the work of the conference has been the publication of *The Development of Library Resources and Graduate Work in the Cooperative University Centers of the South,* by Davidson and Kuhlman (1944); of *Higher Education in the South,* by the Committee on Work Conferences on Higher Education of the Southern Association of Colleges and Secondary Schools (1947); and of *Graduate Work in the South,* by Mary Bynum Pierson (1947). All these publications deal realistically with many phases of the subject and present specific blueprints for improvement.

Three other major developments in graduate and professional study have taken place which mark significant advances in the field. They are the development of four university centers, described in a book under that title published following the dedication of the Joint University Libraries at Nashville in 1941; the region-wide study devoted to the subject of graduate and professional education for Negroes since the United States Supreme Court in 1938 rendered its decision in the Gaines Case requiring the admission of Negroes to white graduate and professional schools unless equal facilities were provided separately; and the organization of the Board of Control for Regional Education in the South in 1949. During the quarter-century 1925–50 cooperative arrangements among the universities and colleges of Chapel Hill-Durham, Athens-Atlanta, Nashville, and New Orleans were perfected which have given graduate work a sounder basis than it had previously through the cooperative provision of library resources, union catalogues, and other library facilities and apparatus. The Board of Control for Regional Education in the South is coming to grips realistically with the problem of providing graduate and professional training for both whites and Negroes through regional support which cannot be provided through the individual effort of institutions. And since the decision of the Gaines Case, southern legislatures, educational foundations, the Conference of Deans of Southern Graduate Schools, and Negro educators have cooperated in projecting graduate programs for Negro students.

The most compelling influence, however, has been the sharp upswing in the number of students seeking graduate and professional training of a high order. In 1936 the enrollment of graduate students in the institutions covered by the Conference of Deans of Southern Graduate Schools stood at 5,521. In 1944, when enrollment reached its lowest point in the war, it dropped to 2,121. But in 1949 it had climbed to 22,090, including Negro institutions, and in summer sessions in 1949 it reached a total of 31,451 for both races.

A demand for increased graduate and professional training at higher levels has come from another quarter. Today the idea of research is more firmly established in the South than formerly, and colleges and universities are being urged to increase their staffs and facilities in order that they may supply an adequate number of research workers to man the institutions, laboratories, and industries of the region. The location of plants for the production of war material contributed greatly to this impetus.

The colleges and universities themselves have established a number of research institutions with fine records of achievement behind them. In the social sciences the Institute for Research in Social Science at the University of North Carolina and the Southern Regional Training Program in Public Administration at the University of

Alabama, with which the Universities of Kentucky, Georgia, and Tennessee are associated, are cases in point. The Southern Association of Science and Industry, established in the early 1940's, listed in its monograph, *Research in Southern Regional Development* (1948), the following separate research agencies in southern colleges and universities: 13 in agriculture, 15 in engineering, 25 in natural science and medicine, 8 in social science, 11 in government and public administration, 12 in education, and 14 in other unclassified fields. In the humanities the Carnegie Foundation for the Advancement of Teaching and several of the national associations have stimulated research through grants-in-aid and through the establishment of regional divisions of their organizations. The Carnegie Foundation in 1947 made a grant to four university centers for a five-year period. Each center associated with itself four colleges, the funds from the Foundation and the institutions totalling $180,000 annually. The American Council of Learned Societies has assisted the Southern Humanities Conference, organized in 1947, in the promotion of research in humanistic fields.

Research in industry has also been greatly extended. The organization of the Southern Association of Science and Industry marked the conscious public development of this movement, and the publication by the Association of monographs on research, forestry, industry, and other subjects has made clear the impressive role research is to play in the region. The Association has also furnished a medium or sounding board for the promotion of regional research. In 1945 the University of North Carolina held a three-day symposium on various aspects of research, the papers presented before which were published in *Research and Regional Welfare*. The Southeastern Research Institute began the publication of its *Journal* in 1949, and industrialists generally have associated themselves directly or through a considerable number of newly established foundations with land-grant colleges and universities in providing funds for research professorships, research assistantships, and fellowships and scholarships in agriculture, business administration, ceramics, chemical engineering, dairying, insurance, textiles, and other fields. For example, the University of North Carolina has four foundations, in commerce, journalism, medicine, and pharmacy, all of which aid in

providing expert personnel and funds for fellowships, library resources, and research.

The Federal Government has also greatly increased and intensified
its program of research in various fields in the South. The agricultural and engineering experiment stations of the land-grant colleges
and laboratories of the Department of Agriculture have undertaken
the solution of many problems in the various branches of agriculture
and forestry. Well-equipped laboratories, with skilled staffs and extensive libraries, are scattered widely throughout the area. The
United States Public Health Service has promoted an intensive program of professional study including fellowships for study and research in the field of public health and public-health education. At
the University of North Carolina alone, which has been designated
as the public-health center for the Southeast, 1,300 fellowships have
been provided in the past ten years for graduate training for sanitary
engineers, public-health educators, nurses, doctors, and other medical
and public-health experts. They have been provided by a wide variety of organizations, such as state departments of public health, the
Public Health Service, and the Kellogg and Rockefeller Foundations
and the Commonwealth Fund.

Of even greater importance, possibly, is the influence that the Oak
Ridge Institute of Nuclear Studies and the Tennessee Valley Authority—two of the greatest research laboratories developed in any
country—have exerted in centering attention upon research as a
means of increasing the wealth and general well-being (or utter de-
struction) of the citizenry of the region. The Tennessee Valley Authority, from its beginning in 1933, has carried on a vast program
of experimentation and research in both the social and natural sciences. It has integrated this program closely with the program of
graduate study and investigation of the land-grant colleges and universities of the valley states, and has stimulated research on every
campus it has touched. The Institute of Nuclear Studies has worked
out a cooperative program of training and research for prospective
scholars and investigators. The faculties of fourteen southern higher
institutions have been included in it, and unusually well-qualified
students from these institutions are enabled through fellowships and
grants-in-aid to go to Oak Ridge and work under the direction of
some of the most noted scientists in the world. The fellows also have

the opportunity of consulting with the faculties of their own institutions and using their laboratories and facilities.

This is the general situation in which the universities and professional schools of the region find themselves. The pertinent question may now be asked, how are the libraries and presses of higher institutions in the South going to aid in dealing with the problem which this development of graduate study and research poses? I bracket these two agencies because both are indispensable in meeting the situation. The libraries must undergird all sound graduate study and investigation, and the presses must aid in directing it into channels of scholarly productivity. The way these two basic university agencies can cooperate effectively is splendidly illustrated in the publication by the Princeton Press and Library of the *Papers of Thomas Jefferson*.

The question for which the libraries of the region have been and are now attempting to find the answer may now be asked of the presses. What, specifically, is their role in this situation? In his article, "Twenty Years of Southern Publishing," in the *Virginia Quarterly Review*, W. T. Couch dealt with a situation which existed here twenty-five years ago, when the University of North Carolina was making the transition from a liberal-arts college with several professional schools to that of a full-fledged university, a state of development now being experienced by many of the institutions of the region.[1] He vividly described the difficulties with which the University of North Carolina Press had to cope in helping the University to make the transition: lack of funds, staff, and publishing know-how; real or imagined emphasis upon senatorial or professional courtesy; compliance with budgetary procedures which failed to meet its requirements; dependence upon printing establishments with limited experience in bookmaking; little knowledge of effective methods of distribution; fluctuation of university and state support during periods of administrative change and national depression. Possibly the greatest difficulty of all, though one not mentioned by Couch, was the apprehension that freedom of thought and publication, if engaged in as they should be by the Press, might draw down public wrath upon the University. No southern university had run the gauntlet of publishing extensively in a region in which the then cur-

[1] For notes, see page 319.

rent problems of farm tenancy, racial discrimination, labor and management relations, prohibition, and the conflict between science and religion would almost inevitably have to be dealt with in every manuscript. Seemingly, the only "safe" manuscripts were those that harked back to the bygone days of slavery, to the nostalgic glories of southern plantations, and to the daring actions of the matchless heroes in gray who laid down their arms at Appomattox! And, as if this were not enough, Couch had to educate his Odums and Bransons and other faculty members, including myself, on all the know-how of publishing! The basis for apprehension of public reaction against the University was to be found in such instances as the storm of indignation directed against Charles W. Stiles in 1910 when he stated that 30 per cent of all rural Southerners suffered from hookworm disease—a charge which, though demonstrated to be true, was resented by most of the southern state departments of public health and characterized generally as a typical Yankee defamation by an outside meddler! It was for this reason that I insisted, when the Institute for Research in Social Science was founded here, that funds be included in the grant to the Institute for the publication of the results of its investigations, and that the Institute should publish them through the local press, so that they could not be dismissed by the public as worthless misrepresentations, as might have been the case had they been published by a commercial publisher outside the region.

Today, many conditions such as these confront the recently founded presses at Alabama, Miami, Tennessee, Vanderbilt, and other institutions in the region, both within and without the Association, as they gird themselves for this new enterprise. How are the university presses to deal constructively with these conditions? How are they to perform the "historic tasks of scholarship" which Lottinville asserts "have been to criticize and re-evaluate the literary, intellectual, and scientific performances of the past and the present, and to provide new concepts indispensable to the forward movement of mankind?"[2]

The experience of the University of North Carolina Press, and of the presses at Duke, Louisiana State, and Oklahoma, may furnish part of the answer but not more than a part, because only a few of the behind-the-scenes discussions and decisions concerning the problems of maintaining satisfactory public relations in an atmosphere characterized by sensitiveness and emotionalism have been revealed. The public generally does not know, for example, why the Board of Governors of the University of North Carolina Press was incorporated separately from the University, or why Williams and Wilkins are asked to assume responsibility for financing *Social Forces*,[3] or why Couch wrote the special "Publisher's Introduction" to the volume *What the Negro Wants*.[4] Revelations concerning these matters would not only be extremely interesting but they would be enlightening as well. So far they have not been made.

Another part of the answer to the question is to be found in the survey recently made by the Association, and in a number of earlier articles by Brandt, Colwell, Couch, Donaldson, Hemens, and Lottinville which the survey suggests should be made required reading for any institution considering the establishment of a press. These articles emphasize the function of university presses in promoting scholarly publishing, regional, state, or local, and in bringing the best works of scholarship ot the attention of an increasingly wide scholarly and lay public. They not only emphasize such publishing as basic to the proper functioning of a university, but they analyze the whole process of university publishing, with practical details covering every aspect of the subject. What a godsend this body of experience and suggestion would have been to me and my colleagues twenty-eight years ago. However, if I may venture a comment, the recent survey and these articles seem to me to stop somewhat short of exploring the ways in which new presses might play a more constructive role in areas like the South, when faced with such a situation as I have described. They present comparatively few generalizations and recommendations concerning the means presses can employ in enabling universities to perform each of their highly important functions of conserving knowledge, of revitalizing and transmitting it through teaching, of discovering new truth through investigation, and of interpreting and communicating ideas, both old and new, through publication and extension service. The formula or program proposed, if I understand it correctly, smacks a bit of aloofness from university connections and is not greatly differentiated from that of commercial publishing, except that scholarly content is demanded, that subsidization by the universities is essential, and that, for most publications, comparatively small printings will be the rule. According to this formula, the press should emphasize managerial and editorial know-how, minimize dependence upon faculty initiative and effort, look critically at the publication of journals and monographs, and keep a weather eye out for subsidies and manuscripts that will sell. This formula, if too strictly adhered to in the graduate study-research situation, in which graduate faculties, special laboratories, and extensive library resources must be acquired and in which the whole university must plan and work together, may fail to provide the stimulation and assistance the institutions of the region should receive.

What I am saying is that in this region, and possibly in other parts of the nation, the universities and professional schools have felt the impact of new forces released by the Second World War and are on the march to higher levels of instruction and research. Because of this fact, university presses will find one of their greatest opportunities for usefulness in publishing the results of research and thereby increasing the intellectual alertness of scholars and laymen, even though the obstacles in the way may be many and extremely difficult to overcome. In this situation the presses should demonstrate the skill and understanding and wisdom of publishing engineers. Shoulder to shoulder with the faculties and administrations, they must do their part in this challenging enterprise. I have not attempted to formulate a program, but, if I did propose one, it would contain such steps as the following:

First, the university presses must look up from the housekeeping processes of publishing long enough to see how graduate study and investigation are developing. They must study the situation, as I think Greenlaw, of the Graduate School, and Odum, of the Institute for Research in Social Science, did at the University of North Carolina in the early twenties, and discover how publishers can aid presidents like Chase and Graham in bringing their universities to full performance. This is what I think Lottinville means when he says "scholarly presses must not only welcome the appearance of taking a hand in the direction and progress of scholarship; they must be capable of doing so in fact."[5]

Second, the university presses must study the types of publication that provide the widest outlet for this rising tide of graduate and research interest, within the institution and without. In addition to books, this means journals, possibly some studies in series, or cooperation with societies or research organizations that lack skill in successful publishing and distribution. I can think of two journals which were of importance to the region that have ceased publication in the last-half-decade with the passing of their faculty editors. One was in dramatic art; the other, in education in the South. Both were needed, and still are needed, for the development of the artistic and educational interests of the region. It is no little accomplishment to have stimulated the developing talent of authors such as Thomas Wolfe, Paul Green, and Betty Smith by having furnished the medium for the publication of some of their early works, or to have furnished a medium through which various aspects of the graduate-research program in the South could be presented and developed from quarter to quarter. I know of two other potentially important journals, subsidized by universities, that are now being published without the benefit of press support and guidance, from which, because of this lack, the institutions receive no commensurate return for their expenditures. In such situations the function of a university press is obviously one of wise guidance and expert assistance. The handling of its journal program in full cooperation with the faculty by the Cornell Press in the past decade illustrates what I have in mind.

Third, as I have read the survey of the Association of American University Presses and a number of the earlier articles by some of its major statesmen, I have sensed a seeming lack of what, for want of a better term, I shall call the philosophy of university-press publishing. The survey is rich in quotations as to the purposes of the 35 presses in the Association. It also analyzes the product of the presses in the survey year. But the student from another field, like librarianship, which is also short on fundamental theory, fails to find the clear enunciation of purposes and goals to which the universities of the region could look for guidance, not only when they contemplate the establishment of presses, but also when they encounter difficulties after their establishment. To the admirable handbook of best practice should be added a handbook of guiding principles. The articles in the issue of the *Saturday Review*, by Malone, Lottinville, and others,[6] illustrate the thought I have in mind and point in the direction which such a publication should take.

Fourth, when the University of North Carolina Press was first established, one of the educational foundations that has contributed extensively to the development of bibliographical apparatus and library resources in several centers in the South was also interested in discovering whether university publishing could be channeled through a single press in a given region. In fact, at the outset the University of North Carolina Press hoped that scholarly publishing in the region would follow this pattern. But that idea, which Donald Bean explored in his story of presses in the twenties, seems not to have had sufficient vitality to cope with institutional ambition and individuality. Libraries have been more successful in carrying out regional bibliographical projects in four university centers and the Southeast generally, though much yet remains to be done cooperatively which could be of the greatest benefit to them. Today it might be advantageous for the Association to broaden its interest in cooperative enterprises to include a study of how best to help the institutions within a given region find a sounder, more effective procedure than they will be able to work out unaided and acting individually. The Southeastern Library Association, the Conference of Deans of Graduate Schools in the South, and, more recently, the Board of Control for Regional Education in the South have found this type of cooperation abundantly rewarding. University presses might also find it so.

Fifth, and finally, while these things are being done, the others on which I commented earlier should not be left undone. Let the university presses frown, if they wish, on the publication of monographs and studies issued in series, provided they do not thereby put a brake on interest in research. Let them discourage professional courtesy if it leads to the publication of inferior manuscripts, but only after having made every effort to suggest constructive measures for improving them. Let them see to it that every manuscript stands or falls on the basis of its merits or in the light of the functions of the university rather than commercial publishing. Let them apply all the publishing know-how they can to all aspects of the complex publishing process, set up accounting systems in keeping with their needs, and watch out for the manuscripts that will bring in golden harvests. But, in addition, they must do two other things. First, constantly criticize the product of the university presses. If, for example, scholars are too preoccupied with certain aspects of American history as

contrasted with the history of other countries or with American social or economic problems, such limitations must be pointed out and
subjects sought that will more adequately cover the special fields of
university publishing. Second, it must always be remembered that
the presses, in cooperation with the administrative officers and faculties of the colleges and universities with which they are associated,
are working together toward one supreme end—progress in intellectual attainment and culture of a region and its people, and thereby
of the nation and the world.

NOTES:

[1]Virginia Quarterly Review: XXVI (Spring, 1950), pp. 171–185.

[2]"Midway between Scholar and Society," *Saturday Review of Literature,*
XXXIII (May 6, 1950), p. 28. (This is an editorial in a number devoted to the
discussion of university presses.)

[3]Chapel Hill, North Carolina: University of North Carolina Press.

[4]Logan, Rayford W., editor. Chapel Hill, North Carolina: University of North
Carolina Press, 1944.

[5]Lottinville, Savoie, *loc. cit.*

[6]XXXIII (May 6, 1950).

The Forward Thrust in Publication

PUBLISHING AT THE UNIVERSITY OF NORTH CAROLINA underwent
three stages of development, which may be characterized as incidental, conscious, and planned. The first or incidental stage was participated in by the University, on the one hand, and by the Dialectic
and Philanthropic Literary Societies, on the other. It began in 1795
and ended a century later in 1893.

The publications of this incidental period fell rather logically into

Reprinted from Louis R. Wilson, *The University of North Carolina, 1900–1930,*
Chapter XXXV, pp. 483–488, 496–500 (Copyright ©1953, University of North
Carolina Press), by permission of the publisher.

three categories. The first included the official *Catalogues* and announcements of the University. The second included rosters of the members of the Societies and the addresses of prominent speakers who appeared before the Societies on special occasions, and, beginning in 1844, the *North Carolina University Magazine*, which served as a medium for the publication of important papers and reports in the fields of literature, history, and science by students, members of the faculty, alumni, and trustees and members of the Historical Society of the University of North Carolina, also established in 1844. The third included literary and historical articles in several short-lived weekly papers, an occasional report or textbook by members of the faculty, and in 1884 the *Journal of the Elisha Mitchell Scientific Society*, the first of the University's learned journals. The *Journal of the Shakspere Club* was issued in 1886–87 for one year only, although a long succession of scholarly papers dealing with Shakespeare and early English drama appeared later in the *Magazine*.

The second period, that of conscious or purposeful, publication, began in 1893 and ended in 1922. In 1893 five members of the faculty, Professors John Manning, Francis P. Venable, J. W. Gore, Collier Cobb, and R. H. Whitehead established the private printshop which they called the University Press, already described in Chapter I. It served as a commercial printery until 1901, when it was taken over by the University and was operated directly by it under an expert printer and student assistants. In 1912 it was continued under lease by the University, and in 1920 it was removed from the campus to an office downtown where it was operated privately under the new name of the University Printery.

The publishing in this period may be thought of as conscious, or purposeful, because the Press was set up to issue the official publications of the University and the growing number of journals which came into being during the period. This second period witnessed an extensive expansion of publication interests. The *Tar Heel*, student paper and organ of the Athletic Association, was established in 1893. It was followed in 1894 by a short-lived, non-fraternity rival, the *White and Blue*. In 1894–95 the Alumni Association, largely through President Winston and members of the faculty, published two issues of the *Alumni Quarterly*, which was then discontinued. In 1896 the

University began the publication of the University of North Carolina *Record*, the medium through which the official publications of the University appeared. Then followed the *James Sprunt Historical Monographs* (1900), the *North Carolina Law Journal* (1904 and 1905), *Studies in Philology* (1906), the *North Carolina High School Bulletin* (now the *High School Journal*, 1910), the *Alumni Review* (1912), the University of North Carolina *News Letter* (1914), *Research in Progress* (1920), the *Extension Bulletin* (1921), and the *Journal of Social Forces* (now *Social Forces*) and the *North Carolina Law Review* (1922). By 1912 publication by this establishment had become so burdensome and the quality of the printing fell so far short of meeting the improved standards of the day, that recourse had to be made to commercial printeries elsewhere.[1]

The incorporation as a non-stock company of the University of North Carolina Press on March 13, 1922, ushered in the third or planned period of University publishing. This action was highly significant and stemmed from certain considerations that may now be noted.

The period 1893–1922 had been one of marked expansion in publication. Not only did the number of journals published greatly increase, but the number of copies of publications issued had undergone a corresponding rise. The problems of editing, printing, financing, advertising, and distributing the publications issued became so involved that in 1919 Chairman of the Faculty Stacy had recommended the appointment of a publications officer to take over the work which at that time was handled by a special standing committee of the faculty on publications. It had also become increasingly essential for the University to send out publications attractive in format, which could be compared favorably with like publications from other institutions. In 1919–20, each journal was handled by a separate board of editors. Consequently the responsibility for editing, advertising, mailing, and collecting for the copies sent out was unsystematized and confusing to the public. Altogether, the total expenditure for the journals, not including the official catalogues, amounted to approximately $14,000 annually, which was offset in part by receipts of $5,250. In addition, the Library exchanged extensively such publications as the *James Sprunt Historical Mono-*

[1]For notes, see page 329.

graphs, the Mitchell *Journal,* the *High School Journal,* and *Studies in Philology,* for which it received many valuable publications in return.

The University also maintained two important lecture series and from time to time published single volumes which did not bear the University's imprint. The McNair and Weil lectures appeared under the imprint of commercial publishers, and although they were financed by the University, there was little opportunity for the reading public to discover that the University was connected in any way with the resulting publications. In 1919, the University published *Education and Citizenship and Other Papers,* by President E. K. Graham, but the imprint was that of G. P. Putnam's Sons, not the University of North Carolina. Thus the University failed to gain the favorable publicity to which it was entitled. In another instance a year later, the *Alumni Review* made the following comment under the caption "Failed to Carry Our Trade Mark":

"Some ten days ago THE REVIEW upon the receipt of one of the first copies of the book 'Raleigh, the Shepherd of the Ocean,' by Professor F. H. Koch, professor of dramatic literaure in the University and director of the Raleigh pageant, wrote the firm which printed it somewhat as follows: 'May we congratulate you on having brought out the most attractive piece of bookmaking North Carolina has yet produced?'

"The point we make here is not that we were attempting to say a pretty speech; but rather that through the cooperation of University teachers and a well equipped printing house, North Carolina has produced a book which in its physical makeup was second to none in the country.

"The real point we are getting at is that the book would have been perfect had it only carried on the bottom of the title page the imprint: Chapel Hill, The University of North Carolina Press, 1920.

"Had the University been able last spring to underwrite the University Press idea this book, which becomes the first offering in the great tercentenary celebration now being participated in by America, would have carried the University's imprint, its trade mark, to the four corners of the world. It would have helped sell the University of North Carolina to the scholarly world—a thing certainly to be desired, or rather to be done on all occasions."[2]

A more serious loss, however, was that of the opportunity of publishing scholarly works by members of the faculty which could not be published at a profit by commercial publishers but which, on account of their scholarly nature, should be available to scholars in other institutions. Where such opportunity was lacking, the incentive to carry on research also tended to be lacking—a condition which if not removed, would defeat the purpose of the University in reorganizing the Graduate School and establishing such organizations as the North Carolina Club and the Institute for Research in Social Science.

An equally weighty consideration was that the establishment of a Press at Chapel Hill would not only stimulate the faculty and students of the University to extend their investigations, but it would be equally stimulating to the scholars and writers of the South as well. It would open a door for regional publishing since the South was practically virgin territory for both commercial and university publishing. It would enable Southern authors to submit manuscripts to editors in Chapel Hill instead of New York, and thereby avoid the expense of travel and the difficulties of submitting manuscripts to readers trained in universities of the Northeast who were unfamiliar with the conditions with which many of the manuscripts would inevitably deal. Furthermore, if the Press solicited manuscripts on a national as well as a regional basis, two additional benefits would follow. The University's influence would be correspondingly extended and the members of the Board of Governors of the Press and the editorial boards of the University's learned journals would profit greatly from the steady stream of ideas and data contained in manuscripts received from scholars and investigators everywhere.

Not only did the logic of the situation call for the establishment of the Press, but individual members of the faculty strongly advocated the measure. As early as 1918, Louis R. Wilson, as chairman of the Faculty Committee on Publications and editor of the *Alumni Review*, analyzed the situation which confronted the University and urged that the step be taken.[3] Dr. Edwin Greenlaw, as chairman of a special committee of the faculty representing the publishing interest of the University, drew up late in 1919 or early in 1920 a memorandum or prospectus which set forth in detail the reasons why a Press should be established. It was upon the basis of this memorandum that the Trustees, at their meeting on January 28, 1920, formally authorized the establishment of a Press for the publication of books, journals, and monographs, although the actual establishment was not carried out until 1922. It was also made clear by the Trustees that it was not their intention to provide a physical printing plant, but that the Press should have its publications printed through commercial printeries.[4]

A final influence which contributed to the establishment of the Press was that exerted by the spirit of the times. The University, stirred by the forces that had been released by World War I, was on the march. It had clearly conceived its role as that of a great organic institution created and supported by the State as its principal agency for training the experts who were to serve it in all aspects of its expanding life. The Presses of Oxford and Cambridge abroad and of Harvard and Yale among American universities had demonstrated the importance of publication as a function of the modern university, through which the results of investigation could be carried to the public and interpreted and thereby made to contribute to the well-being and culture of its supporting clientele. The establishment of the Press, therefore, marked the final step taken by the University before its inclusion in November, 1922, in the Association of American Universities.

The signing of the certificate of incorporation occurred on March 13, 1922, with the following incorporators designated as the first Board of Governors: Trustees—Alfred M. Scales (1892), Z. V. Walser (1884), and Leslie Weil (1895); President—H. W. Chase; Professors—W. C. Coker, Louis Graves (1902), Edwin Greenlaw, J. G. deR. Hamilton, Lucius P. McGehee (1887), Howard W. Odum, Chester D. Snell, Nathan W. Walker (1903), and Louis R. Wilson (1899). Lucius P. McGehee served as chairman and Louis Graves as secretary.

The objects for which the Press was incorporated were set forth in the articles of incorporation as follows:

> To publish periodicals devoted to the advancement of learning and produced at the University of North Carolina by or under the direction of the faculty of that University.
>
> To publish, so far as may be agreed between the corporation and the authorities of the University of North Carolina, cata-

logues, bulletins and other documents pertaining to that University or to any department thereof.

To promote generally, by publishing deserving works, the advancement of the arts and sciences and the development of literature.

The record made by the Press from 1922 to 1930, even though clouded in the last year by the effect of impending tightness of funds, was one of notable achievement. Although President Chase did not remain at the University beyond June, 1930, and consequently did not write a report for the year, he considered the establishment of the Press and its growth as one of the most significant contributions his administration had made to the University. In summary, the achievement of the Press during the eight years may be set down as follows:

Although at the outset the members of the Board of Governors of the Press had had no experience in commercial publishing, all of the faculty members had been successful editors of journals and other publications or news services of the University and were frequent contributors to journals in their respective fields. They were keenly aware of the importance of publication in the promotion of research and scholarship. They likewise believed that they and the administrative staff would in time learn how to handle the activities of the organization successfully in a region that had produced no university or commercial press of national distinction. Consequently, in spite of limited experience and funds, the Press had gone far in establishing contacts with authors, in setting standards for the manufacture of books, in providing appropriate channels for their distribution, and in securing their extensive advertising and reviewing in national literary and scholarly journals.

As a working organization, the Press had set up special committees on manuscripts and finance; it had staffed editorial and sales departments; it had determined the principal fields in which it would publish; and it had brought to its support increasing funds from the University, from sales of its publications, from local individuals and organizations, and from national educational foundations. Altogether, in spite of initial lack of knowledge of the niceties of commercial publishing and especially of publishing accounting, it had laid the foundation upon which a more refined superstructure could be erected. Like the Division of Extension and the University Library, it had followed the enforced formula of beginning with a small staff and little financial support and of gaining experience and winning support as it developed capacity—a procedure which the experienced university publisher of today may look at with a critical eye and attribute to well-intentioned but none-the-less blissful ignorance. In these respects it had demonstrated the ability of the University to develop a program of publishing commensurate with its program of teaching, research, and extension, to all of which it gave stimulation and strength.[5]

The Press had likewise demonstrated another important fact. It had proved to the satisfaction of the University that it could deal with controversial problems such as race, tenant farming, and mill villages in such a way as to contribute to the social and economic development of North Carolina and the South without injury to the University. It had boldly dealt with a wide variety of such controversial problems that were demanding careful consideration and investigation. In fact, of the 88 titles published, approximately one-half dealt with specific problems of the South and focused attention upon their proper solution for the advancement of the region.[6]

This policy had been determined upon when in 1924 the establishment of the Institute for Research in Social Science was under consideration by the Laura Spelman Rockefeller Memorial. At that time the Director of the Press made it clear to the representative of the Memorial that if the results of the investigations made by the Institute were to contribute most effectively to the solution of Southern problems, it would be highly desirable that they be published by the University of North Carolina Press with the backing of the faculty, the alumni, and the Trustees of the institution. Published and supported in that way, it would be impossible for those who objected to the nature of the findings to dismiss them without serious consideration on the basis that they were misrepresentations made by meddlesome outsiders for the obvious purpose of discrediting the South! As a result, provision was made in the grant establishing the Institute for $6,000 annually for three years as funds for library materials and for the publication of the results of the Institute's studies through the Press. Later the criticism by the Synod of the Presbyterian Church of North Carolina relating to the McNair Lectures and certain articles in *Social Forces* was met satisfactorily and without destroying either the Press or the University.

Most important of all, the Press had stimulated scholars in the University and in other institutions throughout the South to greater scholarly endeavor and had provided them an open door through which they could present their studies to the public and scholars everywhere. In these respects, it not only laid the foundation for publishing on the campus at Chapel Hill and on other campuses in the region, but achieved distinction in a phase of scholarly development of maximum importance to North Carolina, the South, and the Nation.

The effectiveness of the role of the Press as a medium for dissemination of information concerning the work of the University was vividly illustrated to the Director in four incidents which occurred while he was on a trip to Europe in 1931. One evening when he was writing a letter home after dinner in a hotel in Dublin, he overheard the conversation of three Americans in the writing room. He recognized the drawl of one of the three as that of a Southerner. From a remark of another member of the trio the Director became convinced that the Press had published a book for him. The Director introduced himself to the second speaker and discovered that he was a professor from the University of Wisconsin for whom the Press had published *The Country Newspaper.*

Ten days later the Director was in the American University Union in London and there met a professor from the University of Michigan for whom the Press had published *The Genesis of Shakespeare Idolatry.* The professor had just come from the British museum where he had obtained a permit to use the Reading Room by showing the the Secretary an article by him in *Studies in Philology*, which bore the Press's imprint. At a meeting of the British Library Association in Cheltenham a few days later, the Director was sought out by the Librarian of the University of Birmingham to arrange for the exchange of *Studies in Philology* for a file of the *Hibbard Journal* and the current issues of the English *Journal of Educational Psychology.* On his return to New York, when he was having his suitcases inspected by a customs official, he had an almost incredible experience of being told by the inspector that there was a University Press at Chapel Hill and that he had read a review of one of its boks

in the New York *Times* on the preceding Sunday. When informed
that the suitcases before him belonged to the Director of that Press,
the inspector placed his O.K. on the bags and sent the Director on his
way!

To use a quotation from the blurb on the cover of a book may
seem to be a doubtful device for appraising the book on whose jacket
the blurb occurs. In this instance, however, the quotation is not so
much a "plug" for an individual book as it is a serious appraisal of
the institution from which the book stemmed. The quotation which
follows relates to *Books from Chapel Hill* published in 1946, as the
contribution of the Press to the celebration of the Sesquicentennial
of the University and was distributed without cost to the Press's
clientele:

"Here, in the somewhat sober guise of an annotated catalogue of
books, is an exciting story—the story of the growth of a great institution for public enlightenment, in a region where such an institution
had not existed before and where the services it could give were perhaps more sorely needed than anywhere else in the United States.
The institution is The University of North Carolina Press; its story
is told in the titles and descriptions of the 500-odd books it has published. Implicit in this record is its rise, in the short space of twenty-
four years, to a strength and an influence which make it the unques-
tioned Southern leader in the field of book-publishing and one of the
half dozen great university presses in the nation.

". . . In its first decade, the Press examined annually an average
of forty manuscripts and published an average of twelve books.
Now, hundreds of manuscripts come to the Press every year; its annual list of thirty or more new books represents the work of authors
from all sections of the country and from many foreign lands in
numerous fields of literature and learning. The Press has achieved
size and permanence, the respect of its peers. Its imprint on a book
today is recognized as a warrant of quality.

". . . And though the books it lists fall in almost all fields and
cover a wide range of subjects, the discriminating booklover or bibliographer will find in its pages a fruitful library of two hundred
original publications in one field—the South, with one common objective—the enlightenment and development of the South. These
books, on every phase of Southern history and civilization, are the

Press's reason for being, the justification of its existence. Distinguished as may be the 'books from Chapel Hill' on other topics, those books could have been issued as effectively by other publishers. Without The University of North Carolina Press, many of the greatest books on Southern subjects would never have found their way to the printed page.

"Here . . . is a record of achievement, a distinguished part of the offering of a great University to its people, a book for those who love, serve, and wish to know the South."

NOTES:

[1]For the development of publishing, 1795–1922, see "Foreword" by Louis R. Wilson in *Books from Chapel Hill: A Complete Catalogue, 1923–45* (Chapel Hill: The University of North Carolina Press, 1946), pp. v–x.

[2]*Alumni Review*, November, 1920, p. 45.

[3]Editorial comments appeared in thirteen numbers of the *Review* from March, 1918, to March, 1922, when the Press was incorporated. Wilson also wrote a memorandum for Dean Greenlaw, later embodied in the latter's memorandum or prospectus submitted to the Trustees in January, 1920, citing the publishing activities in which the University was then engaged, the cost of the individual journals and lecture series then published by the University, and the advantages which would result from the establishment of a Press that would systematize and extend the University's publishing program.

[4]Trustee Minutes, 1917–1924, p. 201. See also papers of Louis R. Wilson, 1919–1920, 1920–1921, and Minutes of the University of North Carolina Press, 1922–1929. The memorandum by Greenlaw is undated and unsigned but it is included in the Press Minutes and antedated the action of the Trustees on January 27, 1920. It is also referred to in the University *Record*, December, 1920, p. 52.

[5]Couch, writing in Knight and Adams, eds., *The Graduate School: Research and Publication*, expressed the opinion that at the beginning the faculty members of the Board were reluctant to criticize severely or reject manuscripts submitted by their colleagues until the depression forced the Press to reject unacceptable manuscripts, or to have them rewritten after careful criticism by the staff. Such reluctance, if actual rather than seeming, might well have been attributable to the inexperience of members of the Board and staff alike in the pioneering stage before expertness in all the complicated procedures of publishing had been acquired. The important fact is that they established the Press, that they set up an administrative organization and gave it support, and adjusted the procedures of the Press to changing conditions in the light of experience gained.

[6]Russell Kirk in his *Academic Freedom*, An Essay in Definition, 1955, p. 90, says: "When Mr. Couch began his work at North Carolina in 1925, he had been told that the Press there would destroy itself if anything was published which dealt seriously with race, religion, or economics." Actually, the University *News Letter* and *Social Forces* had been dealing with such problems for several years and the Press had published such books as Dinsmore's *Religious Certitude in an Age of Science*, Poteat's *Can a Man Be A Christian Today?*, and Odum and Johnson's *The Negro and His Songs* when Couch joined its staff.

Subject Index

Name Index